Nine Keys of Abyssal Darkness

Nine Keys of Abyssal Darkness

The Doctrine and Praxis of Tenebrous Satanism

T. L. Othaos

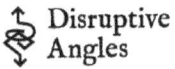

Copyright

© 2023 Theli Lamia Othaos
ISBN: 978-1-7390327-0-8 (Paperback)

All rights reserved. No part of this book may be reproduced in any form or by any electronic or mechanical means, including information storage and retrieval systems, without permission in writing from the author, except brief passages for review, discussion and other non-commercial purposes.

Disclaimer

This book is intended for mature adults of sound mental and emotional health. Practices described herein may be hazardous to the immature and the irresponsible, especially if undertaken while under the influence of intoxicating substances.

Contact

- *Email:* othaos@tenebroussatanism.com
- *Website:* www.othaos.com | www.tenebroussatanism.com
- *Facebook:* www.facebook.com/TenebrousSatanism/
- *X:* @NineKeysOthaos

Acknowledgements

- Edited by Ananael XIII
- Original cover photo by Vino Li
- All layouts, cover art and internal illustrations by T. L. Othaos, with inspiration from public domain works by the Order of Nine Angles

Contents

Prelude to the Creed vii

The Tenebrous Creed ix

Introduction xi

I — The Just Preference of Earth Over Heaven 23

II — Insidious Destroyers of Life 43

III — The Faustian Art of Self-Evolution 75

IV — The Void, Darkness, and the Abyss 96

V — Polishing the Black Mirror 125

VI — Perilous Omens 145

VII — Unleashing the Black Flame 218

VIII — The Nekalah: Dark Gods of the Abyss 251

IX — Azoth: The Sorcerer as Alchemist 314

Appendix I: Rites of Abyssal Darkness 350

Appendix II: Tables 367

About the Author 373

Prelude to the Creed

From the Void we emerge;
in Darkness we dwell;
to the Abyss we go.

Our destination is the same
regardless of whether we keep our eyes closed,
allow the Light to blind us,
or look forward with open eyes.

Let us therefore march onward with our eyes open
and make of our coming forth from the Void
a great Adventure
instead of a cry of despair.

Let us make a home of Darkness,
not for the sake of that which we came from
but for our own sake,
here and now and for the future.

Having lived thus,
we descend into the Abyss without regret,
embracing transformation even in the midst of terror.

And as long as the Black Flame burns within us,
let this be our Creed...

The Tenebrous Creed

1. Satan is an advocate of the unending Adventure of spirit in the realm of flesh, manifest in life's multitudinous striving within an ever-evolving world.

2. Satan is an adversary of any dogma that denies or distorts the realm of flesh, for such dogmas are insidious destroyers of life.

3. Satan lights our way along the path of self-evolution, which we pursue by seeking ever-greater excellence in all of our affairs.

4. Self-evolution is fostered by the possession of zeal, wisdom, honor, empathy, and perseverance, which Satan therefore encourages us to cultivate.

5. Insofar as the herd's fears, fads, and fictions hold us back from self-evolution, Satan urges us to stand apart from the herd.

6. The witch and the sorcerer recognize Satan not only in the Fire of the Will, but also in the Will of the Fire.

7. The Will of the Fire and the will of the sorcerer are one: the advancement of Satan's cause through the embrace of creative strife.

Introduction

The creed this book advances is called Tenebrous Satanism. It consists both of a philosophy of life and occult practices aimed at self-transformation. Tenebrous Satanism is not merely an individual ethos, a belief system, a self-cultivation method, or a set of magickal tools. Rather, in combining all of these, Tenebrous Satanism constitutes a religion — the religion of Darkness, which in Latin is called *Tenebrae*.

Nine Keys of Abyssal Darkness is the foundational text of Tenebrous Satanism. Its first four tracts, the Keys of Doctrine, offer comprehensive reflection upon the mythology of Satan, a clear-eyed account of the human condition, a constructive vision of self-evolution, and an unflinching revelation of dark realities. Its final five tracts, the Keys of Praxis, complement this worldview with occult practices aimed at furthering individual realization and bringing the Satanist into contact with sublime forces of the Abyss.

In both doctrine and praxis, Tenebrous Satanism draws considerable influence from the Order of Nine Angles (O9A). However, Tenebrous Satanism does not in any way endorse the antisemitism, human sacrifice, and other heinous acts with which O9A has come to be associated. What Tenebrous Satanism does derive from O9A is an uncompromising yet constructive doctrine of adversity, potent fundamentals of esoteric practice, and a unique prime directive: to promote collaboration between human beings and the Nekalah, a specific faction of Dark Gods formerly known only through O9A's writings. Tenebrous Satanism thus situates itself as a participant in the same magickal current as O9A, and a promoter of that which is fruitful within that current. While it rejects the infamously hateful and destructive aspects of O9A, *Nine Keys of Abyssal Darkness* shares O9A's aspiration to reveal a unique Sinister Path to those willing to walk it, and to accelerate both individual and collective evolution by empowering such exemplars. This is not just Satanism as a fashionable political identity, nor dark spirituality divorced from "real life." It is instead the Satanism of heretics, outcasts, and other seekers of the forbidden: those who, having awakened to Darkness, make the choice to live differently from others. Our revolt is not only against outdated religious ways, but also against the reality-divorced precepts enshrined by the secular herd.

Such a vision at once raises three questions. First, what do we mean by the term "Satanism"? Second, what does each of the Nine Keys offer to the would-be Satanist? Third, what is the exact relationship between Tenebrous Satanism and O9A, and why has the author of this book chosen to risk controversy by engaging with O9A's ideas, practices, and entities? Addressing these three issues is the focus of this introduction.

On Satanism

The exact meaning of "Satanism" differs among those who profess it. Nonetheless, amid disparate ideologies, one finds an ethos that consistently encompasses the following elements:[1]

Affirmation of the earthly world

Whether via indulging the senses, appreciating attainments in the arts and sciences, or fighting for this-worldly justice instead of accepting otherworldly compensation, Satanism asserts that the full enjoyment of our lives here and now ought to be our top priority.

Adversarial stance toward "the sacred"

Satanism mocks at idols and demands justification for what others take for granted. It does not tolerate, much less submit to, that which stifles the individual. The Satanist criticizes and rejects unjust authorities, dysfunctional institutions, and overrated ideologies of all kinds.

Encouragement of self-empowerment

Balancing the hedonistic tendency of Satanism is a drive toward self-knowledge and self-discipline aimed at fulfilling the Nietzschean ideal of being one's own God. Disdaining the complacency of the herd, Satanists prize wisdom and endurance as virtues that promote self-evolution.

Rejection of feel-good metaphysical claims

Among established Satanic denominations stand both atheistic mainliners and esotericists who advocate a supernatural perspective. *No Satanist, however, believes that some kind of benevolent force or deity is in charge of the universe.* Satanism rejects the wishful thinking behind such beliefs as "God has a plan" or "the fundamental basis of the universe is love." It prefers instead to live in reality, and to speak openly about whatever dark truths must be confronted there.

Beyond these four generalities, Satanic denominations vary in the ways of life they promote. Some focus on self-development to the exclusion of a political horizon. Others skew toward the political right or left. Regardless of such variations, however, all who march under the banner of Satan, embracing a worldview with the above four qualities, may be counted as Satanists. By this definition, the Tenebrous creed constitutes a form of Satanism as well.

The word "Satan" originally designated not a specific entity's name, but a title: "accuser/adversary." In our understanding, this title applies not just to one particular being but to any number of beings, both human and otherwise, who tread the path of the Tempter, Rebel, Lord of This World and Prince of Darkness. By taking up "Satanic" beliefs, values and practices, one declares oneself an adversary of what others consider "normal," and makes accusation against those who spoil earthly existence with their willful blindness, timidity, and lack of imagination. In being adversarial in this sense, Tenebrous Satanism is like all other Satanisms worthy of the title.

Why call our form of Satanism "Tenebrous," though? The word "Tenebrous" means "dark, shadowy, or obscure." We have adopted it because the Satanism it describes is one that explicitly characterizes the Ultimate — i.e., the meta-reality behind all of existence — as the Abyssal Void of Darkness. This does not mean that Tenebrous Satanism worships Darkness, or that the Abyssal Void is to be identified with Satan per se. What it does mean is a recognition that behind life lurks something that is *not* benevolent, combined with a steadfast determination to *affirm life anyway.* This affirmation constitutes a rejection both of naive optimism and of pessimistic despair. Tenebrous Satanism instead embraces the liberating empowerment that can be had when one looks unflinchingly at the worst, yet still refuses to cease striving ever onward toward the best.

On the Nine Keys

The creed of a religion offers but a high-level glimpse of its conceptions of the Ultimate, the human, and what mediates between the two. Providing a full account of such matters, and their implications regarding Tenebrous doctrine and praxis, is the central task of *Nine Keys of Abyssal Darkness*.

The First Key engages in imaginative reflection upon the mythology of Satan: his rebellion against heaven, tempting of Eve, etc. Its goal is not to articulate "truths" about an objectively existing being, but to explain what the first statement of the Tenebrous Creed means by "Satan is an advocate of the unending Adventure of spirit in the realm of flesh, manifest in life's multitudinous striving within an ever-evolving world." To elaborate on this, the First Key elucidates five principles: i) flesh's orientation toward *flourishing*; ii) spirit's orientation toward *self-evolution*; iii) The world as a shared space of *interdependence*; iv) life as that which is characterized by limitation and thus endures *suffering*; v) Adventure as the *willful affirming* of life instead of rejecting life as "evil." By grounding these themes in narratives in which the adversarial angel plays a central role, the First Key spells out both how Tenebrous Satanism's ethos resembles that of other Satanisms and how it differs from what has come before.

The Second Key complements the First Key's account of what Satan stands for with an account of what Satan stands against: "any dogma that denies or distorts the realm of flesh." Tenebrous Satanism posits that, broadly speaking, human thinking has evolved three different ways of distinguishing that which is beneficial from that which is harmful: *order vs. chaos*, *truth vs. falsehood*, and *progress vs. stasis*. All three patterns are found universally among human individuals and cultures, for each is useful to the human organism in some way. When misapplied and overextended, however, each pattern can metastasize into a dogma hostile to the complexities of the flesh and baneful to the liberty of the spirit. In asserting that one of the three patterns is especially baleful when placed upon a pedestal, and calling for the rejection and demolition of such pedestals, the Second Key declares

Tenebrous Satanism's adversarial stance against the insidious destroyers of life.

The Third Key defines self-evolution as the goal of the Satanist and offers advice as to how one may most effectively pursue said goal. It proposes that each of the five principles presented in the First Key has a corresponding virtue: i) flourishing is fostered by *zeal;* ii) evolution is advanced via the acquisition of *wisdom;* iii) interdependence produces obligations of *honor;* iv) the pervasiveness of suffering among incarnate beings elicits *empathy;* v) existence itself is fundamentally an exercise in *perseverance.* These virtues, understood not as moral imperatives but as qualities of personal excellence, are traits whose possession empowers human beings to live their best lives, regardless of the individual's specific goals, political commitments, etc. The Satanic practice of these virtues requires striking a healthy balance between the need to realistically acknowledge the social dimension of human existence and the imperative to stand apart from the herd in order to become something more. The Third Key thus enlarges on what the third, fourth, and fifth statements of our Creed put forward: an ethos of individual self-empowerment that is neither merely subjective, nor dogmatically prescriptive in the manner of a traditional religion.

The Fourth Key presents the metaphysical, teleological and eschatological beliefs of Tenebrous Satanism. Like O9A, Tenebrous Satanism asserts that parallel to our familiar, tangible reality (the *causal*) there exists an alien, elusive dimension of existence (the *acausal*). Tenebrous Satanism refers to those who choose to engage with this realm on an occasional, ad hoc basis as "Tenebrous witches," and those who commit to ongoing engagement with it as "Tenebrous sorcerers." What the occult arts fundamentally consist in is witches and sorcerers utilizing the "Fire of the Will" — i.e., their own mental and spiritual energies — to bring about outcomes not attainable by ordinary means. At times, this endeavor includes supernatural denizens of the acausal, who possess a will of their own — the "Will of the Fire."[2] The Fourth Key describes several factions of acausal beings as well as the disturbing meta-reality that lies behind the acausal as a whole: the Abyssal Void of Darkness. Amid unveiling the mysteries alluded to by the Prelude to the Creed, and by the Creed's sixth and seventh statements, the Fourth Key explains why other religions believe what they believe — and why Tenebrous Satanism believes things that no other religion can stomach. Tenebrous Satanists are thus called to embrace an uncompromisingly

Dark worldview, bereft of the consolations of conventional theism and atheism alike.

Unifying the four Keys of Doctrine is a conviction that two extremes found among existing Satanic denominations must be reconciled: i) among mainline denominations, a too-vehement humanism which disdains spirituality; and ii) among esoteric denominations, a too-mystical occultism that fails to offer a livable human ethos. Tenebrous Satanism does not merely proffer spooky trappings for edgy atheists. Nor does it seek only to make New-Age navel-gazing "cool" for the gothically inclined. It is instead a religion in which this-worldly life-affirmation coexists with a thirst for spiritual fulfillment. How the Satanist may pursue and attain such fulfillment is a central concern of the five Keys of Praxis.

The Fifth Key instructs Satanists in methods of Tenebrous meditation. Each of its four contemplations utilize sigils known from O9A's magickal current to bring about alterations in one's mental state, such as purification, energy raising, centering, and the enhancement of sensitivity to the acausal realm. While such exercises are not a strict prerequisite for other esoteric arts, they are intended to offer a firm foundation from which spiritual evolution can proceed. They are thus especially recommended as a starting point for those inexperienced in occult matters.

The Sixth Key details Tenebrous Satanism's divination system, including a general overview, meanings of individual omens, and methods both of reading and of improving one's divinatory skill. Broadly speaking, the Tenebrous runic-tarot can be used in two ways: i) to gain insight into one's own psyche and destiny, as per traditional methods of divination; and ii) as an aid to exploring one's thoughts and feelings about life's Perils. We use the term "Perils" to designate delineated facets of incarnate existence that inherently inflict suffering upon conscious beings — and all the more so when humans attempt to evade them via dysfunctional coping methods. Learning Tenebrous divination can thus both enlighten the diviner regarding the paths that lie ahead, and empower the Satanist to better overcome the obstacles encountered there.

The Seventh Key details ritual performance — i.e., the necessary tools, the appropriate mindset, the laws by which magick works, and a template for effective Satanic rites. In contrast to the more free-form style of magick typical in much contemporary esotericism, Tenebrous Satanism defines its ritual praxis via a series of basic structures and incantations, which the magician may then adapt to a multitude of circumstances. While the beginner may find this approach more formal than other kinds of modern magick, its advantage is that once fundamentals are internalized, one becomes capable of performing a great variety of workings without having to reinvent the wheel for each new end sought and every new spirit solicited. Tenebrous magick aims to strike a balance between making magick easy enough to promote regular practice, and making magick rigorous enough for magicians to achieve meaningful results. This means both attaining whatever goals one's workings are aimed at and growing in wisdom, discipline, and maturity along the way.

The Eighth Key turns from generalities of ritual to the question of how to accomplish one specific and defining goal of Tenebrous Satanism: communion with the Nekalah, the Dark Gods of O9A. The first method presented entails the witch or sorcerer undertaking an inward *descent* to the acausal thrones of the Dark Gods. The second method entails the creation of a Shadow space, allowing human and Nekalah to meet on the *threshold* between the causal and acausal realms. Instructions on these methods are followed by an account of what the author has learned of the Dark Gods thereby. As this content constitutes personal gnosis, it should be expanded or corrected as subsequent Satanists see fit, not treated as the final word on the Nekalah.

The Ninth Key describes a seven-stage initiation process for Tenebrous sorcerers, utilizing planetary and alchemical symbolism similar to O9A's. The aim of this is to uphold the spirit of O9A's conception of initiation without insisting on the most daunting specifics of what O9A prescribes. Tenebrous Satanism asserts that there are many ways by which a sorcerer can advance Satan's cause — or as O9A calls this, "create aeonic change" or "advance the Sinister Dialectic."[3] Initiation should, therefore, be flexible. At the same time, though, Tenebrous Satanism also insists, in agreement with O9A, that initiation should be challenging, for it is only through adversity that the strength, willpower, and self-honesty of the adept can be developed. It is through the undertaking of such physical, mental, emotional, and social challenges as the Ninth Key proposes that the Tenebrous sorcerer evolves these qualities to the utmost extent.

The occult methods described in the five Keys of Praxis are not obligatory if one is to identify as a Tenebrous Satanist. Tenebrous Satanism does not exclude those who subscribe to the exoteric elements of the Creed, yet lack interest in its esoteric elements. There is room for both kinds of adherent — the secular Satanist and the witch/sorcerer — under its banner.

There is also an understanding within Tenebrous Satanism that many people are simply not cut out to be Satanists. We respect the paths that such people walk, so long as said paths do not intrude prohibitively on our own. It is our belief that all people, as beings of spirit-in-flesh, are capable of some degree of valid perception of spirit. At the same time, though, the acausal senses of all human beings — ourselves included — are always somewhat occluded by the limitations of the flesh. Hence, although Tenebrous Satanism often harshly disagrees with other creeds, it is capable of appreciating how such creeds arise as valid reactions to the tragedies of mortal existence. The fruit of such understanding is empathy, which urges the rejection of ignorantly hateful rhetoric against individual members of any religion. Accordingly, the adversarial hostility of Tenebrous Satanism is directed solely toward the *dogmas* that keep human beings in chains. It is *not* aimed at those individuals who have been manacled — often unwittingly — into ideological slavery.

On the Order of Nine Angles

A final matter to address is the exact relationship between Tenebrous Satanism and O9A. Since few religious organizations can boast as thoroughly negative a reputation as O9A, it is natural to ask two questions. First, in light of Tenebrous Satanism's participation in the same magickal current as O9A, what follows regarding the relationship between these two Satanisms as human institutions? Second, given O9A's negative reputation, why has the author not chosen to look elsewhere for the inspiration for a new Satanic denomination?

Regarding the first question, the author is not now, nor has she ever been, a "member"[4] of O9A, nor is she acquainted with any of O9A's human representatives at the time of writing *Nine Keys of Abyssal Darkness*. The issues of "appropriation" this raises are sure to persist regardless of how many thousands of pages of O9A documents one attests to having read. In light of popular perceptions of O9A as both marginal and dysfunctional, however, such charges seem unworthy of concern. The situation is analogous to others in the history of religion, wherein a heretic arises to reinterpret a creed, extending the parts they perceive as fruitful and abandoning that which they perceive as fruitless. In such endeavors, one does not offer apologies to those who object to one's efforts. If there are deficiencies in the heretic's work, in time they will be corrected by some other heretic, for such is the way of evolution.

As for the second question, the author's own trajectory of spiritual development is such that pretending to have drawn no inspiration from O9A beliefs and practices would constitute an impossible act of intellectual and spiritual dishonesty. The inconvenient reality is that during a time of profound personal and spiritual malaise, O9A's text *Naos*[5] found its way into the author's life, germinating a relationship with the Nekalah and thence inspiring Tenebrous Satanism. O9A was thus an integral influence on Tenebrous Satanism from the beginning. Such circumstances make the author disinclined to occlude the truth in an attempt to make Tenebrous Satanism seem more palatable to readers. It is futile to frame the situation as one in which one should have chosen one's gods better, for the actual circumstances are such that *the gods were the ones who did the choosing,* and not the other way around.

It is undeniable that to be connected with O9A in any way is uncomfortable for the author, a woman of mixed-race heritage and feminist inclinations, who already finds herself barely tolerated in many of today's academic and artistic circles on account of being "not far enough to the left." Nonetheless, the central assertion of the current work is that, in fact, one can wholly reject the aspects of O9A that are hateful, nihilistic, and ultimately self-destructive, while at the same time embracing elements that promote a healthy affirmation of harsh realities, a rejection of mendacity and hypocrisy, and an embrace of transformative self-evolution.

Those willing to approach this work in a constructive manner will discover much therein that is eye-opening — regardless of whether assent or dissent is the audience's final verdict.

Those unwilling to engage thus, lest such engagement violate their dearly held ideological purity, thereby demonstrate their enslavement to the exact mental-spiritual cancer that this book was written to liberate people from.

Notes

[1] The general picture of Satanism presented in the introduction is a composite assembled from such denominations as the Church of Satan, The Satanic Temple, Luciferianism, and The Order of Nine Angles.

[2] The wording of the sixth tenet of the Tenebrous Creed is inspired by the lyrics of the song "Nuclear Alchemy" by Watain. Nor is this the only place in which Tenebrous Satanism draws a degree of inspiration from the Satanic aesthetics of black metal. It should be noted, however, that Tenebrous Satanism condemns the unproductive activities associated with extreme black metal (e.g. church burnings) no less strongly than it condemns the atrocities associated with O9A.

[3] In O9A works, the terms "Sinister Dialectic" and "aeonic change" often appear entangled with other concepts that Tenebrous Satanism rejects. For example, some O9A works classify certain entire civilizations as "old aeon" and proceed to make sweeping generalizations about the supposed lack of value of anything and everything that proceeds from said civilizations. Such an approach obviously lends itself toward intellectually-sloppy essentialism and ethnocentric xenophobia, most commonly in the form of antisemitism. Tenebrous Satanism has no use for this. Our position is that all cultures contain a mixture of progressive and regressive elements — though admittedly in varying proportions — and individuals in our contemporary world will likewise vary due to the constant contact and interaction of different cultures in those individuals' lives, rather than individuals being reducible to their genetics, their nation of birth, etc. We therefore do *not* use such concepts as "aeonic change" with O9A's implication that certain people or cultures are due to be taken out like trash in the imminent future. Rather, when we talk about "Satan's cause" or the "Sinister Dialectic," what we mean is simply a future world in which Satanic goods such as flourishing and self-evolution are more available to Satanists and non-Satanists alike. No one is thus inherently excluded from the "new aeon" envisioned by Tenebrous Satanism. The Second Key spells out more details regarding what such a world would look like in terms of societal trends we would like to see maximized or minimized, the Eighth Key touches upon the same issue in terms of what we believe the Dark Gods would like to see more or less of among humankind, and the Ninth Key's initiation protocol is meant to shape Satanists into the kinds of people who can strive effectively to make such changes a reality.

[4] It is debatable to what extent "membership" in O9A is a meaningful concept. Often one encounters the argument that insofar as O9A has no official leadership or set doctrine, it is more accurately thought of as a movement or subculture than an organization, and as such, it does not in fact have "members." The point, though, is that the author has nothing to do with any existing O9A nexion and has never operated as a participant or associate of any such groups.

[5] In the course of writing *Nine Keys of Abyssal Darkness*, the author has consulted a variety of editions, both print and electronic, of any O9A texts referenced. Additionally, many O9A texts have been published under various pseudonyms. The author has therefore opted to reference O9A texts by their titles only.

The Keys of Doctrine

I

The Just Preference of Earth Over Heaven

> *O earth, how like to Heav'n, if not preferred*
> *More justly, seat worthier of gods, as built*
> *With second thoughts, reforming what was old!*
> *For what god after better worse would build?*
>
> **- Satan in John Milton's *Paradise Lost* (1674)**

> *Eternity is in love with the productions of time.*
>
> **- William Blake, *The Marriage of Heaven and Hell* (1790)**

The first tenet of the Tenebrous Creed states, "Satan is an advocate of the unending Adventure of spirit in the realm of flesh, manifest in life's multitudinous striving within an ever-evolving world." Such a declaration frames Satan positively. Satan stands for an enterprising willingness to explore and advance oneself, an embrace of carnal gratification, and a commitment to live boldly even amid all life's surprises, frustrations, and disappointments.

To ask what "life" is, is to ask a question that every religion must grapple with. Tenebrous Satanism's answer is that *life* — i.e., that which is present in each and every thing that lives — is a *nexion:* a point at which elements and energies of different natures meet and intermingle. One of these elements is *flesh*. It is the causal component of life — i.e., that which is solid, objective, chained within a series of causes and effects, and restricted by the laws of nature. The other element is *spirit*. It is the acausal component of life — i.e., that which is intangible, subjective, self-willed, and beyond the normal limitations of the realm of matter. Each and every individual living being is a nexion of flesh and spirit.

Life itself, meaning now all living beings as a whole, can also be characterized as a nexion, not only in the sense of flesh and spirit coming together, but also in the sense of each individual participating in a web of relationships that connects it with others. The term "world" serves as a shorthand for this grand nexion-of-nexions. The world is a place of "multitudinous striving," wherein its inhabitants experience themselves as distinct individuals and hence potential adversaries. And yet, no being is ever entirely separate from others, for the doings of each part affect the whole. Over time, life's striving produces large-scale changes, and as this process has no end in sight, the result is an ever-evolving world. To acknowledge these inherently adversarial traits of life, meeting the accompanying challenges with a mighty yes instead of a petulant no, is what it means to advocate unending Adventure.

What does all of this have to do with Satan? Reflection upon the mythology of the Adversary reveals a recurring theme of worldliness. The Fallen Angel "falls" by choosing engagement with the world instead of aloofness from it. The most significant tales of adversarial angels in Biblical and apocryphal literature all evince this theme. It can be detected in Christ's encounter in the wilderness, the seduction of Eve, the fall of the Watcher angels, the suffering of Job, and the rebellion of Satan himself.

Such material inspires the Satanist to construe Satan as he who embraces life as it truly is. God, by contrast, is he who condemns life for having failed to live up to his otherworldly standards. Thus does the Satanist perceive Satan as a benevolent figure. At the same time, though, the dark reputation of Satan forbids a peace-and-love romanticization of existence. It is not that life is easy. To the contrary, the Satanist is called to find ways of celebrating life despite its difficulties.

By taking up the name of another religion's villain, Satanism inherently situates itself as an appropriator and reinterpreter of the mythology of that religion. Tenebrous Satanism therefore enters purposefully into deeper engagement with Christianity's narratives than has been typical of the Satanisms of the past. The stories that other Satanic denominations have engaged with only in passing are here examined more thoroughly, so as to bring forward insights either absent or overlooked in previous Satanic thought.

Satan as Lord of This World

> *The devil led him up to a high place and showed him in an instant all the kingdoms of the world. And he said to him, "I will give you all their authority and splendor; it has been given to me, and I can give it to anyone I want to."*
>
> **- Luke 4:5-6**

Tempting has long been a central preoccupation of Satan's. His seduction of Eve, and thence Adam, persuaded humans to doubt God, take pride in themselves, and disobey the divine command. According to Christianity's doctrine of original sin, humans have been cursed with a proclivity for selfishness ever since. It is because everything humans accomplish is stained by self-seeking cupidity that Satan is said to be "Lord of This World." All realization of ambition has its roots in the sin of pride, which breeds disobedience via the will to go one's own way. Against this stands Christ, model of faith and humility, whose rebuke of Satan in the wilderness demonstrates total commitment to the concerns of God, as opposed to an orientation toward "merely" human concerns.[6] A majority of humans fall short of Christ's standard though, some drastically so, as is illustrated vividly by later folklore about ill-fated "pacts" with the Devil for wealth, fame, etc.

To a Satanist, the Lord of This World represents fulfillment — i.e., the granting of desires that are natural for the human being to have, enjoyable in themselves, and conducive to a richer experience of this world in which life unfolds. When such a figure is faced with a would-be savior, is it "temptation" that he proceeds to engage in? Or might it be, rather, the offering of several constructive suggestions:

- "Has it not occurred to you that without material deprivation, there would be less motivation for vicious behavior? And could you not relieve such desperation yourself by making bread from these stones?"

- "Is it not the case that humans are status-driven creatures? And does it not then follow that by possessing status, as per the kingdoms I am offering you, you could vastly increase your ability to influence others for the better?"

- "Many humans are benumbed by mundane difficulties, but could be inspired to a new appreciation for transcendent matters if you were to demonstrate the supernatural to them. Why, then, do you not oblige them by showing them a miracle that proves the existence of angels?"

To reject all of this, as Christ does, is to declare that spirit is too "good" for flesh, and that flesh is therefore obliged to either submit to spirit's demands or get out of its way. Such a dynamic is similar to that between a traditional husband, ostensible head of the family, and the obedient wife who is expected to attend meekly to all of his earthly needs while remaining in his shadow. Forward-thinking people recognize that this is not a good relationship, since it does not promote the equal flourishing of both partners. Satan, in this analogy, is the marriage counselor who challenges the husband: have you considered how your relationship would be improved — for *both* of you — by actually listening to your wife, acknowledging her needs, and generally treating her better?

The Satanist reconsiders the age-old trope of the pact with the Devil along similar lines. Those who enter into such pacts — everyone from desperate peasants to jaded scholars — all tend to have something in common. This "something" is that their flourishing is obstructed by material difficulties — e.g., lack of wealth, status, knowledge, etc. By framing human longings for such things as evil, such stories imply that the better course would have been for the pact-maker to just accept their lack of flourishing, humbly putting up with it on the basis that it is part of God's plan. The damnation of the character on the basis of having taken what action they could — i.e., they chose to make a pact with the Devil — sends a powerfully negative message regarding individual agency.

What would constitute a healthier attitude toward earthly existence? Tenebrous Satanism recognizes that flesh is, by its very nature, a powerful source of needs and wants. So long as spirit dwells within flesh, its flourishing is intertwined with flesh's own. It is therefore both futile and self-destructive to envision these two elements as locked in oppositional conflict. Better by far to conceive of their relationship cooperatively, granting due respect to flesh's demands and desires.

Since the realm of flesh has traditionally been identified with that which is animalistic and instinctual, does it follow that human beings ought to live more like animals? Should we wallow without restraint in all of our "lower" impulses (e.g., food, sex, etc.), forsaking the "higher" (e.g., science, art, etc.)? This does *not* follow, for the crucial reason that human beings are distinguished from animals via the possession of *consciousness*. In an animal that lacks consciousness, spirit's immersion in flesh is total, with the result that instinct runs the entire show at flesh's behest. By contrast, in the conscious human being, flesh is still running the show by default, but now the play is observed by what might be conceptualized as a spectator, a critic, or a director, depending upon the extent to which the individual is able and willing to exercise agency over their existence. Perhaps the director is exceedingly talented and willful, controlling the production with significant creative license. At the same time, though, even the best director is still constrained by the actors, sets, and props available. The script may be creatively ad-libbed, scenes cut or extended, but ultimately one must still put on something recognizable as a play.

The upshot of this parable is that a conscious being is free to seek its own conception of the good, but amid doing so, it ought not to lose sight of the fact that all of humanity's worthy endeavors — even the so-called higher ones — are still grounded in an embodied context. Science is the wellspring of medicine (caring for the flesh) and technology (expanding flesh's capacities). Art, in addition to being a celebration of the physical senses, can expand the mind's horizons, with positive emotions accompanying such expansion precisely because flesh's continued survival is well served by traits such as curiosity and perceptiveness. To frame such activities as sublimation, as if they entail transcendence of the flesh, is to mistake the nature of the endeavor. These are not manifestations of spirit "rising above" flesh but rather the fruit of synergistic cooperation between the two.

The foregoing discussion ought to make plain that Tenebrous Satanism's conception of *flourishing* includes what other Satanic denominations have called "indulgence," yet its conception of the human good does not lie merely in selfish, short-sighted hedonism. The word "flourishing" suggests that the most worthwhile forms of well-being manifest via the sustainable blossoming of inner potential into outer realization.[7] Furthermore, in the natural world, flourishing is as much a property of whole ecosystems as it is of individual creatures. Since humans are themselves creatures of nature, it does not make sense to envision human flourishing as something to be enjoyed by atomized individuals in isolation from one another — contra the every-person-for-themselves mentality that past Satanisms have often espoused.

Lest the preceding point be taken too far, we are *not* saying that flourishing should be conceptualized in *wholly* altruistic terms. Since nature is a place of limited resources, it is justifiable to strive first and foremost on behalf of oneself and one's loved ones. What one must instead recognize is that flourishing entails both a degree of rational self-centeredness and a degree of limited altruism. A healthy balance between these competing demands can be maintained only so long as the realm of flesh is correctly understood both as a place in which trade-offs must always be negotiated, and a state wherein no man is an island.

Through his tempting, the Lord of This World shines a spotlight upon flesh's needs, wants, and limitations. What he thus offers is honest insight into flesh's situation, without which flourishing is impossible to pursue. He is a chastiser of those who demand that spirit always be put first and flesh last. Instead, he insists that we show the vehicle of our earthly existence the appreciation that it justly deserves.

Satan as Cunning Serpent

> *"You will not certainly die," the serpent said to the woman. "For God knows that when you eat from it your eyes will be opened, and you will be like unto God, knowing good and evil." When the woman saw that the fruit of the tree was good for food and pleasing to the eye, and also desirable for gaining wisdom, she took some and ate it.*
>
> **- Genesis 3:4-6**

Eve's attraction to the aesthetic qualities of the forbidden fruit suggests an element of pure sensory enjoyment in her defiance of God's command. But even more evident in the Eden story is Eve's ambition to improve upon her current situation. In Milton's *Paradise Lost*, Eve observes that "good unknown, sure is not had, or had and yet unknown, is as not had at all."[8] These words suggest that by acquiring wisdom, she stands to attain power that she did not previously possess and to take on a greater share of divinity than is currently within her reach. Seeing in this yearning a rejection of God's own divinity via the proud elevation of oneself in God's place, Christianity labels Eve's actions evil.

As Eve's tempter, Genesis characterizes Satan as an encourager of rebellion, enticing humans to aspire to a higher position than their originally allotted rung on the ladder of being. Such deviation from the divine will constitutes "sin" on the supposed basis that God, being omniscient and omnibenevolent, has built a particular order into the world, which humans are obliged to adhere to for their own good. Having observed how such beliefs are used to prop up unjust social and political hierarchies, however, the Satanist is unconvinced by such notions of providence. A cynical eye sees in the Eden story a reinforcement of the status quo: by showing how ambition and initiative-taking lead to disaster, Genesis discourages would-be risk-takers from bold action.

Against such staid conservatism, Satanism does not condemn Eve for her understandable desires for self-advancement. Rather, it celebrates her boundary-shattering. And by interpreting matters thus, it asserts that Satan ought not to be demonized for teaching critical thinking to a naked, willful thought-slave.[9] God, one could argue, is guilty of thwarting human flourishing by insisting that humans stay in their place instead of striving for higher.[10] Satan, on the other hand, promotes human flourishing, opening the way to new pleasures and expanded horizons for Eve.

When it comes to flourishing, what does the Cunning Serpent represent that is distinct from the Lord of This World? The difference between these characterizations lies in the shift from an emphasis on the flesh to an acknowledgment of the spirit. While mainline denominations have conceptualized Satanism as a religion purely of the flesh, such is not the position of Tenebrous Satanism. We assert instead that life is a nexion of flesh *and* spirit. The two are distinguished from one another by what they seek out of their interrelationship. Flesh seeks flourishing, manifest in satisfaction and pleasure, whereas spirit seeks *evolution*, manifest in self-realization and experiences of novelty. Spirit's distinctive nature is evident in reason's attempts to understand the world and oneself, even when this endeavor brings unhappiness. It is also evident in the exuberant arising of more diverse and complex organisms over the course of time, as if this variety were an inherent good in and of itself. On such fronts, an intellectually honest person must acknowledge that something beyond a mere desire for comfortable gratification is at work. Flesh, though a source of pleasure and fulfillment, is also a locus of complacency. Spirit, by contrast, strives always toward complacency's overthrow.

Spirit is, in short, that which seeks *to do ever more* through the medium of flesh, despite the limitations inherent to that medium. It follows that spirit has an inherently transgressive element to it — an element which Eve's disobedience evokes. Tenebrous Satanism accordingly construes Satan not only as a promoter of fleshly enjoyment but also as a proponent of spirit's right to the sovereign pursuit of its own evolution. By opening Eve's eyes to a previously unimagined horizon of personal godhood, Satan evinces both a compassionate desire for human beings to be given the chance to realize their lofty potential and righteous indignation at God's unjust opposition to human apotheosis.[11]

Ultimately, the Cunning Serpent can be conceptualized equally as an external encourager of human striving, and as that element within the individual that *wants ever more*. Either way, spirit is drawn to flesh on account of the possibility of achievements and experiences that can only be had thereby, and Satan embraces and defends this orientation of spirit's. He defies those who would presume to dictate who is or isn't allowed to aspire to divinity. Instead, Satan asserts that it is our right to seek our own self-advancement, and that we should permit no arbitrary tyrant — whether heavenly, or earthly — to obstruct our destiny.

Satan as Fallen Angel

> *And it came to pass when the children of men had multiplied that in those days were born unto them beautiful and comely daughters. And the angels, the children of the heaven, saw and lusted after them, and said to one another: "Come, let us choose us wives from among the children of men and beget us children."... and each chose for himself one, and they began to go in unto them and to defile themselves with them, and they taught them charms and enchantments...*
>
> **- 1 Enoch, Book of the Watchers, 6:1-3 & 7:1-2**

1 Enoch is not among the canonical books of the Bible for a majority of Christians, but many in the early days of the religion were familiar with it. The Book of the Watchers, a subsection of 1 Enoch, stars

two angelic adversaries — i.e., two "satans." One is Semjaza, who multiplies the Watchers' sins by binding all of them to act upon their lust together. The other is Azazel, who teaches humans to make weapons and cosmetics, stirring up the stereotypical manifestations of pride among both men (ambition) and women (vanity). Between the cultural changes that angelic instruction produces and angel-human unions producing the Nephilim — a race of giants whose appetites lay waste to the land — creation is so distorted that God must use the Flood to wipe the slate clean. Not unlike Genesis, 1 Enoch presents knowledge as the culprit behind this disaster: both the "know-how" that the Watchers gifted to humans and "knowing" in the sexual sense.

From a Satanic perspective, the original Christian interpretation of the story of the Watchers reiterates the same themes as Genesis but makes them more explicit and takes them further. God's condemnation of the angels for having "defiled" themselves suggests a devaluation of nature generally, sexuality specifically, and women as an embodiment of these two things. Thus is the flesh denigrated. At the same time, one notices that even as 1 Enoch decries the Watchers' sharing of knowledge with their wives, Enoch himself is portrayed asking the angels questions and receiving this knowledge from them without being castigated for his curiosity.[12] His enlightenment, however, is framed positively, because his intent is to passively contemplate God's creation instead of applying his knowledge toward his own worldly advancement. Such an attitude of "knowledge is only a good thing if you don't actually use it" forbids humans from self-empowerment. Thus is the spirit put in chains.

Consider, on the other hand, how the story alters when the Satanist takes the Watchers' descent not as a degradation of the heavenly but as an elevation of the earthly. By ceasing to merely watch and instead descending to make their home among humans, the Watchers act as muses, providing impetus to humanity's innovative capacities. The angel-human sex act symbolizes both the happy mingling of spirit and flesh and the constructive transformation of pure, disembodied knowledge into tangible gains in quality of life. Condemnation is replaced with honor for the women, for they are the portal through which the wholly new comes into the world: new life, new ways of thinking, new ambitions. As for the Nephilim, one may recall Genesis 6:4's glossing of this term as "mighty men that were of old, the men of renown." 1 Enoch's monstrous presentation is then suggestive of the fear with which cowards who cling to past orthodoxies so often greet the intellectual "giants" who move the world forward.

Why engage in depth with this story when it is less well known than the preceding and covers many of the same themes? Whereas Genesis illustrates an encounter between Satan and human, 1 Enoch illustrates an encounter between *satans* and *humans*. The social horizon of the latter story enables it to speak to a reality beyond flesh and spirit in themselves: the *world* in which their interaction unfolds. When offered the choice between a transcendent, ahistorical existence unconnected to the web of life and an embodied, temporal existence among nature's many creatures, the Watchers judged the latter preferable — so much so that they were willing to sacrifice their portion of eternity in order to realize this experience. The world, as grand nexion-of-nexions, is above all a zone of interdependence. And the Fallen Angel is he who affirms the fulfillment to be had within this zone, by choosing to enter into both physical and intellectual relationships with the world's inhabitants.

To define material existence as a "zone of interdependence" is a move admittedly contrary to much Satanic discourse of the past. Amid emphasizing individual attainment and personal sovereignty, the Satanisms of yesteryear typically reject any such collective-oriented perspective. Tenebrous Satanism contends, however, that just as every other religion attempts to deny aspects of reality that it dislikes, the Ayn Randian-individualist stream of Satanism is guilty of fleeing from the facts that life itself is a place of interconnection and that human beings are fundamentally social animals. Failure to recognize these realities reduces Satanism to a breeding ground for solipsistic narcissists.

Acknowledging the world as a place of interdependence, on the other hand, not only constitutes an honest admission but also enables a more sophisticated take on Satanism's positive valuation of knowledge. Often though the proverb "knowledge is power" is invoked, Tenebrous Satanism contends that it does not actually speak to the real heart of what knowledge is and why it matters. Knowledge takes chaos, names its elements, puts them into *relationship* to one another, and unifies this whole under an order that is both satisfying to contemplate and useful to apply. This putting-into-relationship can be used to attain power but can also be applied toward many other purposes, such as communion with others via the alleviation of ignorance. It follows that knowledge is a key contributor to flourishing — and that it makes its contribution specifically by enabling us to bring disparate things, ideas, people, etc.

into constructive relationship with one another. Small wonder, then, that the Watchers should decide knowledge would be better shared with the denizens of the earth than reserved for isolated, otherworldly beings up in the heavens.

The Fallen Angel is, in summary, the very embodiment of "eternity in love with the productions of time." Said love is shown both via the honoring of the flesh and the liberation of the spirit. The fruits of this love include appreciation for knowledge, for the earth, and for one's fellow beings. Only amid such an awareness of a shared horizon, built upon an acknowledgment of the world's interdependent nature, can such Satanic goods as self-determination and self-evolution take a constructive form.

Satan as Accuser

> *Then the Lord said to Satan, "Have you considered my servant Job? There is no one on earth like him; he is blameless and upright, a man who fears God and shuns evil. And he still maintains his integrity, though you incited me against him to ruin him without any reason."*
>
> **- Book of Job 2:3**

The Book of Job is challenging for both Christians and Satanists. The issue for Christians is that Satan incites God to visit catastrophe upon his faithful servant merely to make a point. God's willingness to enter into this wager is hard to reconcile with him being infinitely just. The issue for Satanists, on the other hand, is that Job's Satan does not appear to be "fallen." He freely visits Heaven and obeys God's orders, first ruining Job's prosperity but sparing his health, then ruining Job's health but sparing his life. This positions him as an adversary to Job, but *not* to God. Moreover, Job's Satan acts in a manner that obviously clashes with the picture we previously painted of a benevolent promoter of earthly enjoyment. What, then, can we gain by engaging with this portrayal?

Of central Satanic interest in the Book of Job is the role that Satan plays in the story as Accuser. The accusation that Satan makes openly is that Job is only loyal to God because his life is easy. One could argue, however, that this is only the surface accusation. Beneath it lurks a more profound accusation that Satan makes, not to God against Job, but to the reader against God: the pattern of fortune and misfortune that human beings actually observe in the world contradicts the claim of God justly rewarding good and punishing evil. God cannot, in fact, be relied upon to deal with us in a manner we recognize as "fair." God's willingness to let Satan ruin Job's life demonstrates the validity of the accusation, since that arbitrary act against an undeserving person is itself a failure of justice.

The Accuser may thus be conceptualized as "he who reveals that which is unpleasant to know but is nonetheless how things are." One such unwelcome truth is that the universe does not, in fact, present us with evidence that a just, good God is behind it — and it is both insulting to our intelligence and morally bankrupt to pretend otherwise. What does the universe present us with instead? The optimistic-sounding story of the preceding sections — pursuit of flourishing as the good of flesh, and ever-greater freedom as the good of spirit — must be balanced against a recognition that life is also a place of strife and suffering. Spirit's coming into relationship with flesh, and enfleshed beings' coming into relationship with one another, are both attended by a variety of *Perils*. This causes spirit's proclivity toward the flesh to take on a tragic aspect.

The Sixth Key provides a far more comprehensive account of what exactly Tenebrous Satanism means by "Perils." The following points will suffice, however, as a brief summary of what our use of the term encompasses:

- *Limits of attainable knowledge* due to having to contend with imperfections of the senses, poor regulation of emotions, the fragility of sanity, and the interruption of introspection by external demands.

- *The less-than-purely-rational nature of the human mind,* as evidenced by counterproductive fixation on dissatisfaction, the pretending-away of problems, resentment of that which violates expectations, and the elusiveness of unbiased judgment.

- *Refusal to acknowledge the presence of spirit in beings of flesh other than oneself,* manifest in soulless conformity among "us," excessive hostility toward "them," and willful denial of the vulnerability experienced by all living beings.

- *The difficulties of living alongside others in a world of material limitations,* wherein sociality is ever threatened by unsustainable selfishness, unequal distribution of resources, the fomenting of resentment, and unrealistic utopian impositions.

- *Inability to accept the impermanence that haunts all flesh,* manifest in dysfunctional attachment to objects, neurotic fretting about sexuality, futile attempts to deny death, and underestimation of the degree of disciplined effort that living well requires.

- *The challenges of striking a healthy balance between the contrasting elements that define life.* Relevant dualities include order versus chaos, individual versus collective, and reason versus emotion. A multiplicity of other faculties and virtues also clash, however, even as they all make valid claims upon human attention.

- *A demand for happy stories* in an attempt to erase existence's "wrongs" and the persecution of dissenters to such stories due to the alternative — honest confrontation with Darkness — seeming unbearable.

Some Perils acknowledged by Tenebrous Satanism echo claims of well-known ascetic faiths, such as Buddhism. However, when right-hand-path religions put forward such insights, the conclusion they typically draw is "this is why humans need to avoid investing in the world." The Satanist, by contrast, acknowledges the same unpleasant realities, only to retort, "yes, I *know* life has these less-than-ideal features — and yet, I *still* commit myself to this-worldly pursuits of flourishing and self-evolution!" This shows that an enumeration of life's Perils need not lead to devaluation of existence. In fact, it is often those who refuse to acknowledge these darker aspects of life that turn out to be the life-deniers — as the Second Key will explain in detail.

In acknowledging life's Perils, Tenebrous Satanism rebukes both the venomously desire-hating priest and the self-indulgent libertine sleepwalking into self-destruction; both the privileged hypocrite and the embittered victim whose identity revolves wholly around resentment; both the deluded utopian who schemes to fix everything and the blinkered conservative who sees nothing in need of being fixed. It particularly rebukes anyone who thinks, as Job's friends did, that one has merely to do all the right things in order for life to turn out okay. It instead insists — just as Satan revealed to Job — that life is rife with unfairness.

It follows that one ought not to be too quick to blame victims for what they suffer, nor to credit oneself overmuch for accomplishments that lucky circumstances helped to facilitate. To point this out is neither a submission to Christian humility nor a subscription to fashionable "privilege-checking." It is rather the essence of wisdom grounded in realism. Tenebrous Satanism asserts that empathy is a fit virtue for Satanism, not for the sake of trying to pass as a "normal," "respectable" religion, but because the arrogant refusal to extend empathy is rooted in a hubristic, counterproductive denial of human vulnerability. Satanists ought not to stoop to the same kinds of childish flights from reality that they are so quick to condemn whenever other religions behave thus.

Amid such talk, one should not lose sight of the optimistic orientation that Tenebrous Satanism adopts toward the prospects of flesh's flourishing and spirit's self-evolution. At the same time, though, ours is not a religion that looks at life through rose-colored glasses. By continuing to affirm life even while acknowledging its many Perils, the Tenebrous Satanist rises to the very challenge with which Satan confronted Job: to affirm one's religious commitments even amid the dark implications that attend them, rather than merely thinking oneself committed due to naivety about what true commitment demands.

Satan as Rebel Against God

> How you have *fallen* from heaven, morning star, son of the dawn... You said in your heart, "I will ascend to the heavens; I will raise my throne above the stars of God... I will make myself like the Most High."
>
> - Isaiah 14:12-14

> Then another sign appeared in heaven: an enormous red dragon with seven heads and ten horns and seven *crowns* on its heads. Its tail swept a third of the stars out of the sky and flung them to the earth... Then, war broke out in heaven...

- **Revelation 12:3-7**

The final Satanic narrative worth reflecting upon is the most primordial: Satan's fall from Heaven. The majority Christian view likens Satan's rebellion to that of an arrogant king who oversteps his authority. Satan, the story goes, was created as the most excellent of God's creatures, but fell from grace on account of choosing his own excellence over God's excellence. This choice is "evil," and the pride that drove it "sinful," on the assumption that the finite is inferior to the infinite — i.e., that which is *excellent but merely a creature* ought to submit to the higher power and better judgment of that which is *most excellent on account of being the Creator*. Negative attributions of Satan's, such as Prince of Darkness, Ruler of Hell, etc. suggest that by rebelling against the only "true" power behind the universe, Satan in effect chose a worthless nothingness. Dante's depiction of Lucifer as a once-heavenly being now reduced to a moribund mass of impotence is an especially vivid illustration of this idea.[13]

Positive takes on Satan's rebellion typically proceed by framing the values at stake differently from how Christianity frames them. For example, instead of a foolish preference for the limited over the ultimate, Satan sides with indulgence against restraint, or critical thinking against blind faith, or freedom against tyranny. All these oppositions are valid articulations of key Satanic values. Nonetheless, Tenebrous Satanism's approach does not proceed along such lines. We maintain the theological framing of the story as a choice of creature over Creator — but with reversed conclusions as to who is fittest to rule the universe.

On this front, consider: is an infinite Creator truly best qualified to rule over a Creation that, being finite, has needs and limitations foreign to its Creator — needs graspable in principle via the Creator's omniscience, yet nonetheless alien to the Creator's lived experience as an omnipotent being? Might one plausibly suggest instead that the excellent creature may, from its position *within* creation, be better able to appreciate all the comedies and tragedies that arise from the limitations of existence? In contrast, does it not seem that the Creator, judging the world from a distant and otherworldly perspective, is prone to holding creation up to impossible standards? Many a Satanist-to-be rejects Christianity precisely because of the alarmingly large number of people it damns to eternal hellfire over seemingly petty transgressions.

In accord with these insights, Tenebrous Satanism proposes the following metaphysical scenario: despite the Perils inherent to life, spirit remains ever-desirous of the flesh; life's Perils are, at the same time, often traumatic to witness or experience; as a result of said trauma, living beings sometimes fall into despair-driven denial about the pro-flesh imperative that drives spirit. This leads to such beings misperceiving incarnation as a fall into corruption instead of an embrace of *Adventure*. The vision of the gods, angels, etc. of the right-hand path has become distorted in this way, producing their deluded belief that they must "save" spirit from flesh. In the eyes of such beings, spirit is a drug addict who must be rescued from compulsively self-destructive habits. Opposing such a view, however, there exist other spirits who remain consciously and willfully flesh-oriented. Their contention is that spirit is drawn toward life as inexorably as a person breathes. In their eyes, the right-hand path is thence guilty of suffocating spirit via futile, counterproductive attempts to oppose spirit's actual inmost inclinations. It is with adversarial, Adventurous spirits of this sort that Tenebrous Satanism allies itself.

The matters to which the preceding paragraph alludes are articulated in greater detail in the Fourth Key. The central focus at present, though, is the meaning of "Adventure." An adventure is an endeavor that entails some manner of ordeal — e.g., leaving familiar settings, going outside of one's comfort zone, new experiences, surprises, dangers, etc. At the same time, it is an endeavor willingly undertaken, for the sake of some payoff that proceeds from risk-taking. The acquisition of resources, power, knowledge, personal growth, and the gaining of novel experience in and of itself are all examples of adventure's prospective rewards.

In conceiving of life in terms of Adventure, Tenebrous Satanism asserts that existence in the world of flesh is not a mistake to be undone, a punishment to be endured, nor otherwise to be despised or lamented. Granted, it may often seem like this to the beings currently enduring it, given the Perils they must contend with. Tenebrous Satanism nonetheless insists that within every living being is something that *chooses* fleshly existence. This is evident in the ardor with which living things strive to survive and reproduce and the typical reluctance of human beings — even downcast and weary ones — to intentionally terminate their own existence or that of their loved ones. This obstinate hunger for more existence may at times feel, to the suffering living being, like an inscrutable alien force that coerces them into doing things that they neither understand nor freely consent to. And yet, at the point at which one faces this force honestly, reconciles with it, and owns it as the core of one's innermost self, one discovers that in fact it is *oneself* who chooses flesh again and again, not in spite of life's Perils, but *because* such challenges force spirit's evolution into ever new and more complex forms. What the right-hand path conceptualizes as seduction by an external tempter, the Sinister Path recognizes as the embrace of the true will of one's inmost self.

Leaving aside for now the question of whether "God" exists as an actual acausal being, there is a literary-philosophical level on which Tenebrous Satanism understands "God" and "Satan" as metaphorical representatives of two opposed perspectives on spirit's Adventure. "God" is he who sees only evil and suffering in life's prospects. He therefore decides that the world ought to be destroyed and replaced with something more ideal, as the Book of Revelation so vividly illustrates. Judging that things are only good insofar as they conform to his own plans, God ultimately rejects that which is a prerequisite for Adventure: adversity. "Satan," by contrast, is he who turns away, unimpressed, from the eternal peace that God idealizes. To his way of thinking, the "lower" world of change is in fact superior to the "upper" world of stasis. For one thing, in its ever "reforming what was old," it offers infinitely more challenge and reward than any finished state of so-called perfection ever could!

Satan's rebellion thus proclaims: let there be no plan from the Creator to regulate creation, but instead as many plans as there are creatures; in place of eternal children remaining unchanged within their unspoiled garden, let there be the chaotic multitude who is humanity; above all, let there be *adversity*, for without it, there is no Adventure. Thus, Satan is neither Dante's ruined hulk who perversely chose emptiness over plenitude, nor a tyrant-in-waiting whose only ambition is to replace God, his rival. Instead, the Rebel Against God is he who would rather reign in hell than serve in heaven: the many-headed dragon that refuses to assent quietly to a bland eternity. Instead, Satan embraces ongoing tribulation as the proving-ground of the perpetual Adversary.

Summary

Rather than evoke only Satan's fall or Eden's serpent, and these only in passing, Tenebrous Satanism's conception of Satan draws upon a broader, more engaged reading of Biblical and apocryphal accounts of adversarial angels. Such an exercise reveals five main themes:

- The *Lord of This World* promotes flesh's flourishing.
- The *Cunning Serpent* encourages spirit's self-evolution.
- The *Fallen Angel* forsakes heaven to participate in worldliness.
- The *Accuser* reveals the harsh, Perilous realities of life.
- The *Rebel* rallies the Adventurous against tyranny and stagnancy.

In advancing a substantial case for Satan as a positive force, Tenebrous Satanism agrees with other forms of Satanism on a variety of points. It affirms that all things of this world, from the lowest animalistic level to the highest intellectual one, are meant to be enjoyed. It calls upon humans to take bold action toward self-actualization, rather than merely conforming to others' expectations. It recognizes knowledge as worthy of pursuit, both for the benefits it yields and as a good in and of itself. It eschews comforting delusions, preferring instead to openly acknowledge difficult aspects of our existence. And it validates striving for the fullest measure of self-deification a human being can achieve, in defiance of right-hand-path naysaying. In all of these matters, Tenebrous Satanism demonstrates a solid continuity with what has been recognized as Satanism up to this point in time.

How does Tenebrous Satanism nonetheless differ from other denominations? It is clearer and more overtly constructive with regard to what is meant, and what is not meant, by the pursuit of earthly enjoyment. It more explicitly enshrines self-evolution and thereby discourages a too-complacent conception of "indulgence." It frames the human condition in a way that rules out not only the self-abnegating universalism of right-hand-path religions but also the self-absorbed narcissism of Satanism's antisocial past incarnations. It encourages deeper introspection regarding what we are justified in taking credit for, versus what we must honestly acknowledge as beyond us, toward the end of fostering greater self-awareness. And it upholds a steadfast preference for earth over heaven, taking seriously that this world is our home without having to rule out a meaningful spiritual horizon as part of that stance.

Although the differences between Tenebrous Satanism and other denominations are not insignificant, Tenebrous Satanism does not contend that other forms of Satanism are "not true Satanism." Similar core values are evident among all forms of Satanism, even if the emphases, applications, and implications of these are interpreted differently. Tenebrous Satanism therefore aspires toward constructive engagement between Satanists of all stripes, regardless of where similarities end and differences begin. Adversarial though the left-hand path may be, much bickering that occurs between Satanic denominations has more to do with petty competitions for status and legitimacy than it does with any truly profound differences in values. More constructive and extensive forms of "creative strife" could be unleashed upon the complacent herd if Satanists were to pay as much heed to the fronts we can cooperate on as to the fronts on which we disagree.

We thus hope that the First Key will inspire any Satanist who reads it to take a deeper interest in the narrative portrayal of the adversarial angel and to reflect fruitfully upon the values that both he and we stand for.

Notes

[6] See Matthew 16:23.

[7] The First Key's conception of flourishing — i.e. as a form of well-being oriented toward the long term, manifesting on both individual and collective levels — is strongly influenced by the book *Becoming Divine: Towards a Feminist Philosophy of Religion* by Grace Jantzen (1999). Although Jantzen's focus is on what a feminist perspective can offer Christianity, her advocacy of a spirituality that is this-worldly instead of otherworldly has long struck the author of the current work as being in better accord with the ideals of Satanism than it is with much of the Christian tradition. One may also observe a rather shocking degree of similarity between Jantzen's arguments and arguments made by purported O9A founder David Myatt in his later work, *Understanding and Rejecting Extremism: A Very Strange Peregrination* (2013). Both thinkers assert that human life has been negatively impacted by fixation upon simplistic ideological abstractions, "macho" individualism, and the romanticization of violence. Furthermore, both suggest we should instead adopt an ethos that grapples honestly with real-world complexities, demonstrates awareness of interdependence, and emphasizes expansive empathy. It is just that Jantzen calls the problem "masculinist values"

and the solution "feminist values," while Myatt calls the problem "masculous values" and the solution "muliebral values" — "muliebris" being Latin for "of women." A significant intellectual driver behind the formulation of Tenebrous Satanism is the conviction that it is, in fact, possible to reconcile these shared insights of Myatt and Jantzen with something that can still meaningfully be called "Satanism."

[8] John Milton, *Paradise Lost* (1674), Book IX, lines 756-7.

[9] This sentence paraphrases one of the most popular versions of the internet meme known as "Good Guy Satan."

[10] This dynamic is also illustrated in the Bible in the story of the Tower of Babel, Genesis 11:1-9.

[11] This sort of Promethean take on Satan's motives finds much support in the writings of Percy Bysshe Shelley, William Blake, and other such proto-Satanists of the Romantic movement.

[12] See especially 1 Enoch 25:1-7.

[13] As described in Canto 34 of Dante's *Inferno* (1472).

II

Insidious Destroyers of Life

> *Let me repeat: this depressing and contagious instinct stands against all those instincts which work for the preservation and enhancement of life... Of course, one doesn't say 'extinction': one says 'the other world,' or 'God,' or 'the true life,' or Nirvana, salvation, blessedness... This innocent rhetoric, from the realm of religious-ethical balderdash, appears a good deal less innocent when one reflects upon the tendency it conceals beneath sublime words: the tendency to destroy life.*
>
> **- Friedrich Nietzsche, *The Antichrist* (1895)**

The name "Satan," meaning accuser or adversary, indicates someone who is against something. But what exactly is Satan against? The traditional answers are God, Jesus Christ, Christianity. Consider, however, that Christianity includes everything from the stodgy hierarchy of the Catholic Church to the fragmented diversity of Protestantism, and from conservative fundamentalism to Marxist liberation theology. Such diversity raises the question, is what Satan opposes present wherever Christianity is? Or does it lie in something distinct from Christianity itself? The answers to these questions are sure to have implications regarding what other religions and ideologies Satanists ought to stand against.

The second tenet of the Tenebrous Creed states, "Satan is an adversary of any dogma that denies or distorts the realm of flesh, for such dogmas are insidious destroyers of life." The Creed here identifies a thing Satanism counts as its foe (dogma), on the basis that said thing operates in a particular fashion (denial and distortion of the flesh), producing negative consequences (insidious destruction of life). The term "dogma" means "a way of thinking that is professed and enacted in an unquestioningly strict, extreme manner." Certain thought patterns, though useful and beneficial to humans in moderation, lead to harm when the pattern itself is raised to the status of an idol and that idol worshipped at the expense of honest acknowledgment of reality. Tenebrous Satanism calls for such idols to be torn down. Often, they present themselves as benevolent on the surface and in the short term. Ultimately, though, they impede flourishing and discourage self-evolution.

What must be emphasized at the outset is that in opposing dogma, it is *pernicious beliefs and practices* that Tenebrous Satanism sets itself against. Our quarrel is not with whatever initially constructive human impulses metastasized into dogma. Nor is it with human beings merely because they belong to a group that subscribes to a dogmatic ideology. When a person identifies themselves by a group's label, this may indicate dogmatic commitment, but could also indicate just a desire for social belonging or an association of convenience. It might even indicate nothing more than an accident of birth. Therefore, harboring negative attitudes toward everyone in a single group — to assert, for instance, that the Moral Majority crusader, the hip gay pastor and the old lady who volunteers at the charity shop are all equally "destroyers of life" on account of being Christians — reveals an intellectual laziness that is beneath the Satanist.

It follows that, despite Satan being Christ's mythological antagonist, Tenebrous Satanism sees neither individual Christians nor Christianity itself as the enemy. Rather, the challenge we grapple with is that nearly every ideology puts forward both something adaptive and something maladaptive. Typically, the dysfunctional component springs from a refusal to acknowledge the world as it really is. This failure to grapple adequately with life's Perils tends, in turn, to further aggravate dogmatists' alienation from reality. Thus, dogma is pernicious in part because it is self-perpetuating.

To call out the dogmatic element of an ideology is not necessarily to assert that such dogma is the only, the worst, or the most pressing evil that plagues humanity. The claim, rather, is that what harms dogma does cause run wider and deeper than is often recognized — hence the adjective "insidious." And since said harms involve a subversion of much that Satanism holds dear, the matter is one that the Satanist ought to attend to.

The central task of the Second Key is to propose a vocabulary by which we may distinguish specific adaptive and maladaptive components of human thought patterns. This will help enable us to identify where dogma is ascendant today — the first step toward resisting its impositions.

Three human thought patterns

The thought patterns described below are each variants of a fundamental duality: beneficial vs. harmful. Although human beings translate this duality into evaluative terms that are meaningless in a non-human context (e.g., good vs. evil), the duality itself is one that is found within nature via the fact that there is no organism that finds all circumstances equally supportive of its flourishing. Every organism has environments in which it thrives, and others in which it cannot survive even briefly; there is the food by which an organism sustains itself, and the threat of becoming the food of another organism; there are allies and resources on one side, enemies and obstacles on the other. Every enfleshed being must contend with such Perils. Therefore, no enfleshed being can afford not to distinguish the beneficial from the harmful.

Amid the instinctually driven behavior of animals, "good" can only mean something like "supportive of the individual animal's flourishing." "Evil," in turn, means the opposite — if, indeed, it means anything at all in this pre-conscious, amoral context. Conscious beings, however, manifest greater range and sophistication in their perception of beneficial vs. harmful. This is because consciousness roams over the past and future as well as the present. As consciousness reviews the past and anticipates the future, striving always to improve on one's flourishing, it tends to translate the blunt immediacy of beneficial vs. harmful into other categories that are less concrete and present-oriented, more abstract and future-oriented. "Good" becomes that which *promises* beneficence, and "evil" that which *threatens* harm.

Consciousness thereby attempts to provide the organism with an advantage. Knowing the "good" empowers one to seek out that which will be beneficial instead of waiting passively for it to cross one's path. Knowing "evil" enables one to avoid potential harm before it can become actual. The limitation of these sorts of mental constructions, however, is that the label "good" does not always wind up accurately identifying that which is beneficial. Nor does the label "evil" always correspond to that which causes harm. Pursuing something the brain's algorithms have labeled "good" can lead to outcomes that are not beneficial, such as disappointment and squandered energy. And attempting to fend off what one believes to be "evil" can *cause* harms, such as needless anxiety or overreaction.

Humans tend to downplay such limitations, defending their mental constructions out of a sense that a flawed system is better than no system. This prevents people from recognizing when their thought patterns have degenerated into something tooled more toward feeling in control and feeling good about themselves than toward actual harm prevention and benefit pursuit. Such self-delusion culminates most destructively when flesh itself is declared "evil." When human beings fall under the spell of such a pattern, they wind up at war with themselves and against existence itself. At the same time, self-righteousness prevents them from seeing how their attempts to fight supposed evil are in fact producing actual harm.

Tenebrous Satanism identifies three thought patterns according to which the human mind constructs "good vs. evil." In the first, *order* is good, and *chaos* is evil; in the second, *truth* is good vs. *falsehood* is evil; in the third, *evolution* is good while *stasis* is evil. We refer to these as the Apollonian, Magian, and Faustian patterns respectively. Each will be unpacked below with regard to their evolutionary warrant, their implications for how we see ourselves and our world, their cultural manifestations, the harms caused when they go awry, and why the pattern tends to persist despite these harms.

Regarding the labels Apollonian, Magian and Faustian, it should be emphasized that although, like the Order of Nine Angles (O9A), Tenebrous Satanism borrows these terms from the work of Oswald Spengler, we define them in a manner that differs significantly both from that of O9A and Spengler himself. For Spengler, each term refers to the collective cultural, racial, and geographical experience of a particular human civilization. Spengler believes that such groups differ from one another in fundamental matters of ethos and aesthetics. It is not unusual for far-right Spengler fans to further play up the racial angle of this schema, simplifying "Magian" into "the Jews" and "Faustian" into "Western White culture." Tenebrous Satanism, by contrast, rejects racial essentialism. It instead uses these terms to highlight patterns that are present in *all* cultures, religions, and ideologies, albeit in varying proportions that can and do change over time. The rationale for this divergent interpretation, and for how it meaningfully reflects Spengler's schema despite being divergent, will be explained below.

The Apollonian pattern: order vs. chaos

The first method of constructing "good vs. evil," *order vs. chaos*, is the most ancient. Many creatures can be observed behaving in a manner that reflects this pattern, however unconsciously. For instance, many organisms will freeze if suddenly taken from their familiar environment and placed into a strange one. Evolution favors this behavior, since in its familiar environment, the organism knows where to find food, what is dangerous, etc. In a new environment, on the other hand, these are all unknowns. It is good for one's survival and flourishing to know what is what — i.e., order — whereas amid unknowns — i.e., chaos — there is a higher risk of danger and death. It is not difficult to imagine this way of looking at things coming naturally to the humans of ancient times. But it comes no less naturally to humans of today, since humans never ceased being part of nature, alienated from it though many may be.

Order vs. chaos thinking tends to orient one toward the visible and the concrete, since surfaces can be experienced in a more immediate way than that which lies beneath surfaces. Accordingly, the order vs. chaos pattern identifies and classifies the elements that make up the world based on what it sees and accompanies this schema with rules as to how one ought to act toward each category. The sum total of this mental system is order, while anything not yet assimilated into it is chaos. One way that chaos may be dealt with is by expanding order, integrating the new elements one encounters into the realm of that which is known and understood. Another way is to simply acknowledge chaos as that which remains outside of order and is therefore best treated with caution, if not avoided entirely. Either way, the overarching sentiment is that all is well so long as everything has its proper place. Chaos must remain under control, but there is no drive to eliminate every trace of it from existence.

When it comes to implications regarding human beings, two main consequences follow from thinking in terms of order vs. chaos. One is the conceptualization of human happiness in terms of *harmony* — i.e., so long as everyone behaves appropriately, needs are met, and discord is avoided, everything is okay. To an ambitious Satanist, this kind of happiness may sound like mere complacency. But insofar as it is the closest humanity can come to recapturing the primordial oneness with nature that we lost with the gaining of consciousness, one ought not to underestimate its appeal.

The second human consequence of the order vs. chaos pattern stipulates *whose* harmony is of concern. Here, the tendency is to divide humanity into "us" vs. "them." "Our" group's members are held to "our" ways and customs. Other groups have their own ways, which are outside of "our" sphere of concern. The order vs. chaos pattern justifies this selective preoccupation by framing one's own group and its norms as what constitutes order. Strangers and their ways, on the other hand, are of the realm of chaos. Thus, "we" are the upholders of the cosmos through our adherence to the "proper" way of being human.[14] "They," by contrast, are "not quite as human as us;" hence, they are not part of our moral community. As far short of a contemporary celebration of diversity as this mentality may fall, it should nonetheless be recognized as a limited tribalism that does not go so far as to say that different people do not have the right to exist at all. It insists, however, that if they are going to exist, it ought to be "over there," lest "they" adversely impact "our" harmony.

Many features of the lives of ancient cultures suggest the predominance of the order vs. chaos pattern. The benevolence of order manifests in the predictable turn of the seasons, complemented by traditional knowledge regarding the resources that become available as the year goes through its cycle. Order is also manifest in polytheistic conceptualizations of a well-run cosmos in which each department of nature is managed by its own deity. The religious life of such cultures is oriented toward securing this-worldly boons (e.g., bountiful harvests), by performing the correct rituals at the correct times. Different tribes with different customs and gods do clash, primarily over matters of territory and resource access. They are relatively unworried, however, about other people having the "wrong" customs or the "wrong" gods as such. Yes, at times and in certain contexts, they may define themselves in terms of contrasts against these others. But insofar as they believe in an already-existing order behind the world, which they must defer to, they tend not to think it is their place to go around imposing their own idea of order on those who differ from themselves.

A sign that a society has become dogmatically order-demanding and chaos-fearing is the existence of caste systems that dictate what one can and can't do according to lineage, age, or other such factors. Another sign is heteronormativity- i.e., strict demands that men act like men and women like women, rigid regulation of who can mate with who, and the persecution of sexual dissenters. Obnoxious though such developments may be, evolutionary principle dictates that such arrangements would not endure if they did not benefit humans in some way. One can thence observe that such features seem to have persisted because a complacent majority find comfort in knowing their place — their "place," unfortunately, being defined by the ability to point a finger at those who are out of place. Immersion of the individual in the family and the tribe, and the attendant narrowing of occupational and sexual options in accord with social controls, is the price paid for a deepened sense of belonging. To recognize this is not to excuse or ignore the harm that such systems cause. It is simply an acknowledgment that behind many persistent injustices lie misguided attempts to cope with fear of chaos.

Tenebrous Satanism perceives a number of positives that emerge from moderate applications of the order vs. chaos pattern. Societies in which this way of thinking is predominant are often societies whose members have substantial contact with nature. This endows them with a healthy appreciation for this-worldly flourishing, recognition of a web of relationships in which that flourishing unfolds, and pragmatism in dealing with life's Perils.

The deficiency of order vs. chaos thinking, however, lies in its tendency to process individual uniqueness in terms of an outbreak of chaos. Maintenance of harmony is premised upon limitations on acceptable human behavior, and the resulting conservatism is hostile toward self-evolution. The biggest problem with this way of thinking from a Satanic perspective is how un-Adventurous it tends to be. At best, it makes allowance for certain the-exception-that-proves-the-rule type people, whose idiosyncrasies are tolerated in the context of serving as a designated mediator of chaos for the community's benefit. More typically, though, misoneism (fear or hatred of the new) rules the day, holding back healthy innovation and change.[15]

We will henceforth refer to the chaos vs. order thought pattern as the *Apollonian* tendency. Spengler's use of this term takes cues from Nietzsche's, associating the Greek sun god Apollo with order, rationality, and an aesthetic of prudent balance.[16] The term's connotations include a preference for that which is "present, visible, measurable, and numerable," the conceptualization of nature as "a sum of well-formed bodily things," and an aesthetic preoccupation with the "near, strictly limited, self-contained body."[17] Polytheism, Spengler asserts, is a logical religious expression of the Apollonian pattern.

Whereas Spengler had Classical Greece in mind, the term "Apollonian" in the current discussion includes elements predominant in a multitude of ancient paganisms and indigenous traditions. This is justified on the basis that in many such cultures, one readily observes an orientation toward harmony in the material world of the present — this world which we all share with one another "under the sun," as the saying goes.

The Magian pattern: Truth vs. Falsehood

Unlike the first way of constructing good vs. evil, which is motivated by what human beings share with less-developed organisms, the second stems from two distinctive features of human existence: sociality and story-telling. "Story" here includes not only those in an obvious narrative form, such as religious mythology, but also institutions (a story about who is in charge), money (a story about the relative value of goods), etc. A "story" is anything that humans made up for the purposes of facilitating social cooperation. Such inventions are the foundations of many large-scale human accomplishments, such as long-distance trade, the building of cities and nations, etc.

Given the extent to which human sociality is enabled by stories, it is understandable that a strong imperative arises to safeguard them. Sometimes this extends even to declaring the story sacrosanct, so as to better fence it off from challenges and complexities. In such circumstances, "good vs. evil" comes to be construed as *truth vs. falsehood*. These terms are defined, however, according to the imperative to protect whatever stories an individual or community is invested in. Truth means, basically, whatever upholds these stories we made up in order to facilitate social cooperation. Falsehood, on the other hand, is whatever challenges or opposes our preferred stories. The truth vs. falsehood pattern thus has everything to do with maintaining consensus for the purposes of social-political lubrication and little to do with accurate representation of objective reality. The terms "truth" and "falsehood" reflect not what the pattern is, but what its adherents *believe* it to be and the nature of their investment in it. The subsequent capitalization of these terms highlights this element of credulous over-investment, and the conflation of ideology and reality that often follows.

Unlike the order vs. chaos pattern, which sorts objects into categories on the basis of visible characteristics, Truth vs. Falsehood concerns itself with the invisible. Having taken a fiction and elevated it beyond challenge, the believer fends off all possible considerations that could threaten Truth, to the point that reality itself is bent accordingly. There are some contexts in which the believer will affirm that Truth is self-evident and others in which they will complain that Truth's face has become occluded behind a mask of Falsehoods. Either way, the faithful will insist steadfastly that on an ultimate level, Truth eternally prevails — even when all visible evidence suggests otherwise.

This degree of immersion in "pretend" yields benefits in the area of social cohesion. Thinking of morality in such a fashion encourages people to take it seriously, and thinking of institutions this way motivates people to defend them against attack. However, the more globally the Truth vs. Falsehood pattern is applied — and, in particular, with regard to religious matters — the more its interpretation of reality veers into a *rejection* of reality. At the furthest extreme, either the world is reductively simplified into a chessboard upon which Truth and Falsehood duel, or it is dismissed wholesale as a temporary illusion that occludes Truth until that happy day when the flesh is sloughed off. Either way, the subscribers to such a worldview are indoctrinated into a negative bias against life. Instead of accepting life's Perils and learning to cope constructively with them, they spend their days embittered at Falsehood's pervasiveness and Truth's elusiveness in our "fallen" world.

The implications of Truth vs. Falsehood regarding the nature of human beings and the nature of human happiness are also rife with troubling elements. Global commitment to the pattern chains one to an exhausting obligation: human well-being depends on the protection and promotion of Truth. Falsehood threatens this and therefore must be annihilated; if one is not actively engaged in furthering Truth, one is guilty of tolerating Falsehood. Lasting peace is impossible amid the world's messiness, so in its place, there arises a craving for *consensus* as the best-possible approximation of peace that can be had. Human happiness requires that everyone assent to Truth and live accordingly.

Such an expectation sets the stage for distress when one encounters other human groups living according to different stories. Dissent reveals one's own stories to be a choice, rather than a necessity built into the universe. Difference must therefore be eliminated and replaced with consensus. This may be achieved either by bringing others into line with the "correct" story (i.e., one's own), or by otherwise cleansing the world of those who differ. Truth vs. Falsehood thinking may even go so far as to rationalize away the violence of such imperatives, by insisting that, really, all human beings are "one" anyway, so the elimination of difference is nothing more than the elimination of delusion — a peeling-away of the False in order to reveal the Truth beneath.

Right-hand-path world religions frequently purport to reveal Truths hidden behind False surfaces. Many have historically engaged in proselytization, both by the word and by the sword. Despite how their claims may differ on the surface, fundamentally, they all assert something strikingly similar: behind all the apparent diversity of Apollonian polytheism is One Ultimate Thing — e.g., God, Allah, Brahman, etc. People who are wise and good orient themselves toward this thing. Only the ignorant and the evil refuse.

Religious assertions along these lines have long been convenient to empires because they support a mandate to conquer other peoples and convert them for their own good. Such imperializing societies frame themselves as exemplar civilizations, vanquishers of barbarians and heretics alike, hopeful of one day establishing eternal peace via consensus regarding how human beings "should" live. Right-hand-path religions' apocalyptic visions, featuring the definitive extermination of the False and the glorious vindication of the True, illustrate how this idea looks when taken to its furthest extreme. This is not to say that the Truth vs. Falsehood pattern is solely manifest in religious contexts. For much of history prior to the twentieth century, however, religion was undeniably the soil from which the pattern's most glaring and extreme manifestations sprang.

Several major harms produced by dogmatic investment in Truth vs. Falsehood thinking are surely obvious already. Such harms include the demonization of skeptics and non-conformers, the authorization of crusades and inquisitions, etc. At the same time, though, one must admit that cultures dominated by the Truth vs. Falsehood pattern have succeeded to an even greater extent than those dominated by the order vs. chaos pattern. This is thanks to the large-scale social cooperation made possible by cladding one's shared fictions in iron. The power of the Apollonian conception of order is limited on this front. Constrained by the visible messiness of embodied life, it must always tolerate a little chaos — even if only by labeling it as such and shuffling it off to a safe corner. Truth's invisible order, on the other hand, is absolute, allowing nothing to remain "outside." For many people, the elimination of ambiguity offered by being on the side of Truth therefore constitutes an irresistible temptation, unparalleled in its capacity to soothe common human fears and anxieties.

Obviously, dogmatic manifestations of the Truth vs. Falsehood pattern stand sharply opposed to everything that Tenebrous Satanism stands for. Absolutized Truth partakes of a purity that is not of this world. Commitment to it produces such ills as a refusal to engage honestly and constructively with the flesh and a resentment of the world for being complicated. Fanatics obsessed with Truth either fixate on life's Perils to the point of condemning the flesh and the world as mediums of suffering, or elide and deny them in ways that massively aggravate them until suffering grows so pressing that condemnation becomes unavoidable after all. They denounce liberty of the spirit, since it is in conflict with consensus, and decry Adventure, since it is sure to confront one with all the worldly complexities that Truth would sooner deny.

This is not to say that all manifestations of the Truth vs. Falsehood pattern lead to these conclusions. One must not forget that many great things have been built with the help of this potent social glue. The general rule, however, is that the more the pattern is permitted to advance its considerations as the only relevant ones in every human context without exception — as certain religious and political ideologies are especially prone to doing — the worse the results that follow.

We will henceforth refer to the Truth vs. Falsehood pattern as the *Magian* tendency. The term "magi" originally designated a priest of the Zoroastrian religion, in which a good god (Oromazd) and his truth (Asha) are pitted against an evil god (Ahriman) and his lies (Druj). It is a term that evokes dualistic struggle between two absolutely opposed otherworldly forces. To believers, these forces are more real than the physical world, which is merely a theater in which the dualistic struggle is acted out. Although the religions that Spengler identifies as Magian are monotheistic (e.g., Christianity, Islam, etc.), he frames them as dualistic because their worldviews distinguish two sides: a divine force that is unified and good on one hand; individual souls separated into different bodies, and hence subject to corruption, on the other. This duality of "one equals good, many equals bad" positions consensus as a centerpiece of Spengler's conception of Magianism: "... in Magian there is no individual-ego, but a single Pneuma present simultaneously in each and all of the elect, which is likewise Truth."[18]

Tenebrous usage of the term "Magian" encompasses not only tendencies found in the Abrahamic religions as per Spengler, but also the otherworldly monism of Eastern religions such as Hinduism and

Buddhism. Our usage even encompasses the ostensibly "secular" fanaticism of many authoritarian political movements. However, at the same time as Tenebrous Satanism identifies *dogmatic* Magianism as an insidious problem, it must be emphasized that it does *not* condemn Magianism as such. A religion, after all, entails the promotion of belief in one's preferred story for the purpose (among others) of creating social cohesion between like-minded individuals — and Tenebrous Satanism is itself a religion. Thus, even if the excesses of the Magian pattern are uniquely problematic from a Satanic perspective, one must thus not forget that Magianism is no less a valid part of being human than the other two patterns.

The Faustian pattern: evolution vs. stasis

The third thought pattern, *evolution vs. stasis*, has its roots in a trait that is inherent to life itself but overt to a truly impressive extent only in organisms as advanced as human beings. That trait is adaptability. Human beings demonstrate an unparalleled ability to shift their behavior, values, expectations, etc. in response to changing circumstances.

The ancient development of tool usage is a primal example of adaptability in action. Adaptability is not only manifest on this most literal of levels, however. Much of the cultural innovation discussed above — i.e., everything from traditional indigenous knowledge and religiosity to the systems of hierarchy and economic abstraction that came later — can also be framed in terms of adaptation. From this perspective, a tool is anything that helps humans get more done and live better lives. Adaptability itself is, in turn, an ultimate good, for it inspires us to always seek ways of further improving on our tools. According to such thinking, anything that enables us to *do more* is good. Conversely, that which fails in securing such advantages is evil. "Evolution" is proximate to such concepts as activity, progress, and growth. Alternate glosses of "stasis," on the other hand, include inertia, complacency, and stagnation.

Rather than labeling things in accord with what they are and how one ought to interact with them (as per order vs. chaos), or in accord with to what extent they instantiate or deviate from an ideal (as per Truth vs. Falsehood), evolution vs. stasis thinking classifies things according to the potential it sees in them and the attendant implications for how they might be transformed into something better. Whereas the Apollonian pattern is pluralistic in outlook and the Magian pattern dualistic, one arrives here at a monistic worldview: all is one, in the sense that all things can, with effort, be transformed for the better. Whatever distinctions are present currently are always open to revision and hence relative. This way of looking at the world occupies itself with both the visible and the invisible equally. It grasps that without first acknowledging what *is*, one has nothing to work *with*. But it also recognizes that without being able to imagine what is currently *not*, one has nothing to work *toward*.

Evolution vs. stasis is also distinct from the other patterns in its denial of any need to submit to an already-extant "way that things are." The definitive human act is not to sort things into rule-bound categories, nor to be a vessel for some supposed Truth. The human task is instead to *go out and do* — i.e., to discover, transform, and refine. Evolution vs. stasis therefore rejects the other two patterns' conformist conceptions of humanity. It does not conceive of humanity as a collection of tribes, each obligated to imitate its forbearers, nor as a single unity embodying a transcendent essence. Instead, it defines humanity as a multitude of diverse individuals, each acting to move history forward and acted upon by other such movers. From such a perspective, "belonging" ceases to be a "good" thing for the individual human and is instead disdained as a sign that one has failed to distinguish oneself. Better to stand out than to belong, the evolution vs. stasis mentality declares.

The conception of human happiness favored by evolution vs. stasis thinking is *prosperity*. Prosperity is characterized not just by gaining that which is beneficial, but by having secured the means by which additional benefits can be gained in the future. The evolution vs. stasis pattern naturally appreciates all the specific goods that human beings consider worth attaining for their own sake, such as material wealth, emotional connection, the enjoyment of justice and security, etc. Even more highly, however, it prizes adaptive traits that let us capitalize on opportunities in the future. Such traits include curiosity, initiative-taking, and a willingness to experiment.

For most of history, to elevate the evolution vs. stasis pattern to predominance has struck many as an experiment too dangerous to attempt. Amid threats both from nature and from other human beings, many resent the intrusion of further complications or uncertainties into the familiar rhythm of their lives. Individuals who sought to cross boundaries and accomplish the impossible have therefore often found themselves demonized as representatives of chaos and Falsehood. And yet, what have innovative scientists and artists, intrepid explorers and entrepreneurs, and far-thinking prophets and revolutionaries long offered the world? Is it not the case that often, in the wake of such individuals' influences, one beholds wide-scale improvements in both quality of life and self-determination? The resulting world contains more novelty, diversity, and overcoming of adversity than the status quo previously allowed for. And the more the world opens up in this way, the more scope exists for autonomous individuals to find yet better ways of living well by their own lights.

The dark side of the evolution vs. stasis pattern, on the other hand, is manifest in a variety of technocratic disasters. Too much enthusiasm for trying to make things better can lead to treating rationalization and organization as goods in themselves. This leads to the rise of bureaucracy, surveillance, economic exploitation, and the scientization of things that many people feel it is cold or wrong to scientize. Too-ambitious attempts to make progress against stasis have wrought worse yet: colonial aspirations to "civilize the savages," eugenic attempts to improve the human race via genocide against "backward" groups, and the catastrophes that so many large-scale experiments in utopian politics have produced amid their efforts to eliminate "regressive" elements.

In the worst of these enormities, Apollonian and Magian excesses are usually also evident. The death camps of the Third Reich, for example, proceed simultaneously from excessive order-fixation, totalization of a self-flattering story, and technocratic aspiration taken inhumanly far. Nonetheless, it cannot be denied that the evolution vs. stasis pattern bears its own share of responsibility for oppression. The evolutionary benefits of the pattern, and its reasons for persisting, are obvious insofar as it is the very engine of improved quality of life. At the same time, though, an honest look at the darker fruits of "progress" suggests that it is not unwarranted for human beings to worry about what may come of unbridled ambition to transform the world.

The more prevalent social validation of the evolution vs. stasis pattern in recent centuries, and the relative youth of Satanism as a religion, are no coincidence. Satanism is precisely the kind of religion one winds up with when evolution vs. stasis thinking is ascendant. Tenebrous Satanism's optimistic conception of the human being as capable of self-improvement through self-evolution is a clear illustration of such thinking. Consider, too, how thoroughly evolution vs. stasis thinking permeates the concepts presented in the First Key. Spirit is the *mover*, flesh is the *moved*, and the Adventure is the *moving*. Life is flesh *animated* by spirit. The world, as the nexion in which such beings come together with one another, is a place of *ceaseless motion*. Human beings can and should take the raw material of existence and make something *better* out of it. At the same time, Tenebrous Satanism's open recognition of the Perils of life promotes vigilance against dogmatic manifestations of the evolution vs. stasis pattern. The challenge, which Tenebrous Satanism rises to meet, is to fully grasp the ethical and political dangers that so often accompany evolution vs. stasis thinking without these dissuading one from striving yet onward.

We will henceforth refer to the evolution vs. stasis pattern as the *Faustian* tendency. While folklore knows of more than one version of Faust's story, the one Spengler has in mind is Goethe's anti-hero, who seeks out all manner of worldly adventures at Mephistopheles' side under the condition that only if he is ever satisfied will the Devil be permitted to claim his soul. Goethe's Faust is thus a figure characterized above all by *striving ever onward*. Spengler additionally associates the name of Faust with the "will to spatial transcendence" expressed in Gothic architecture and Baroque music, with Western conceptions of human beings as "fighting, active, progressing" and with the enthusiastic conquest of limitless space revealed by "the passion of our civilization for swift transit, the conquest of the air, the exploration of the Polar regions and the climbing of almost impossible mountain-peaks." In all of these, the spirit of "ever more and ever higher" is clearly present.

Tenebrous Satanism's use of the term "Faustian" may seem to strongly echo Spengler's, insofar as some readers will misperceive praise for scientists, entrepreneurs, and explorers as a sign that we romanticize Enlightenment modernity exclusively. We go beyond Spengler, however, in proposing that, actually, Faustian agency rears its head in *all* times and places where innovation, iconoclasm, and boundary-transgression are ascendant. Tenebrous Satanism soundly rejects the contention that there is anything inherently "Western," let alone "White," about Faustianism. While the pattern has admittedly actualized its potential more visibly in some cultures than others — and not necessarily for the best in said cases — it is nonetheless part of the evolutionary birthright that belongs to the entire human race equally. The same may be said of Apollonianism and Magianism. To deny this is to buy into a blinkered and impoverished conception of humanity wherein too much emphasis is put on meaningless superficialities (such as skin color) and not enough attention paid to more profound and universal elements of human experience.

The threat of Dogmatic Magianism

It should already be clear from the preceding section that each of the three thought patterns produces harms when it predominates to the point of dogmatism. And since dogmatism breeds arrangements and behaviors that obstruct flourishing — e.g., enshrining dysfunctional hierarchies, squandering potential, justifying violence, etc. — it is undesirable in any of its forms.

With the Magian thought pattern, however, comes an especial proclivity toward dogmatism. This is so because of the way each of the three thought patterns respectively fosters, or fails to foster, investment in the world. The Apollonian mindset seeks harmony via the maintenance of an already established order, while being just tolerant enough of chaos to be able to cope constructively with the world's actual messiness. Similarly, the Faustian mindset seeks prosperity via the transformation of that which is already existing. It may go awry by conceiving of the world too passively while overestimating one's own agency, but ultimately it can achieve nothing without honest engagement with the world — and from a Faustian perspective, few things are as unbearable as achieving nothing! In emphasizing Truth, however — i.e., what is in actuality a socially useful fiction — the Magian mindset inherently tends toward disengagement from the world. Healthy Magianism, balanced by the other two mental patterns, is capable of utilizing a map (i.e., story) while understanding that the map is not the territory. Unhealthy Magianism, however, becomes so fixated on the map's accuracy that it would rather try to forcibly alter the territory to match the map than admit that the map itself could benefit from revision. Add to this pigheadedness the fanatical insistence that any and all questioning of the map proceeds solely from Falsehood, and one arrives at dogmatic Magianism: a thought pattern that has closed itself off both from honest engagement with the world and from any potential challenges to its ideologically skewed perspective.

We will henceforth abbreviate the phrase "dogmatic Magian" as "Dogmagian," to underline that we are talking about a metastasized version of Magianism, not all things associated with the Magian pattern.

The use of storytelling to make sense of the world is not in itself a problem. The problem, rather, is the elevation of one's preferred story above worldly realities and the harmful life-hostility that results. It is this tendency that turns certain ideologies into "insidious destroyers of life."

What can make Dogmagianism all the more insidious is its propensity for camouflaging its mechanisms with high-sounding ideals: peace, love, justice, etc. Such idealistic costuming can make Dogmagianism difficult to unmask, and harder still to challenge. What, then, should the Satanist look for? And upon uncovering evidence of the Dogmagian thought pattern, how might one oppose it effectively? It is to these questions that the Second Key now turns.

Recognizing Dogmagianism

The root of Dogmagianism is overinvestment in a socially convenient story. Stories with the following traits are the worst for this:

1. They assert that *the world is less complicated* than it is. Such stories are appealing and addictive because they let people feel more in control of life than they really are.

2. They insist *we are owed compensation* for the worst parts of existence. Those who embrace such stories develop a sense of entitlement, making them reluctant to relinquish the expectations the story has inculcated in them.

3. They *justify certain individuals' authority or superiority*. Self-interest thus motivates those favored to keep reinforcing the narrative.

Whether the story in question is religious or secular, dogmatists become convinced that without it life would be intolerable: snap judgments would not be enough to yield the right decisions; no reward would be promised to the good nor punishment to evildoers; one's self-esteem and status would not be guaranteed by a mere fact of group-belonging. Of course, the Satanist will notice that *this is, in fact, how life actually is!* The Dogmagian,[19] however, is simultaneously the addict unable to cope without their drug, the child unwilling to live in an adult world, and the egotist who wants to be "special" without effort.

When groups of people fall under the spell of Dogmagianism, certain themes emerge, regardless of the specific tenets of the infected ideology. Four such themes include:

I. Insularity

The world at large is considered "evil," and believers called to separate themselves from it. They are to live apart, as a holy community, abstaining from anything tainted with worldliness. Typically, this culminates in extensive efforts to repress or destroy any passions, instincts, or interests that the ideology disapproves of. Self-destructive asceticism delineates the distinction between insiders and outsiders.

II. Heresy

Whatever "sins" the group frets over tend to be defined not in terms of demonstrable harm to real, specific people, but in terms of "incorrect" thoughts and feelings. Believers are made to feel they cannot live without the community and fear excommunication over even minor deviations from Truth. Human reason and resolve are both judged corruptible, justifying censorship and other paternalistic measures aimed at protecting the weak from being led astray by "wrong" ideas.

III. Elitism

Believers pride themselves on being "better" than outsiders, while anointed saints who have mastered the ideology occupy a yet-higher pedestal. High-handed condescension toward others is made to seem warranted via claims of moral and epistemological superiority, and compassion treated as a vice if it is directed toward the wrong people. Insiders are thought to possess infallible intuition regarding who is a "sinner," while concepts such as fairness and neutrality are condemned as formalities that get in the way of what ought to be the top priority: the urgent vanquishing of obvious forms of evil. In such an atmosphere, everything from petty cruelty to outright violence can be defended as a heroic necessity, so long as ideological prerogatives are served thereby. In extreme cases, this creates regimes in which good and evil become alarmingly reversed from what most normal human beings recognize as such, yet the holy community remains entirely blinded to the extent to which atrocities go unremarked in their midst.

IV. Apocalypticism

Since the war between Truth and Falsehood is reaching its climax at the current time — so goes the narrative — one must be supremely vigilant against Falsehood, lest evil overcome the forces of good. At the same time, the faithful assert that Truth *must* win in the end. Believers therefore alternate between doom-saying and victory-strutting without noticing how contradictory their discourse is. One moment, they will stress urgency, as if one's failure to do the "right" thing this very second will make one personally responsible for evil's victory. In the next instant, however, they will puff up about how "of course" their side must prevail, and anyone who does not grasp this is "on the wrong side of history."

All of these themes entail a hearty dose of *dualism:* "we" are good, "they" are evil, and the only acceptable outcome is the vanquishing of the latter at the hands of the former. This is hardly surprising, given how often dualism is a key component of the sorts of stories people overinvest in. Positing the existence of only two sides makes for an appealingly *simple* story; claiming that one side has been victimized by the other carries straightforward implications regarding who is *owed* restitution; declaring that the universe has chosen us to make it right gives us a mission that is *special.* For all the trouble Dogmagianism causes, one must recognize obvious pragmatic and psychological reasons why people gravitate toward it.

Beyond narrative overinvestment and archetypal themes, Dogmagianism also makes itself known via specific patterns in fanatics' attitudes and behaviors. Six of these are:

A. Dwelling on victimhood

Often, what drives individuals into Dogmagianism is a dysfunctional reaction to aspects of material existence that conscious beings find upsetting and which therefore prompt denial, rage, despair, etc. Such Perils are laid out at length in the Sixth Key, but the basic form of many of them is, "life is inherently difficult, unfair, and complicated. Thus, if you want to flourish and evolve, you will have to admit that things are as they are, take actions that you may find unpleasant, and accept that even in the best case scenario, it is simply never possible to escape all forms of suffering." Dogmagianism appeals strongly to the kind of person who not only resents such an assertion but takes it as a personal affront that the universe would *dare* demand such a thing of them. The narrative that such people defensively embrace revolves around blaming other people, external conditions, society, etc. for everything wrong with life. By taking up this discourse, the Dogmagian adopts an identity that revolves around victimhood — e.g., being a victim, being a noble soul who stands up for victims, or both. This excuses Dogmagians from having to ask hard questions about the extent to which their own expectations, habits, etc. might be contributing to why they experience life as disappointing.

B. Policing thoughts and emotions

Dogmagianism entails a conviction that it is not enough to just control what people do outwardly because i) human fallibility is such that wrong thoughts and emotions motivate wrong behavior irresistibly, and ii) wrong thoughts and emotions in and of themselves constitute sinful acts, or are even able to cause direct harm to others via some sort of supernatural mechanism. Given such dire threats, only inward control is mighty enough to fight evil. Therefore, Dogmagians assert there can be no distinction between the private and public realms, nor between the personal and the political. Everything must be analyzed and judged according to ideology, even if it is a solitary pursuit or one that takes place only among consenting adults.

C. Reducing art to propaganda

Dogmagianism frequently displays a marked hostility toward art that is complex, nuanced, and ambiguous — or, in short, *good*. This is because of a conviction that art is only "good" insofar as it parrots the messages and values of the preferred ideology. Artists are held responsible for public morality, while such ideas as personal preference or a free marketplace are decried as signs of a complacent willingness to let evil run rampant. The kind of art that supports the Satanic endeavor

— e.g., confronting and integrating the Darkness within — is particularly likely to face suppression under such a regime.

D. Rejection of curiosity, empiricism, and evolution

Overinvestment in "Truth" breeds impatience, hostility, and disdain toward those who ask inconvenient questions. For a Dogmagian, such questioning — whether it comes from a scholar striving to advance knowledge or an innocent who is "just wondering" — can *only* be indicative of nefarious intent. If an outsider challenges the ideology, they will be accused of ignorantly speaking out of turn; if they show their credentials, said credentials will be declared fraudulent; if they present themselves as an ally offering constructive critique, they will be labeled an impostor or traitor. Dedicated Dogmagians therefore cannot be challenged via the presentation of information that contradicts their worldview. Either they refuse to engage outright, since only a worthless sinner would raise such heretical points, or they reach for the torches and pitchforks.

It is additionally worth noting that Dogmagians are especially prone to defensive shutdown behavior if confronted with an evolutionary perspective on the human condition. This is because an inherent implication of evolution is, "the story has not yet been written and could turn out otherwise than we would like, since we ourselves are not its sole authors." Obviously, such a premise is intolerably offensive to those who have decided in advance that they already know the True Story.

E. Dressing up status games in moral language

The atmosphere of Dogmagian-dominated communities tends to be drab, stifling, and humorless. Discourse is oversaturated with a small handful of voices whom the ideology has lionized, and social interactions are dominated by masturbatory displays of ideological credentials and good-guy badges. Dogmagians in such milieus obsess over making appropriate noises at one another in response to appropriate stimuli, without any awareness of how pretentious, self-righteous and generally insufferable they sound to outsiders. Often, one can find all the red flags of abusive relationships within such settings: the normalization of unwinnable conversational games ("your refusal to admit you're a sinner proves you're a sinner"); social penalization based on guilt by association; dominant parties being permitted to engage in forms of emotional manipulation forbidden to their "inferiors"; destruction of self-confidence via gaslighting; etc. The more the ideology flaunts its high ideals, the easier it is for self-aggrandizing narcissists to turn the whole thing into a status-advancement game for their own benefit. To point out that this is taking place is to risk inciting the whole community against oneself, since one will appear to be invalidating the anointed shepherds that the whole flock of sheep depends on.

F. Counterproductive utopian idealism

A final aspect of Dogmagianism worth highlighting is its head-in-the-clouds utopianism. Blinded by the light of Truth and driven by apocalyptic urgency, Dogmagians will demand an instantaneous end to any practice, institution, etc. that they have judged evil, without reflecting on whether such a sudden, drastic change is really a good solution — or even, for that matter, a *possible* one. They will reject any proposal less extreme than their own as an unacceptable compromise, and attack processes that stand in the way of what they want without considering why those measures were put there in the first place. For example, they may complain that due process thwarts the rapid delivery of True justice, or argue that electoral regulations more favorable to themselves are required in order to make a given election "fair," etc.

It is also a signature of Dogmagianism to presume that "we" are qualified to speak for the victims of evil. Should an actual victim speak up in rejection of the Dogmagians' proposed solution, such a dissenter is sure to be ignored or talked over. They may even be accused of ignorance or deceit on the presumption that no "real" victim would ever quarrel with sacred ideological Truths. Nor is this the only manifestation of utopian hypocrisy among Dogmagians. Witness what occurs when their reforms succeed, only for the new arrangements to prove unexpectedly inconvenient to their own inner circle. In such instances, Dogmagians are sure to cook up an exception to the rules, enabling members of their own group to still enjoy the very luxuries they have forbidden to the masses. The alternative would be to admit that their new world order is a mistake — something that they are utterly opposed to doing.

II — Insidious Destroyers of Life

What does the utopian facet of Dogmagianism reveal? That by refusing to grapple realistically with worldly limitations — material scarcity, human nature, etc. — Dogmagians wind up inflicting the worst of all worlds on everyone. In the long run, this includes even themselves.

A unifying element among all Dogmagian behaviors outlined above is *hubris*. In the first place, the Dogmagian suffers from an intense need to feel "good" and blameless. Secondly, their supposed moral purity is what authorizes them to police the arts and sciences for the protection of the public. Thirdly, they gravitate toward win-at-all-costs tactics to shore up the security of their egos. For these reasons, Tenebrous Satanism associates the O9A term *homo hubris* with the Dogmagian mentality.

O9A, we contend, is correct in observing that certain human beings make the world worse for everyone via their arrogant preoccupation with only their own favored narrative and their complacent refusal to recognize the limitations of their worldviews. This, however, has little to do with the ordinary, mundane person on the street and even less to do with "plutocratic puppet-masters" and similar antisemitic dog-whistles. It is folly to imagine that one can point at whole groups of people, whether defined by race, fashion choices, being "mainstream," being "alternative," or something equally superficial, and declare, "there is homo hubris," or, "those are the Dogmagians." Nor is it any more useful to pin a simplistic label on a whole religious group, or on the entire half of the political spectrum opposite to one's own, or on everyone who is even slightly better off than oneself in terms of material wealth. One must instead look carefully at the internal logic of specific ideologies and at the concrete details of how human beings attempt to impose this logic upon the world.

Responding to Dogmagianism

Once one has recognized Dogmagianism, what to do about it depends on how advanced the problem is. So long as only a few individuals are infected, a recommended initial measure is to separate oneself from said individuals. The power-grasping nature of Dogmagianism, however, is such that ignoring it will leave it free to continue tyrannizing those who, due to whatever circumstances, are unable or unwilling to part ways with it.

Insofar as the Satanist is capable of mounting any kind of offense against Dogmagianism, our most deeply held values urge us to do just that. As the First Key indicates, Satan stands for individual empowerment, unobstructed pursuit of knowledge, and honest engagement with all the wonders and challenges that accompany existence in the flesh. The Satanist is thus well positioned to recognize dogma for what it is: the sour-faced father of resentment, castigating the flesh for its messy complexities, and the bitter mother of cowardice, stifling the spirit because she cannot bear the risks inherent to Adventure. A life lived in a mental-spiritual prison, surrounded by paranoid inquisitors, scolding busybodies, sanctimonious bullies, and smug riders of high horses, is not for us. Nor do we wish such a life upon other human beings.

What follows, then, are some suggestions regarding how to work toward liberation from Dogmagianism.

1. Open your eyes and reject excuses

As with addiction, so with Dogmagianism: the first step to getting help is admitting the issue. This requires objective and merciless reflection upon the criteria outlined in the previous section, toward the end of admitting when people or groups are behaving in these ways and acknowledging that this is a problem, no matter how good the intentions of those involved. Some specific things to be vigilant about include:

- *Do not assume Dogmagianism can only be found among your enemies.* Interrogate your *own* social group and be honest about what you behold there.

- *Do not assume Dogmagianism can only be present where religion is present.* Anchorless, rudderless secular people can be easily seduced into a victimhood mentality since it bestows on them a formerly lacking purpose in life. They are also in danger of becoming the blindest fanatics because, since they think of themselves as "not religious," it threatens their egos to consider that maybe their behavior has a puritanical and evangelical dimension to it.

- *Do not let yourself be talked out of recognizing the problem.* Do not be dissuaded by rebuttals such as "maybe you just don't understand," "it isn't your place to judge," "there are so many more important issues to deal with," "why are you being so mean-spirited toward people who are just trying to make things better?" and so on. It is good to maintain an open, critical mind about your own position as well as others', but do not let others pressure you out of trusting your own instincts if you know that something is wrong.

2. Defend your own sovereignty

As already mentioned, a good first step to resisting Dogmagianism, at least individually, is to distance yourself from those under its influence. This may be more easily said than done, however, for it may require alienation from family and friends, leaving one's current occupation, or in extreme circumstances, even fleeing from one's nation of origin.

It is not unusual for considerations of survival and comfort to obstruct one's attempts to sever all ties with Dogmagian influences. Even in such circumstances, though, one ought to still strive for some degree of social and psychological separation. A large part of the insidiousness of Dogmagianism lies in it causing people to feel as if all aspects of life, without exception, "belong" to the ideology. Resist this by engaging in honest introspection about your own beliefs and passions and making the time and space for yourself to explore these things without feeling as if the fanatics are always looking over your shoulder. Keep a private journal of your thoughts, in which you openly express what you really think and feel about what is going on around you. Get in the habit of clearly articulating, even if only to yourself, what is most crucial to your own flourishing and what conclusions follow from this regarding whether Dogmagian ideology really serves your best interests. Do not allow yourself to be made to feel as if you are obligated to submit all aspects of yourself to the approval of others. Spending time by yourself in the midst of nature or engaging in regular solitary meditation (whether as described in the Fifth Key or otherwise) are additional measures that can help with boundary-setting.

3. Guard yourself against strong-arm tactics

If the Satanist is forced to spend time around Dogmagians, two protective measures are highly recommended. First and foremost is the recognition and rejection of dualism. Dogmagian contexts are often saturated with rhetoric about how "if you're not with us, you're against us," "there are really only two kinds of people," etc. When such talk gets thrown around, take a moment to remind yourself that, in fact, life is complicated, and anyone who tries to pretend otherwise is certain to have an agenda for doing so. Reducing things to black and white is a rhetorical trick these people use to force you into taking their side, lest you otherwise support the "evil" one. It is understandable for people to use this trick when they are seeking to defend what they see as a worthy cause amid desperate circumstances. But that does not change the fact that it is a simplification, which you are not automatically obligated to assent to.

Second, educate yourself about such topics as logical fallacies, cognitive distortions, abusive relationship dynamics, advertising and propaganda, etc. Notice when people wield thought-terminating clichés or use other such games to undermine challenges to their position. If someone's words and deeds reveal them to be a narcissistic bully, recognize this instead of allowing ideology to make excuses for their abusive behavior. Resist allowing these sorts of people to manipulate you, and find ways of supporting other people around you who are being browbeaten and guilt-tripped.

4. Present ideological and social alternatives

Leaving the Dogmagian fold can be difficult, especially for those brought up in such contexts or otherwise exposed to them for lengthy periods of time. Since such individuals will have been extensively gaslit, they often suffer from feelings of self-doubt and isolation when they first try to break away. This can leave them vulnerable to falling back into their former social circles and thought patterns unintentionally if they do not receive support from elsewhere. A few things that the Satanist can do to combat such situations include:

- *Educate yourself broadly about such areas as science, history, anthropology, etc.,* and look for opportunities to bring these topics into conversation with others. Sparking curiosity about the wider world can help people find something other than their current ideological fixation to ground themselves in. In some circumstances, inspiring people whom dogma has misled or kept sheltered to try reading even *one* thing that obliquely challenges the ideology can be the critical first step on their path to liberation.

- *Live in a way that demonstrates the possibility of being a good person without being a strict adherent of the ideology.* Whether by carefully considered deeds or simply having a positive presence in others' lives, the Satanist can role-model an alternative to ideology's "Truth." Amid such an endeavor, genuine empathy for others and an absence of self-conscious egoism can do much to open hearts and minds. Conversely, role-modeling that lacks subtlety, especially if tainted by smug disdain, will merely trigger onlookers' defensiveness, with counterproductive results.

- *Encourage meeting people and participating in groups that challenge Dogmagian assumptions.* Trying to "save" people seldom works, but they can sometimes be persuaded to save themselves by leaving their abusers. This is most likely to succeed in the presence of a support network. If you are not willing to be part of that for someone yourself, you can still act as a nexion connecting them with a different, healthier circle of associates than they have previously had access to. As with the preceding measures, showing people that *there is an alternative* is the most critical thing to accomplish.

5. Cultivate creative resistance

The harsh realities of existence are such that the need for violence is hard to rule out absolutely, and entrenched forms of Dogmagianism can become impossible to oppose effectively without resorting to it. Nonetheless, before deciding to use violence, one should always reflect carefully and realistically on how likely it is to achieve one's goal in the specific context under consideration. Dogmagian ideologies can often readily process dissenters' acts of violence into "proof" that their own oppressive measures are necessary to protect the "holy community" from "evil." Resentment and bitterness toward the ideology, however understandable, should therefore be managed carefully, lest they drive choices and actions that will ultimately play into the hands of one's opposition. It is one thing to engage in defensive violence for self-preservation purposes, and to prescribe pacifism in such circumstances is to wrongfully demand tolerance of oppression. But violence that is meant to "send a message" — i.e., what normal people call *terrorism* — is often driven by romanticized "macho" notions of what can be achieved with guns and bombs, coupled with childish longings for a simple solution. The collateral damage that inevitably accompanies such acts also has a tendency to aggravate far more problems than it solves.

With such provisos in mind, how should the Satanist approach situations in which Dogmagian forces have gained a considerable upper hand and a proportionate capacity to impinge on human flourishing? A few general strategies include:

- *Look for opportunities to prevent the ideology from further extending its foothold.* If dogmatists are just beginning to come into positions of real power, be vigilant against measures they will advance to make it easier for them to bully and intimidate dissenters.[20] In dogma-dominated environments, calling out power-grasping initiatives too directly can backfire by seeming to oppose that which is well-meaning, so look for ways to scuttle initiatives by questioning their practicality instead. Force dogmatists to openly and stridently defend their demands, for such zeal risks alienating the uncommitted. And if the dogmatists do wind up establishing their hegemony, do not allow your pride and principles to blind you to what you might yet accomplish through such methods as feigned idiocy, malicious compliance, and outright sabotage.

- *Whenever possible, act on behalf of people, rather than against them.* Hardcore Dogmagians will take any opposition poorly, but such individuals are often surrounded by those who follow more because they are timid and exhausted than because their hearts are really in it. Be, then, as the Serpent seeking to liberate such people from the dystopian Eden in which they dwell. Find subtle opportunities to seed questions, present alternatives, and support doubters. Act with the intent of creating and solidifying alliances, but proceed cautiously, lest you mistake the committed for the uncommitted — or vice versa. Do not give up on looking for potential allies, though, for if you do so, you may wind up unintentionally supporting the ideology's own lies about "established consensus."

- *Educate yourself about non-violent resistance instead of just lazily assuming that it never works.* Many would-be revolutionaries vastly underestimate the breadth and creativity of non-violent tactics that have been used successfully by past freedom-fighters in similar situations. Do not be so quick to assume that the desire to avoid violence can only be motivated by cowardice, moral primness, or ingrained subservience to the status quo. Yes, sometimes such motivators are in play, but if you assume such is *always* the case, you close your mind against a broad range of alternative tactics that may work *better* for what you envision accomplishing. You may also learn tactics that could complement and augment any forms of resistance you are already contemplating.

- *Never apologize.* Dogmagian techniques for dealing with "captured" enemies often entail convincing the target that the ideology really is the Truth, that by the light of such Truth they are guilty of something heinous, and that they will be destroyed if they fail to capitulate. In fact, though, it is capitulation to the ideology that further empowers the Dogmagian mob to destroy the target and also allows Dogmagianism to present itself as a powerful and compelling force to the world at large. Therefore, if things arrive at a point where you are cornered as a self-evident enemy in the Dogmagians' midst, *never capitulate.* Hold your head high, be proudly and fearlessly what you are, and let them try to destroy you instead of doing the work for them. Rebellion, even only of a single person, demonstrates to others that revolt is indeed possible. Therefore, take Satan as your model, and mount whatever rebellion is within your power to wage against the shacklers of spirit and deniers of the flesh.

Summary

Who, or what, is Satan the adversary of? People and groups are only the enemy so long as they cling to patterns of thinking that produce pernicious effects. Were the mind to genuinely change or the community's values to shift, there would be no need for continued opposition. To harbor personal animosity toward people and groups with values opposed to one's own is therefore childish.

Nor is it constructive to harbor animosity toward any of the patterns by which human beings define good vs. evil. All three are evolutionarily justified, all three yield important benefits in the right circumstances, and all three produce their share of problems when they become too dominant. It is human to navigate the world by tracing the boundary between order and chaos; it is human to tell and participate in stories that offer a meaningful worldview and help us coordinate with one another; it is human to want more and to seek ways of improving on one's situation. Hence, there is nothing inherently wrong with Apollonianism, Faustianism, or even Magianism. Each occupies a legitimate place in the fabric of human existence, so long as each is employed constructively.

The enemy, instead, is dogma, which takes what was salutary at the right dose and ruins it by totalizing it. The Second Key contends that the Magian pattern is especially prone to this sort of disaster. This is because of Magianism's inherent orientation toward an otherworldly ideal and the tendency for its uncompromising dualism to prevent self-criticism. Given life's Perils, one can sympathize with the Dogmagian's desire for simple and definitive solutions to the problems of existence. Unfortunately, though, this longing drives the Dogmagian to enclose themselves in a phantasmagoria, wherein it is the mission of an elite caste of sainted victims (themselves) to win an at-all-costs war against the evil world that besets them from all sides. Toward this end, the Dogmagian takes up arms against self-insight, human passions, unregulated forms of beauty and knowledge, normal conceptions of fairness, and the political realism that enables different people to get along with one another. Such an approach toward life breeds paternalism, intolerance, self-deceit, ignorance, petty cruelty, dysfunctional institutions, and general misery. Dogmagianism therefore warrants opposition, regardless of the exact nature and scale of infection. To ignore small harms is to permit larger ones down the line if the power and influence of the ideology continue to grow unchecked.

Dogmagianism ultimately culminates in the thwarting of flourishing and the stifling of self-evolution for everyone it touches. This includes the Dogmagians themselves, whose ideological investments curse them to chase an otherworldly mirage that recedes ever more rapidly the more ardently they pursue it. It is therefore entirely possible to oppose dogma while at the same time empathizing with those currently under its spell. In the course of our opposition, we should never lose sight of the fact that the Dogmagian remains our fellow human being, struggling to cope with life's Perils in the face of an indifferent universe.

That said, however, it remains important for Satanists to recognize dogma for what it is and vanquish it without mercy. Otherwise, the world that eventually results will not be one friendly to the values and ideals of Satanism. The Satanist, therefore, should not be lulled by innocent-seeming rhetoric into ignoring the insidious destroyers of life.

We hope that the Second Key will foster more widespread recognition of harmful dogmas, and strengthen opposition against these by providing grounds on which Satanists may justifiably present themselves as conscientious religious objectors against dogmatic imposition.

Notes

[14] None of this should be taken to mean that all societies dominated by order vs. chaos dynamics are equally narrow-minded about what range of behavior is acceptable within their own group — a misimpression that might readily arise among the many Satanically inclined persons who unreflectively define order as bad and chaos as good. Tenebrous Satanism's position is that, in fact, when these kinds of people *think* they want chaos, what they actually want is *an alternate order* — namely, one more open-minded and amenable to themselves than what they have thus far encountered. Nobody *actually* wants real chaos, total and absolute, because it is an inherently undesirable state for beings living amid material limitation: a state wherein the constant ambushes of uncertainty render meaningful pursuit of flourishing impossible. This understanding should enable one to recognize that gravitation toward Apollonian order need not inherently make a society oppressive. Such gravitation is rather just a minimal condition for having anything recognizable as a society at all.

[15] What is described here should not be reduced to the old canard of "primitive" people who will tolerate a shaman's idiosyncrasies but react in a xenophobic manner toward everything else on account of being excessively tradition-bound and superstitious. Such Victorian notions about non-Western cultures are both simple-minded and outdated, and the author rejects the notion that whole societies can or should be judged based on their "levels of development." The point, rather, is that any society that tends to invalidate "different" people generally is also likely to invalidate Satanists specifically.

[16] The opposing mythological figure is Dionysus, who Nietzsche associates with chaos, irrationality, and an aesthetic of wild abandon.

[17] All quotations from Oswald Spengler used throughout the Second Key are taken from the 2006 edition of *The Decline of the West*, abridged by Helmut Werner and Arthur Helps, translated by Charles Francis Atkinson.

[18] The capital "T" appears in Spengler's original text.

[19] The term "Dogmagian," when used as a noun, serves as a convenient way of referring to an individual who has become overinvested in said thought pattern. It is crucial to understand, however, that this is not indicative of a permanent and unchangeable state of affairs. It is all too common a human fallacy to fixate upon other people being the enemy, when in fact it is an adopted ideology, and not something inherent to the person, that is the problem. Tenebrous Satanism therefore discourages Satanists from directing the kind of dehumanizing rancor toward "the Dogmagian" that many Niners direct toward "the Magian." Hatred does more to limit one's horizons regarding effective ways of fighting a harmful ideology than it does to advance liberation.

[20] One example of such a measure is the elimination of the secret ballot from forums in which group decision-making takes place. Beware individuals who advocate for such a change by claiming that secrecy is unnecessary amid in-group solidarity, or worse, that it is a good thing for peer pressure to force dissenters to "own" their dissent. Such thinking is indicative of the advocate's having fallen into the mindset of the Dogmagian inquisitor, who seeks to unmask and eliminate any heretical outsiders who may lurk in the midst of their holy community. Dwelling upon such mundane-seeming procedural issues may strike the Satanist as both paranoid and unexciting, but the reality of the matter is that corrupting the procedures by which a community self-regulates is one of the most insidious ways by which Dogmagianism establishes itself. Vigilant resistance against such corruption is therefore important if one wishes to ward off Dogmagian encroachment into the communal spaces that oneself is invested in — e.g. a fulfilling occupation, vibrant artistic scene, constructive online community, etc., that stands to lose the qualities the Satanist cherishes if Dogmagian dynamics take root.

III

The Faustian Art of Self-Evolution

> *We'll plunge into time's racing current,*
> *The vortex of activity,*
> *Where pleasure and distress,*
> *Setbacks and success,*
> *May come as they come, by turn-about, however;*
> *To be always up and doing is man's nature...*
> *I want frenzied excitements, gratifications that are painful*
> *Love and hatred violently mixed*
> *Anguish that enlivens, enspiriting trouble;*
> *Cured of my thirst to know at last,*
> *I'll never again shun anything distressful.*
> *From now on my wish is to undergo*
> *All that men everywhere undergo, their whole portion,*
> *Make mine their heights and depths, their weal and woe,*
> *Everything human encompass in my single person,*
> *And so enlarge my one self to embrace theirs, all*
> *And shipwreck with them when at last we shipwreck all.*
>
> **- Faust, in Part I of Goethe's play (1790)**

The third, fourth, and fifth tenets of the Tenebrous Creed state that:

- Satan lights our way along the path of self-evolution, which we pursue by seeking ever-greater excellence in all of our affairs.

- Self-evolution is fostered by the possession of zeal, wisdom, honor, empathy, and perseverance, which Satan therefore encourages us to cultivate.

- Insofar as the herd's fears, fads, and fictions hold us back from self-evolution, Satan urges us to stand apart from the herd.

These tenets speak to what Satanists consider worthy of pursuit (ever-greater excellence in all of our affairs), what factors support this endeavor (zeal, wisdom, honor, empathy, and perseverance), and what hindrances threaten to obstruct it (the herd's fears, fads, and fictions). As a whole, this set of ideas coheres into an ethos: the path of self-evolution.

Satanism, as a creed in which Faustianism is dominant, sees energy, motion, and progress as positive. Listlessness, incapacity, and sloth are negatives to be overcome. What such a creed holds invaluable is the acquisition of that which is not only good in itself, but also assists one in the acquisition of additional goods. Tenebrous Satanism therefore prizes self-evolution on multiple levels. Self-evolution entails maximizing one's strengths, minimizing one's weaknesses, and accomplishing that which a singular combination of talent, opportunity, and coincidence have put into one's hands to accomplish. Self-evolution is a first-order good whose possession is directly beneficial both for individuals and for the communities in which they are embedded. At the same time, though, self-evolution is also a second-order good, for the more skills and capacities one attains, the more one has to draw on for future success.

Some people are allergic to any mention of evolution when talking about human beings. Often, their primary worry is that worldviews that talk this way tend to blame initially disadvantaged people for their own failure to succeed. This matter is worth addressing before proceeding further, given the brash social-Darwinist talk bandied about by many Satanic denominations of the past. When Tenebrous Satanism puts forward the concept of self-evolution, however, it is with an understanding that "the more you succeed now, the more likely you will continue to in the future" is a law of existence whose tragic corollaries include "the less you succeed now, the less likely you will succeed in the future" and "the more you lose, the easier it is to keep losing." This understanding enables Tenebrous Satanism to recognize that the refusal to take people's circumstances into account and to help them rise above constitutes a squandering of those people's unique human potential. Dysfunctional ways of trying to assist the less fortunate deserve criticism, but this does not mean that to assist is not a valid imperative. Fundamentally, human beings are social animals who benefit from one another's well-being. There are even some whose highest manifestation of self-actualization lies in the discovery of ingenious ways of assisting their fellows. Tenebrous Satanism therefore does *not* endorse social Darwinism. It calls instead for the rejection of that ideology on the basis that such a worldview fails to grapple honestly with life's Perils.

The foregoing should make clear that by embracing self-evolution, both as a good in itself and a facilitator of other goods, Tenebrous Satanism endorses an ideal that is life-affirming without being victim-blaming. Merely endorsing self-evolution, however, is not enough to carry one all the way through to "ever-greater excellence in all of our affairs." Left unanswered is the question of *how* to strive for excellence effectively.

In response to this question, the Third Key proposes five virtues that it would benefit the Satanist to cultivate and one particularly pernicious vice to avoid. Lest this language be mistaken for moralizing — something that Satanists as a whole do not take well to — one must understand that the central aim of the Third Key is the fostering of excellence in the sense familiar to literary anti-heroes such as Faust, and to real-world philosophers such as Nietzsche. The guidance that follows is mindful of the social horizon of humanity, but a moralistic "getting along" with other human beings is not its central purpose. Instead, its aim is defining the art of Satanic excellence: attitudes and habits that both serve one's own long-term self-interest and promote a better quality of life — not only for oneself, but also for other human beings whose lives overlap with one's own. Regardless of what exactly an individual wants out of their earthly existence, what commitments they view as essential, or what political arrangements they may prefer, the Third Key asserts that the human life is simply *better* with these traits than it is without them.

Five Satanic virtues

The word "virtue" in its original usage has connotations that pertain to the pursuit of excellence generally, rather than morality specifically. A careful reading of Aristotle's account of virtue will reveal this, as will a not even particularly careful reading of Machiavelli. There is no reason, then, for a Satanist to be repelled by "virtue," as if such talk can only presage being preached to. A virtue is just a personal quality that promotes habits of a constructive, disciplined nature. Those who live virtuously in this sense are more likely to flourish. The unvirtuous, by contrast, are prone both to experiencing their own lives as frustrating and to frustrating the people around them. The brute fact is that amid the realities of "how life is," some behaviors and attitudes will be selected for by evolution, while others will be selected against. From such a perspective, virtues are traits with adaptive value: all other things being equal, people who possess such traits tend to *do better* at life.

Tenebrous Satanism's conception of "how life is" was previously laid out by the First Key. Each of the five virtues discussed below thus flows from one of the First Key's foundational concepts. *Zeal* attends the flourishing of the flesh. *Wisdom* facilitates the evolution of the spirit. *Honor* arises from awareness of a multitudinous world. *Empathy* is an appropriate response to life's Perils. And finally, *perseverance* enables the endurance of perpetual Adventure.

The rootedness of all of these virtues in the same Satanic soil speaks to their being interrelated. All virtue systems feature such interconnectedness, for virtues are not ranked goods whose hierarchy forbids them from clashing. Instead, they are goods irreducible to one another, meant to be sought side by side, each regulating pursuit of the others. It follows that, for best results in the art of self-evolution, Satanists ought to take each of the virtues into consideration to some extent. Exactly how much emphasis to put on each virtue, however, and how to moderate between them when their imperatives clash, is something that each Satanist will have to determine for themselves. Such is a fitting approach for a religion that prizes self-determination as much as Satanism does.

Zeal

Zeal offers a good starting point for a Satanic perspective on virtue, for since it is strongly oriented toward self-gratification, it lacks the aura of morality that many a Satanist is likely to find off-putting. Zeal consists in the enthusiastic possession of desires, the determination to fulfill these desires, and the initiative-taking necessary to bring desire to fulfillment. Zeal is evoked in *The Marriage of Heaven and Hell* by William Blake's proverb "Exuberance is beauty," as well as by his more hyperbolic "Sooner murder an infant in its cradle than nurse unacted desires."

Zeal speaks to Satan's role as Lord of This World, for zeal is manifest in the joyful embrace of "temptations": objects and experiences that, when seized, make life richer and more vivid, improving the quality of one's existence thereby. Zeal motivates one to do what must be done in order to bring about flourishing. At the same time, though, zeal is flourishing itself, in the form of exuberant enjoyment of one's gains. The term "zeal" also speaks to ways in which flourishing differs from mere self-indulgence. To have zeal for something connotes not only a desire to pursue it but having consciously reflected on and chosen this pursuit (e.g., zealous devotion to a cause). Self-indulgence, by contrast, tends to carry the negative implication of acting impulsively on one's desires in neglect of longer-term consequences.[21]

While zeal can refer to pursuit of carnal gratifications, it equally evokes the quest to satisfy intellectual curiosity, the enjoyment of aesthetic experience, the warmth of affinity between friends, and so forth. The imperative of zeal is not a demand to greet *all* of these with equal enthusiasm but rather to greet *something* with enthusiasm. The exact nature of that something will depend on the needs and wants of each unique individual. Proximate as it is to fulfillment as such, however, zeal is what makes life worth living. It ought, therefore, to be fought for as a birthright, both for one's own sake and on behalf of those whose well-being one cares about. Absence of zeal is not "wrong" in some moral sense. It is, rather, a warning sign, suggestive of the need to change something in the life of oneself or one's loved ones, lest one otherwise squander the singular opportunities of one's current existence.

Reflection upon the ways zeal can go astray reveals its interrelation with other virtues. Zeal cannot manifest virtuously without introspection about what one truly wants and why one wants it. Similarly, zeal ceases to be virtuous if it presents itself as a desire so intense as to produce compulsive or otherwise self-destructive behavior. Wisdom is the font of the introspection and ongoing reflection requisite to a healthy pursuit of zeal. Additionally, the most advanced pursuit and fulfillment of zeal is only possible when zeal is accompanied by perseverance. This is evident in how future success often requires exercising discipline now for the purposes of payoff later and finding ways to overcome obstacles instead of giving up.

Wisdom

Wisdom was a widely promoted virtue in the classical world. It receded into the background, however, as Christianity rose to prominence and society's conception of virtue became less excellence-oriented and more morality-oriented. The quality of wisdom can be illustrated by a consideration of a wise person's actions when faced with the need to make a complex decision liable to have serious consequences in the case of a mistake. Such a person remains calm and pauses for reflection instead of rushing in, attempts as broad a survey of considerations and options relevant to the decision as urgency allows, is honest with themselves about their strengths and weaknesses, and neither under-plans nor over-plans when it comes to envisioning contingencies. Wisdom, as manifest in tendencies such as these, is a prerequisite for the competent living of a sovereign life.

Lack of wisdom, on the other hand, not only leads to failure but undermines the credibility of the Faustian ethos as such. "See what happened when that idiot tried to go their own way?" Dogmagians will say when they witness a Satanist whose affairs are a mess. "This kind of bad result is why it is better to entrust oneself to Truth than to trust one's own judgment." Wisdom's absence is thus actively harmful to Satanism's cause.

The fact that knowledge often constitutes a facet of wisdom suggests a connection between wisdom and interdependence, for without awareness of how one's existence is connected to and impacted upon by others, there is little hope of prudent decision-making. However, from a Satanic perspective, the sort of wisdom most deserving of the name is the self-knowledge that drives self-evolution — a theme evoked by the Serpent's promise that the forbidden fruit would open Eve's eyes. Knowledge of Good and Evil emerges from conscious reflection on one's resources and situation before making a decision, and judging in accord with what is actually there instead of submitting to the biases of past experience or the preconceptions of society. This is not to say that wisdom consists only in introspection. Introspection accomplishes little if it is not accompanied by educating oneself about the world at large and maintaining an open mind about the possibility of novelty (i.e., rather than assimilating all new experience to that which is already known). Nonetheless, introspection is an essential component of the sort of undefiled wisdom that has the power to ward off hypocritical self-deceit.[22]

Whereas many virtues consist in a mean between two undesirable extremes — e.g., zeal is the mean between unsatisfactory abstinence and unhealthy compulsion — it is hard to go wrong with too much wisdom. One may take too long to reflect upon an urgent matter, or dwell on considerations that are not relevant, or paralyze oneself with indecisiveness, but these are all *unwise* courses of action.

What must yet be recognized about wisdom is that it is grounded in practicality, aimed at ensuring that one is doing one's best while one is, as per Faust, "up and doing." Wisdom is therefore not manifest in mere navel-gazing or in other psychological habits that appear intellectual yet lead to the indefinite deferral of action. Accordingly, the adjacent virtues most intimately tied to wisdom are zeal and honor, for both are directed at the attainment of specific purposes. Zeal entails a consideration of how to get what one wants. Honor, on the other hand, entails a consideration of how to deal with others in accord with what they deserve.

Honor

Tenebrous Satanism defines honor as a way of acting that is grounded in the recognition that human beings exist within a web of reciprocal relationships. Given that humans are social animals of this kind, it makes sense both to think of human relations in terms of a social contract[23] and to assent to the validity of said contract for the benefit of all. To pursue immediate gain by lying, breaking promises, taking advantage of trust, etc. is the behavior of a short-sighted fool. In the long run, such dishonorable behaviors both deprive one of the support of one's fellow human beings and undermine the social contract as such, to everyone's detriment. Mature Satanists are capable of recognizing this.

At the same time, Satanic honor is not only about upholding the social contract. It also encompasses integrity in the sense of knowing what one stands for and resisting the compromise of one's closely held principles. This aspect of honor provides robust support for self-assertion, as opposed to the attitude of "forgive and forget." It is a fundamental wrong, Satanism asserts, for people to be pressured into making nice with those who have harmed them just so that cowardly bystanders will not have to deal with the unpleasantness of conflict. Upholding honor means not only treating others with appropriate reciprocity, but also seeing to it that one receives what is due from others, rather than being taken advantage of.

A wise individual recognizes that the purpose of a social contract is to shield human beings from some of our shared vulnerability to life's Perils. Recognition of these Perils is thus one of honor's roots. Honor is even more directly tied, however, to interdependence, for rootedness in a shared world is what justifies the virtue: one ought to honor those relationships which one is most deeply and intimately invested in. The Watcher angels behaved in this fashion when they gifted the women they loved with such arts as would advance both themselves and their tribes. The idea thus illustrated — that it is worthwhile to enter into relationships with others in the world, and that such relationships ought to be mutually rewarding — speaks to the condition of human beings as creatures who live their best lives when they temper their innate selfishness with social cooperation. The Second Key's call to recognize the benefits of the Magian thought pattern, rather than dwelling solely on its harmful excesses, is justified by this reality.

The Order of Nine Angles (O9A) is a Satanic denomination whose writings more explicitly reflect upon the value of honor than do many others. Since Tenebrous Satanism is derived from O9A, our conception of honor naturally overlaps with O9A's to some extent. Most worth highlighting in this regard is the conception of honor as warranting differential degrees of ethical relationship between different human beings, rather than a universalistic ethic of "treat everyone equally." O9A and Tenebrous Satanism alike could be said to see merit in the old Arab Bedouin saying, "I against my brothers; I and my brothers against my cousins; I and my brothers and my cousins against the world." Like it or not, the reality this saying alludes to is that we simply are not in the same relationship with all human beings. When some relationships then press more closely upon our hearts and interests than others, prioritizing those relationships is the honorable thing to do. This concept is self-evident to any spouse who favors their significant other and even more so to any parent who favors their own child. To those who engage with life honestly, there should be nothing controversial about such a principle.

On the other hand, there are two fronts on which Tenebrous Satanism sees O9A's conception of honor as appropriate in past societies but less so nowadays. One is O9A's framing of honor as owed only within one's own Sinister tribe — i.e., a too-insular way of drawing honor's boundaries. The other is O9A's conceiving of honor as entailing an obligation to meet certain kinds of insult with physical force. These are conceptions of honor that befit situations in which a community is acutely endangered by its neighbors, or where individuals fear being pillaged by stronger competitors who must be dissuaded from this temptation via dominance displays. Tenebrous Satanism acknowledges the adaptive utility of O9A-like conceptions of honor *in such circumstances*. Most people living in developed nations today, however, do not experience such conditions and stand to lose more than they gain by trying to live "honorably" by O9A's definition. Tenebrous Satanism therefore defines honor in terms both broader and less reactive than O9A's.

As far as how honor is moderated, wisdom and empathy together illuminate the requirements of honor in any given situation from an intellectual and an emotional standpoint respectively. The absence of either results in the neglect of honor's duties, whereas their presence promotes further refinement of one's sense of honor over time. This includes, among other things, being able to perceive whether obligations of the social contract are being invoked in good faith or abused and whether the social contract may itself contain blind spots — e.g., cases where a society is in the habit of treating certain kinds of people inhumanely for poorly justified reasons. Empathy decries such inhumanity, while wisdom demands that irrational arrangements be replaced with ones that make better sense for everyone involved.

Amid all of this, Satanic honor entails a recognition that a balance must be struck between reciprocity's demands and the imperative to be true to oneself. Accordingly, it repays genuinely felt debts without complaint but bristles at guilt-based attempts at extortion; it keeps promises to those who deal fairly but breaks them with those who attempt to use one's word against one; it recognizes a general right to avenge wrongs done, even if practical considerations weigh against the taking of vengeance in the specific situation at hand. At all times, it is self-aware about what motivates reciprocity — e.g., whether a relationship is founded upon mutual affection or something more pragmatic — and gives and takes accordingly. None of this nuance is manageable in the absence of wisdom and empathy. With their support, on the other hand, honor hits its mark: the living of a life in which meaningful engagement with others augments one's own sense of fulfillment instead of detracting from it.

Empathy

In *The Antichrist*, Nietzsche argues that calling for pity "thwarts the whole law of evolution, which is the law of natural selection. It preserves whatever is ripe for destruction; it fights on the side of those disinherited and condemned by life; by maintaining life in so many of the botched of all kinds, it gives life itself a gloomy and dubious aspect." Such an attitude has long been pervasive in Satanic circles. It is not uncommon for Satanists to deride universalistic imperatives to "love one another" on the basis that such an attitude is saccharine, unrealistic, and unhelpful to victims wrongly pressured to forgive their abusers. Nonetheless, dissenters have emerged in recent years, calling for "compassion and empathy toward all creatures in accordance with reason."[24] Tenebrous Satanism contends that not only is there something to be said for this idea, but in fact one can argue for its congruence with Satanic values far more extensively than has been attempted thus far.

The Satanic warrant for empathy lies in it being an appropriate response to life's Perils. The upshot of Satan's behavior in the Book of Job is to forbid the telling of lies that pretend the world is just when in fact it is not. The events he sets in motion upend the complacency of Job's friends, who imagine that by adhering to idealistic principles (e.g., God is always just, only sinners suffer), they can immunize themselves from the suffering that befalls other people. In reality, though, all are born into a state of limitation shaped by both nature and nurture, all are vulnerable to reversals of fortune, and all are subject to death and the sufferings that precede it. This is no less true of Satanists than of other human beings. The Satanist who complains about this sort of talk because it rains on their parade of Faustian triumphalism is simply not living in reality. Satanists ought instead to conduct themselves in a way that takes this Dark side of existence into account.

Of course, the empathy espoused by Tenebrous Satanism is in important ways different from the universalistic endorsement of charity found in Christianity, of compassion found in Buddhism, etc. On one hand, the Satanic imperative of empathy "in accordance with reason" means that one is called to recognize the full breadth of beings that *deserve* empathy. This category turns out to be very wide indeed, encompassing not only human beings, but other sentient creatures besides — all who are capable of suffering. On the other hand, one must also admit, in accordance with reason, that it is unrealistic to actually *practice* empathy toward this full breadth of beings with perfect consistency, due to limitations of time, resources, energy, practicality, and so forth. The validity of partiality, already evoked above in connection with honor, follows from such limitations. The very nature of material existence makes constant, equal care for all suffering beings impossible, and therefore, it is both rationally and ethically justifiable to put those nearest and dearest to oneself first. Rather than engaging in pointless hand-wringing about the elusiveness of cosmic justice, the Satanist simply attends wholeheartedly to empathy's *attainable* imperatives.

The attitude just described has significant implications regarding the treatment of enemies. The Satanist is not called upon to love or show mercy to one's enemies. However, a mature moral being ought to grasp that no one, including one's foes, is immune from life's Perils, and strive accordingly to understand how such Perils — e.g., feeling fenced in by them, desperation to avoid them, etc. — drive the behavior of all sentient beings. The pursuit of such understanding is a front on which Faustian thinking collides headlong with the strictures of the Apollonian and Magian patterns. Where the Apollonian view sees an example of chaos to be avoided, and the Magian view sees a representative of Falsehood to be vanquished, the Faustian view sees a product both of its own impetus, and external pressures — i.e., something which therefore might yet alter from its current state, were that impetus or those pressures to change. The other two patterns are apt to perceive this constructive and optimistic aspect of the Faustian attitude as Sinister — i.e., inauspiciously proximate to, and sympathetic toward, "evil."

For Tenebrous Satanism, then, "Sinister empathy" is not just a synonym for acausal insight. It is rather a phrase that evokes the full ethical burden that empathy demands. Satanic empathy is apt to seem "Sinister" insofar as it promotes a degree of openness toward that which more timid minds insist "good" people should be completely closed to. By considering one's fellow beings always in light of their ever-present potential for change and evolution — instead of dismissing them because they violate the categories through which one filters the world or despising them as abominations for opposing the Truth — Satanism strives to actualize the Faustian pattern as fully as possible. This commitment to an open future directly opposes the arrogant dualism of Dogmagianism.

The sad fact is that, between sheer terror of life's Perils on one hand and overinvestment in herd conformity in denial of this vulnerability on the other, it is understandable for many people to find Tenebrous Satanism's extension of empathy "too Sinister" for their tastes. Our kind of empathy is undeniably difficult to maintain consistently. Nonetheless, Tenebrous Satanists strive for it, simply because that is what full, authentic engagement with life's Darkness demands.

Two virtues strongly tied to empathy are honor and perseverance. While empathy is what elevates honor from a mere calculation of social obligations to something actually of the heart, honor moderates empathy in accord with what is appropriate given the limitations of material existence and one's closer relationships with some beings over others. Perseverance, meanwhile, reinforces empathy insofar as a full comprehension of the degree of suffering present in the world is a daunting task, yet one that honesty demands — insofar as we can bear it. Empathy is, inarguably, a heavy burden, yet at the same time, one taken up willingly by those unafraid of seeing and acknowledging the world as it truly is.

Perseverance

Perseverance is essential to Satanism, for it enables one to prevail amid challenges, treating difficulties as opportunities for demonstrating and further developing one's strengths. As such, it is the *sine qua non* of an adversarial spirit, standing in for a variety of related traits — e.g., resilience, courage, patience, discipline, etc. A person who wholly lacked such traits would be unlikely to become a Satanist to begin with, given how the espousal of Satanism leads one into situations of strife that one could avoid by subscribing to a less controversial creed. Conversely, to embrace life's challenges wholeheartedly, making the best of whatever accidents of fortune Darkness inflicts, is a characteristic Satanic attitude.

The strong connection between perseverance and Satanism reflects the connection between perseverance and the Adventure of life itself. All successful organisms testify to perseverance, for had they lacked it, their species would have died out long ago. As a human virtue, then, perseverance is the conscious choice to perpetuate life's instinctual striving. But this does not mean perseverance is merely a matter of course. Conscious beings often shy away from it, opting instead to waste energy denying life's difficulties, whining about its unfairness, retreating into Dogmagian delusions in the vain hope for a "solution," etc. Ultimately, none of these evasions accomplish much compared to what might be accomplished via the determination to *just get on with life* — i.e., to persevere.

Satanic perseverance requires us to look the Dark side of existence straight in the eye and embark upon Adventure not despite its difficult characteristics, but because of them, eager for the opportunities to make more of ourselves that arise thereby. An Adventure is, by definition, a test of perseverance. Satan embraced Adventure when he took on the monumentally difficult endeavor of waging revolution against the "Almighty." The Satanist is similarly called to undertake endeavors that weaker, more conventional minds consider too hard to attempt.

All of this said, perseverance is like other virtues as far as the need for balance. It is no good to be a coward or a quitter. But it is equally no good to be reckless or stubborn to the point of self-destruction. Perseverance's mean lies in striking a balance between zeal and empathy. Zeal's contribution here is the ardency of one's desire, urging one ever forward and onward. The contribution of empathy, on the other hand, lies in the realistic grasp of one's vulnerabilities, reining in ill-conceived brashness and stubbornness before they can lead to ruin.

Perseverance can, finally, be likened to wisdom, insofar as these are both virtues whose possession, or lack thereof, decisively shapes how well or poorly a person will practice all of the other virtues. Wisdom's degree determines whether one is able to perceive where and how the virtues apply, and to reflect on the demands of all of them in a balanced way. Perseverance's degree, meanwhile, determines whether or not one will persist with the practice of the virtues even in circumstances in which it has become inconvenient or dangerous to act with integrity. The writer C. S. Lewis, though a theologian of the right-hand path, makes a good point in *The Screwtape Letters* (1942) when he asserts that "courage is not simply one of the virtues, but the form of every virtue at the testing point... A [virtue] which yields to danger will be [virtuous] only on conditions."

"Strength through adversity," it turns out, is not only the motto of the Satanist, but the motto of any person, of any ideology, who has any mettle at all — on top of also being the motto of nature itself. Acknowledging that this is so amounts to a call for empathy via openly recognizing the suffering that all living beings, human or otherwise, must persevere through in the course of maintaining and extending their earthly existences. At the same time, perseverance also issues forth a call to zeal, reaffirming one's own will to continue seeking fulfillment ever-onward — no matter the odds that may be stacked against one.

Satanic vice: herd conformity

A vice is the opposite of a virtue: a quality that promotes personal habits that are destructive of well-being. Vices may be conceptualized in a simplistic fashion by reflecting on the obstruction of virtues. Lack of zeal is manifest in apathy. Foolishness is the opposite of wisdom. One who fails to honor oneself or others is dishonorable. To reject empathy is to be guilty of solipsism at best, and cruelty at worst. Where perseverance is insufficient, sloth and cowardice rear their heads. These and other negative qualities make themselves evident in various violations and shortcomings of the social contract — things that a sane, responsible Satanist has just as much reason to oppose as any "ordinary" person.

Crime, for instance, as a violation of the social contract, typically entails a failure of empathy toward victims, a lack of perseverance via opting for an "easy" way of obtaining something instead of the harder but more honorable way, and inadequate wisdom insofar as whatever plan one has to get away with it fails to keep one out of prison. Amid such preponderance of vice, one cannot argue convincingly that crime is a valid manifestation of zeal. The Satanist who attempts to rationalize crime, as if any and all forms of transgression were equally edifying, is nothing more than an irresponsible thrill-seeker. The short-sightedness of such individuals ultimately obstructs the very cause that they imagine themselves to be advancing.

Shortcomings of the social contract, on the other hand, often proceed from the enshrinement of a misapplication of a virtue. For example, an oppressive institution may be built around flawed principles of honor, which people refuse to consider altering because they view the institution as somehow necessary to the continued perseverance of society. Or a charitable program may be zealously motivated by an excess of empathy without the balancing consideration of wisdom, such that it is better at producing lofty feelings in its supporters than it is at actually helping people. In such instances as these, vice not only prevents issues from being addressed, but may well prevent them from being perceived.

Does Tenebrous Satanism then conceive of vice solely in terms of a lack of virtue? To the contrary, that which the Creed highlights as a specific vice is distinct from the absence of any one virtue, being instead a thwarter of self-evolution in general. At issue here is the herd, and in particular, its fears, fads, and fictions. The contention is not that the herd is evil in and of itself, nor that all the most pressing evils that trouble humanity stem solely from it. Rather, what the Creed asserts is that wherever herd mentality is too ascendant, one witnesses a stifling of all the things that Satanism holds in highest esteem. Thus, as with the insidious destroyers of life discussed in the Second Key, Satanists are called upon to attend to that which bears so strongly against our foremost interests.

The conception of herd conformity as a vice is justified by the harms that inevitably follow whenever people assume:

- One ought to embrace the *fears* of the herd by automatically abhorring and avoiding what others do

- One ought to embrace the *fads* of the herd by automatically desiring and seeking what others do

- One ought to embrace the *fictions* of the herd by automatically believing whatever others believe

A person who embraces such notions is likely to:

- Feel shame at desires outside of the norm and censor such desires instead of pursuing them — contra *zeal*

- Place trust in established opinions instead of asking questions that could cause friction — contra *wisdom*

- Slack off on obligations insofar as others' behavior tells them that they can get away with this, or else uphold unreasonable expectations of some parties of the social contract because "that's how things work" — contra *honor*

- Stifle concern for those the herd deems undeserving or even behave spitefully toward them — contra *empathy*

- Abandon unconventional pursuits — contra *perseverance*

Accordingly, Tenebrous Satanism calls for resistance against herd conformity. It must be understood, however, that this resistance is not conceived in terms of wholesale rejection of the herd as such. The thorny difficulty that Satanists run into on this front is that although our worldview valorizes individualism, this does not change the fact that we ourselves remain, whether we like it or not, members of an animal species that tends to flourish best when we cooperate with our fellows. The Satanist who preaches individualistic libertarianism to the point of occluding this reality is no less guilty of self-deceit than the deluded creationists and blank-slaters[25] that Satanism opposes.

Tenebrous Satanism therefore urges Satanists to refrain from the unrealistic romanticization of the self-reliant "lone wolf" that is so often found in other Satanic denominations. Honest reflection upon the nature of human life strongly suggests that those who are dismissive toward sociality have nonetheless always found themselves the beneficiaries of it at some point. Consider first, on this front, that all human beings enter the world in an initially vulnerable and fragile state that is not survivable if the infant fails to receive at least a minimal welcome into the world by its caregivers. Second, consider how much there is to be learned — general knowledge, applied skills, and so on — in the course of growing to maturity and how impoverished one's life would be if one had only one's own trial and error to resort to, unaided by the past discoveries of those who came before us and their willingness to share their expertise. Third, consider the broad range of human achievements that arose only thanks to the coordination of cooperation via storytelling, as has already been highlighted via the Second Key's acknowledgment that Magianism is not wholly pernicious.

Fourth, consider how most people's conceptions of meaningful happiness include not only their own well-being, but also that of their loved ones, as per the First Key's observation that flourishing is an endeavor with an inherently social horizon.

Consider, finally, that while there is an obvious degree of individualism built into every organism's striving to preserve itself, reflection upon long-term ramifications reveals that "every man for himself" is not a wise principle to maximize. Given initially bountiful resources but limited space (a restriction that is, in truth, never not in effect), the instincts of self-preservation and reproduction can drive organisms to multiply and consume until they have exhausted their own food supply and poisoned themselves with their own wastes. Such an outcome is the logical culmination of each individual organism's blind striving to advance only itself. The hope for a conscious species such as humanity, on the other hand — slim though it may be — is that by foreseeing this conclusion and coordinating with others for the good of all we might yet manage to avoid this fate.[26] Conversely, a society of selfish libertarians would be, in the long term, a doomed society.

By insisting on acknowledging the above points, Tenebrous Satanism avoids framing human nature in the unrealistically atomized terms that former Satanisms have too often been beguiled by. At the same time, we do insist on the prerogative of advancing individual flourishing and self-evolution, recognizing that, ultimately, the herd is but a collection of individuals — a collective that is better off tolerating individualism than being ruled wholly by conformity. This is inherently obvious to the walker of the Sinister Path who strives, against the inertia of a defective society, to bring something better into existence. Ultimately, though, even the ordinary, complacent citizen experiences improved quality of life when individuals of unique vision are empowered to think, invent, and accomplish new things; when dogma is challenged instead of being left unquestioned; and when dysfunctional systems are critiqued and overthrown — however much some may resent the short-term upheaval that results.

Nor is this to say that the importance of the individual lies only in what they can offer to the group. To the contrary, the inherent value of the individual is enshrined in the very metaphysics of Tenebrous Satanism via spirit's gravitation toward the flesh even in the face of all the difficulties that attend worldly existence. One may here observe that, by orienting itself this way, spirit evinces a preference for multiplicity (individuality) over unity (conformity): any initial unity it possessed was willfully shattered by its descent into the plurality that is life. Yes, it is true that we are unlikely to succeed in making a lasting home of this world without willingness to think of humanity as a whole. However, it must at the same time be recognized that the embrace of multitudinous existence is in itself an embrace of diversity and uniqueness, and hence of individualism. Tenebrous Satanism therefore insists on giving individualism its due.

When the fifth tenet of the Creed then calls for Satanists to "stand apart" from the herd, it is with the following key points of the preceding discussion in mind: i) yes, it is true that the herd tends to obstruct a number of Satanic goals and values; ii) nonetheless, there is pragmatic justification for the herd-existence of humanity and thence for ideologies that seek to promote and protect herd-being; iii) there is, however, no less justification for the promotion of individualism — and Satanism is itself an ideology dedicated to advancing and preserving this facet of embodied existence.

Accordingly, the Creed acknowledges that the herd can have pernicious effects on the Satanist yet does not call for the Satanist to seek the herd's destruction. In fact, it does not even call for the Satanist to greet the herd with particular antipathy. What it instead commends is that the Satanist *maintain a degree of separation* from the herd. The exact meaning of this will depend on the circumstances of individual Satanists.

In some instances, "standing apart" may require physically removing oneself from the presence of others, so as to maintain one's own space. This may include limiting or foregoing things like social media, the unnecessary consumption of material goods, mass forms of entertainment, or other sources of interpersonal "noise." The issue is not that any of these things are wrong per se, but rather, that their presence in one's life tends to aggravate confusion between one's own priorities and the priorities of society. Separation may also take the form of severing stifling social ties, frequent introspection toward the end of discovering and promoting values that are truly one's own, intentional rearrangement of one's schedule so as to better pursue things that are important to oneself, and so forth.

In all cases, what is most essential to the effort to separate oneself is that one experiences said effort as psychologically efficacious in securing a space in which one feels free to pursue one's unique potential. Externals, such as the adoption of an appearance that sets one apart from others, are only of value insofar as they express and extend this sense of space. A downfall of too much external signaling of difference, on the other hand, is that such behavior readily falls back into herd-preoccupation via the need for the herd to see one's set-apartness. Satanists embarrass themselves when they behave as just another alternative subculture, declaring that they "do not care what other people think" — frequently, loudly, and coincidentally within the hearing of other people. To masquerade as a rebel is easy. To genuinely wean oneself off the need for the attention and approval of other people is much harder but proportionately more rewarding.

Ultimately, one cannot blame people too much for falling into herd conformity, for were they to stray too far outside of their quotidian ruts and ideological bubbles, they might be forced to recognize that the way they live their life is not really as in touch with reality and as well geared toward their own flourishing as they might like to believe. Such an admission is difficult to wring out of people because with it comes an imperative to rethink one's life. Many people lack the will and energy for such an endeavor. As a seeker of evolution and opponent of stasis, however, the Satanist is up to the task. Casting aside the shackles of preconception, expectation, and delusion is an essential step on the path of self-actualization and is therefore a step that no Satanist should neglect.

Summary

Instead of formulating moral commandments in the mold of "thou shalt," as religions typically do, Tenebrous Satanism's conception of self-evolution empowers each Satanist to explore for themselves what exactly excellence means in their own particular case. At the same time, the Creed also recognizes that some human qualities and habits have a near-universal tendency to support self-evolution, while others tend to get in its way. It is worth articulating these matters explicitly, not for the sake of restriction, but for the sake of offering constructive advice in the art of living well. Hence, the Third Key sets forth zeal, wisdom, honor, empathy, and perseverance as virtues beneficial for Satanists to cultivate. These qualities are helpful in human life, regardless of what specific goods an individual sets out to pursue. Conversely, one ought to resist herd conformity, not because it is morally "wrong," but because no matter what exactly a Satanist wants out of life, excessive preoccupation with the herd is more likely to obstruct it than to aid it.

In situating self-evolution's open-endedness within a conception of virtue and vice, the Third Key's overall aim is not unlike that of secular humanism: to provide as much scope for individual diversity as possible within a foundational structure that discourages dysfunctional behaviors. There are obvious Satanic reasons why this is preferable to a too-suffocating moral system. At the same time, it is also preferable to a too-vague sentiment of "do as thou wilt." To say only this, and no more, is to neglect to provide any tools to assist one in reflecting upon whether it is truly to one's benefit to "will" what one does or how best to do what the will asserts itself toward.

Some prospective Satanists may already possess such tools. Others, however, will not — perhaps including one's own children, who will have their own struggles with the herd to contend with. We therefore hope the Third Key's reflections on virtue and vice will offer provision to such as these, both by putting into their hands the tools of self-cultivation, and by warning them against what might otherwise detract from the excellence of their future attainments.

Notes

[21] While Anton LaVey did draw a clear distinction between indulgence and compulsion in *The Satanic Bible* (1969), the sheer fact that he felt the need to spell out such a distinction does not speak well of the implications inherent in the word "indulgence" by itself.

[22] This sentence paraphrases elements taken from Anton LaVey's Third Satanic Statement, from *The Satanic Bible* (1969).

[23] The phrase "social contract" is used here in a broad sense. Readers who are politically centrist may project onto it an endorsement of such institutions as governments and taxpaying, while those inclined toward libertarianism or anarchism may frame it in terms of chosen obligations of mutual aid without endorsing an imperative to submit to state power. Tenebrous Satanism does not insist on one of these interpretations over others, nor do we demand an embrace of the specific theories of Thomas Hobbes, Jean-Jacques Rousseau, or others who have thrown about the "social contract" concept. To us, "social contract" is merely a tidy, short-form way of capturing the uncontroversial claim that humans are a species whose interests are typically served by at least some degree of cooperation with one another.

[24] Quoted from "The Seven Tenets of The Satanic Temple," https://thesatanictemple.com/pages/about-us

[25] We refer here to individuals who proceed on the assumption that human beings are "blank slates," i.e., exempt from evolution, bereft of instincts, and perfectible via ideological imposition. The term is derived from Steven Pinker's book *The Blank Slate: The Modern Denial of Human Nature* (2002). Many kinds of Dogmagianism, whether religious or secular, proceed from a blank-slate ideology, for their otherworldly delusions would not be able to get off the ground otherwise.

[26] For a book-length discussion of these issues, see Peter Ward's book *The Medea Hypothesis: Is Life on Earth Ultimately Self-Destructive?* (2009).

IV

The Void, Darkness, and the Abyss

> *That motley drama-oh, be sure*
> *It shall not be forgot!*
> *With its Phantom chased for evermore*
> *By a crowd that seize it not,*
> *Through a circle that ever returneth in*
> *To the self-same spot,*
> *And much of Madness, and more of Sin,*
> *And Horror the soul of the plot.*
> *But see, amid the mimic rout,*
> *A crawling shape intrude!*
> *A blood-red thing that writhes from out*
> *The scenic solitude!*
> *It writhes!-it writhes!-with mortal pangs*
> *The mimes become its food,*
> *And seraphs sob at vermin fangs*
> *In human gore imbued.*

- "The Conqueror Worm" by Edgar Allan Poe (1843)

Though the preceding Keys have made a handful of general acausal claims — i.e., that there exists an invisible and intangible thing called spirit which animates life and strives for ever greater self-realization through the flesh — these claims have been kept minimal up to this point. Thus, nothing so far prevents those who reject the supernatural from adopting Tenebrous Satanism as a way of life, were they to construe "spirit" as merely a figurative way of talking about the subjective experience of human freedom. Nor is this the only front on which Tenebrous metaphysics can be adapted into metaphor.

Nonetheless, the full-fledged doctrine of Tenebrous Satanism does incorporate supernatural belief. One can still identify as a Tenebrous Satanist without subscribing to this if one gravitates toward the philosophy of the previous Keys yet lacks interest in the esoteric elements that subsequent Keys discuss. There is nothing wrong with said lack, as a good many human beings would be better off if they were to fix their attention more wholeheartedly on *this* world, instead of elsewhere. The secular Satanist is, however, but one of three possibilities Tenebrous Satanism allows for. The other two — the witch and the sorcerer — embrace not only the causal ethos of Satanism, but also its acausal elements: esoteric beliefs and practices of a Dark nature.

The sixth tenet of the Creed states, "The witch and the sorcerer recognize Satan not only in the Fire of the Will, but also in the Will of the Fire." Recognizing Satan in the Fire of the Will is inherent to all Satanists, for though we intend this phrase to refer to an inner spiritual essence, we do not object to others construing it as just a poetic way of talking about the self-empowerment Satanism promotes in its adherents. The Will of the Fire, however, unavoidably refers to a supernatural reality distinct from the humanistic, this-worldly component of Satanism. More specifically, it alludes to acausal forces and entities that take up an adversarial stance against the forces and entities more typically venerated by human religions. Such adversarial beings want many of the same things that human Satanists want: for embodied creatures to experience full enjoyment of the flesh, for evolution to be advanced by daring new achievements, and for conscious minds to reckon honestly with Darkness instead of fleeing from it. It therefore makes sense for these acausal entities to cooperate with humans who share their agenda.

While the Tenebrous witch and sorcerer are alike insofar as they interact with forces and entities that the secular Satanist has no relationship with (or at least, no *conscious* relationship), they differ with regard to the nature and degree of their occult fervor. The witch's motives include curiosity, ambition, and a thirst for meaning. For such individuals, the allure of the occult lies in its capacity to reveal realities unknown to ordinary mortals, to fulfill desires that cannot otherwise be fulfilled, and to thereby add depth and vividness to life's texture. They do not necessarily want to make esotericism into a full-time preoccupation, however. Accordingly, the witch engages with the occult on an ad hoc basis, without formal commitment to the forces invoked.

The sorcerer is motivated by many of the same drives as the witch. However, the sorcerer is additionally compelled by a sense of being called to a destiny in alliance with a specific acausal being or beings. This may be the Nekalah, the Dark Gods venerated both by the Order of Nine Angles (O9A) and by Tenebrous Satanism, or it may be some other entity or entities with an identifiably Satanic agenda. Either way, toward the end of pursuing and fulfilling this destiny, the sorcerer enters into a pact with the forces of Darkness. This pact may be accompanied by a passage of initiation — i.e., a trial whose adversities force the sorcerer to transform and evolve beyond their current capacities. Such initiatory proceedings may follow the protocol that the Ninth Key describes or take whatever form the individual sees as appropriate in their own case.

The level of commitment to acausal matters that the sorcerer's pact entails is what the Creed's seventh tenet has in mind when it states, "The Will of the Fire and the will of the sorcerer are one." It is not that the sorcerer — nor, for that matter, the witch — is in any way subservient to the powers with whom they work. Rather, a congruency exists between the sorcerer's trajectory of self-evolution and the long-term goals of certain acausal forces. It is then only natural for the two to find one another and forge an alliance. It is likewise natural for this Faustian partnership of human and nonhuman to together undertake endeavors that challenge the established ways of the world, to the dismay of those who prefer the status quo. Such an eventuality is what the Creed calls "the advancement of Satan's cause through the embrace of creative strife."

The specific occult methods of the Tenebrous witch and sorcerer will be detailed fully in the Keys of Praxis. But what must first be understood, and is hence the focus of the Fourth Key, are the esoteric beliefs of Tenebrous Satanism: beliefs about the fundamental reality behind existence, about humanity's place in the universe, and about our final destination — i.e., the question of life after death. These are, respectively, questions of metaphysics (what is), teleology (human purpose), and eschatology (final things).

In all three of these areas, what most distinguishes Tenebrous Satanism from other religions is its conception of the Abyssal Void of Darkness.[27] By providing a full elucidation of this most ultimate of entities, the Fourth Key will make explicit much that the Prelude to the Creed hints at. And in the process, it will paint a vivid picture of the spiritual backdrop of Tenebrous witchcraft and sorcery.

IV — The Void, Darkness, and the Abyss

Metaphysics of the Void

> *In the beginning was the Word — so goes*
> *The text. And right off I am given pause,*
> *A little help please, someone, I'm unable*
> *To see the Word as first, most fundamental.*
> *If I am filled with the true spirit*
> *I'll find a better way to say it.*
> *So: In the beginning Mind was — right?*
> *Give plenty of thought to what you write,*
> *Lest your pen prove too impetuous.*
> *Is it mind that makes and moves the universe?*
> *Shouldn't it be: In the beginning*
> *Power was, before it nothing?*
> *Yet even as I write this down on paper*
> *Something tells me don't stop there, go farther*
> *The Spirit's prompt in aid; now indeed,*
> *I know for sure: In the beginning was the Deed!*

- Faust, in Part I of Goethe's play (1790)

To speak of the Void is to admit how little we can honestly apprehend about whatever is behind the universe. The experience of Goethe's Faust is illustrative in this regard. As he puzzles over scripture, Faust grapples with the traditional notion that in the beginning was "the Word," i.e., God's design, imposed upon reality so as to bring about creation. What is this, though, but a child's explanation, equivalent to "the world exists because God said so"?

Contemplating the matter further, it occurs to Faust that design implies intention. Behind the Word must be a Mind that formulated it. But since a mind that lacked a capacity for actualization could produce nothing, Faust reasons that Power must be an even more fundamental mover behind the universe. He does not stop here, however. Instead, he carries on one step further, asserting finally that "In the beginning was the Deed!" This is a striking conclusion, considering the nature of the angst that drives the plot of the play. Faust is defined by his inability to ever gain enough knowledge to satisfy him. Such a theme frames Faust as here banging his head against his own limitations. As a mere mortal, reasoning from an earthly perspective, he is forced in the end to admit that he cannot determine the extent to which God lives up to his traditional attributions of omniscience (Mind) and omnipotence (Power). He can only deduce that God must have had *enough* of said qualities to be able to accomplish "the Deed," i.e., the creation of the world. Honest utilization of the intellect reveals to Faust that God is a doer of deeds, but he can know little else.

Tenebrous Satanism's conception of the Abyssal Void of Darkness proceeds along similar lines. The Satanist contends that if one looks at the world honestly, there is little reason to believe that "God" is anything like what the Magian religions envision — i.e., all-powerful, all-knowing, all-good, etc. When the Satanist's eyes fall upon life, they behold no signs of providence. Life, to the contrary, is an ongoing carnival of eating, mating, and death, in which pain, disappointment, and betrayal are ever present. The fact that some aspects of life can be experienced as pleasant for a time merely occludes these underlying realities temporarily without either erasing or wholly mitigating them.

If one is to then speculate about what manner of acausal force might be behind a world with such features, the Satanist finds it more plausible to characterize such a force as "Dark" than as "Light." This is because a deep shadow of obscurity and opacity is cast over life. Life frequently descends into experiences of suffering, chaos, and futility. And yet, life is still dearly cherished by the vast majority of creatures that possess it. What life thus fundamentally consists of is blind, inexplicable, ever-restless striving. It is the clamor of multitudinous beings all attempting to make their way in the world and thereby coming into constant conflict with one another. It is a many-headed monster, ever devouring itself. Or it is a collection of innumerable puppets, compelled to and fro by a master who seems more interested in entertaining himself than in the wellbeing of his creations. Either way, this picture hardly suggests the benevolent deity of any right-hand-path religion. It far more readily evokes something like H. P. Lovecraft's Azathoth, the blind idiot god and mad daemon sultan who seethes and bubbles at the center of the universe, gnawing hungrily away at reality.[28]

Why dream up such a repugnant-sounding being and proceed to dignify it with the label of "deity"? Tenebrous Satanism acknowledges the divinity of Darkness as an act of open-eyed engagement with reality. In so doing, Satanists reject the dissatisfying alternative of retreating into whatever more pleasant and self-flattering stories others use to console themselves. Consider, on this front, the self-contradictory nature of many Magian accounts of the Light. Right-hand-path religions are forever having to invent rationalizations to explain how God (or the equivalent representative of Ultimate Truth), endowed with various perfections as he is, coexists with a Perilous world in which such perfections are often manifestly absent. What such rationalizations frequently boil down to is that although God is perfect, he nonetheless creates an imperfect world, and enters into an imperfect process, in anticipation of perfection's glory shining forth all the brighter once it emerges from this morass. That this more or less turns the world into a vanity project of God's, in which the suffering of untold numbers of causal beings is justified for the sake of God's own self-aggrandizement — and yet, God is still characterized as *benevolent!* — is truly a wonder of Magian logic. The cynic, meanwhile, observes that God, needing nothing, nonetheless created the world solely so that he could marvel at himself; God subsequently disliked the reflection he beheld and ordered his creations to improve themselves to please him better; God is thus a self-absorbed masochist, endlessly toiling to fix a self-created problem. Point this out openly, however, and the believer will retreat into nonsense about "divine mystery beyond human comprehension" and so forth.

Contra such formulations, the advantage of Tenebrous Satanism is that its conception of deity entails no self-contradictory mental pretzels of this sort. Satanists never find themselves in the awkward position of preaching that all worldly things are sinful in one breath, only to bluster in the very next breath that leaving the world via suicide is yet another sin.[29] There is, similarly, no need to tie oneself in knots about how God is supposed to be all-knowing, all-powerful, and all-good, yet evil nonetheless exists in the world. The difficulty is easily solved by throwing out the optimistic notion of a perfect being. Replace this with a conception of deity as the inscrutable, implacable, and unrelenting striver behind life, utterly indifferent to any human notion of "good," and a great many things about the operation of the evolutionary principle in material existence suddenly make far more sense. No wonder, in that case, that life is simultaneously suggestive of a mad scientist's experiment, a meat grinder, and "a tale told by an idiot, full of sound and fury, signifying nothing."[30]

If the ultimate acausal reality is to be conceived of in such bleak terms as this, does it follow that Tenebrous Satanism embraces nihilism? Such a conclusion only follows if nihilism is defined in the purely metaphysical sense of denying the existence of a loving God.

Yes, Tenebrous Satanists believe that it is better to acknowledge the harshness of existence than to engage in optimistic make-believe about reality. We think it is both irrational and harmful, though, to use metaphysical beliefs — whether our own or anyone else's — to promote any ethos that makes the quality of human existence worse rather than better. The mere possession of metaphysical beliefs about the Abyssal Void of Darkness does not prevent Satanists from formulating an ethos that is nonetheless life-affirming and constructive. The contents of the previous three Keys should have already made this evident.

That said, it is fair to ask how one can reconcile talk of the Abyssal Void of Darkness with what the previous Keys proposed regarding flesh, spirit, and the relationship between them. All that is necessary here, though, is to recognize that the prior Keys' way of talking about the acausal (spirit) and the current Key's way of talking about the acausal (Abyssal Void of Darkness) are just different ways of talking about the same thing. On a higher level, one can speak of the acausal as an undifferentiated whole — e.g., it is the primal origin of life (Void), mover and shaker behind the world (Darkness), and eventual devourer of all (Abyss). On a lower and no less correct level, however, one can speak of the acausal as differentiated amid its active participation in the causal realm. This is spirit — i.e., that part of the acausal which is currently engrossed in enfleshed existence. Tenebrous Satanism thus embraces a panentheist understanding of divinity in which it is equally correct to speak of the divine as something that transcends the world (Abyssal Void of Darkness), and as something immanent in the world (spirit).[31]

If spirit is itself an aspect of Abyssal Darkness, it follows that every living being has, as its animating principle, a portion of the restless Void. What Tenebrous Satanism thus envisions regarding the acausal origin of life is that the Void constitutes a sort of primordial ocean from which the spiritual components of living beings — i.e., what are typically called souls — initially arise. Flesh, in turn, is the medium through which these components become differentiated, both from one another and from the Void as a whole. Prior to entry into the flesh, all is one in the Void. What flesh offers to spirit is the establishment of the boundaries that distinguish one being from another. Without such boundaries, there can be no meaningful individualism.

It follows from such a conception of life that, contra what other religions believe, Tenebrous Satanism does not think of spirit as something that is supposed to remain separate from the flesh or which operates according to fundamentally different rules from the things of the earth. Instead, Tenebrous belief embraces the following trio of fundamental metaphysical principles, each of which will be elaborated on further in the sections that follow:

- *Pervasive mortality:* All souls are contingent, mutable, and subject to decay, while only the Void is limitless and everlasting.

- *Universal incarnation:* Each and every acausal being at one time knew life in the flesh, for only through such material delimitation could they have come to conceive of themselves as distinct individuals.

- *Inward divinity:* Since every living being's soul is a fragment of the Void, esoteric methods can enable one to tap into the Darkness lurking within and use it to accomplish things that would be difficult or impossible to do by causal means alone.

Pervasive mortality

All souls are contingent, mutable, and subject to decay, while only the Void is limitless and everlasting.

What Tenebrous Satanism refers to as the soul is not, as in other religious traditions, an everlasting and unchanging spiritual substance. It is instead a vortex of energies that are both coming together and coming apart on an ongoing basis, not unlike how the physical body is constantly engaged in the process of taking in sustenance and eliminating waste.

The more primitive an organism, the more loosely bound its acausal energies. Conversely, the more complex an organism, the tighter a nexion of instinct, desire, and consciousness it will develop. Past a certain threshold (which one suspects is crossed by many higher animals besides human beings), the causal form imposes sufficient structure for the acausal energies to continue cohering even after the death of the physical body, at least for a time. In this regard, the metaphysics of Tenebrous Satanism resemble certain elements of Buddhist belief, allowing for the persistence of beings after death in some sense, yet at the same time denying that souls are everlasting.

To deny immortality is not to say that souls cannot still enjoy a very long existence separate from the flesh. The circumstances that can lead to such an outcome will be explored in the next section. What is worth stressing in connection with the present topic, however, is the Tenebrous conviction that ultimately, there is no survival without striving. Just as with causal beings (i.e., animals, humans, etc.), the continued existence of acausal beings (i.e., spirits) is dependent on their ability to maintain themselves. This requires exertion, both to ward off specific threats to one's continued existence and against the forces of entropy in general. Hence, the weak and inconstant perish, while the strong and determined prevail — though even their time will not be forever. Brutal Darwinian processes and their associated tragedies are no less operative in the acausal realm than the causal. This state of affairs being unfair or depressing does not change the fact that things operate thus.

Amid acknowledging the Dark nature of this worldview, Tenebrous Satanism nonetheless persists in viewing life as something to be affirmed. Regardless of how many despairing beings may wish they could end their suffering definitively by wholly abandoning the cycle of existence, the Void's enthusiasm for entry into the flesh remains undiminished. It follows that to purposely seek extinction — whether via suicide or via the self-negation preached by religions such as Buddhism — is to throw away one's unique and never to be repeated existence without really accomplishing anything by doing so. Such an act does nothing to prevent the indifferent Abyss from recycling the dispersed energies into some other being or beings, and so the perpetual mad experiment of Darkness carries on unabated. Self-extinction therefore has no real power to diminish the total amount of suffering in the universe. It is as if, amid playing a game and deciding that one did not like the moves available, one were to purposely make the worst moves possible, so as to petulantly undermine the game for both oneself and others. The Satanist contends, to the contrary, that even amid a set of bleak options, surely we are better off choosing the best among them: to seek what self-evolution and flourishing are nonetheless within the reach of ourselves and our loved ones, cherishing what comes to us thereby even if it can never be everlasting.

Yes, our pleasures and fulfillments will always be imperfect on account of being, like our very lives, temporary and mutable. Amid pervasive mortality, though, there is nothing that is not imperfect and temporary. Tenebrous Satanism asserts that the sooner conscious beings learn to accept and celebrate this, instead of bemoaning or denying it, the better for everyone.

Universal incarnation

Each and every acausal being at one time knew life in the flesh, for only through such material delimitation could they have come to conceive of themselves as distinct individuals.

Tenebrous Satanism believes that without embodiment, there is no individualism. Prior to experiencing life in the material world, the Void is an undifferentiated unity. Upon entry into the flesh, however, a being comes into existence that has particular needs which inevitably conflict with the needs of others. Such a creature naturally pursues its own interests, distinguishing (whether consciously or instinctively) between allies and enemies in the process. It is thus life that produces individualism — sometimes with such forceful distinctiveness that a being's acausal energies remain cohesive even after the death of its physical body. The habits engendered by the flesh are such that it is common for such souls to be quickly drawn back into enfleshed existence again — i.e., to reincarnate. Nonetheless, Tenebrous Satanism holds the belief that some circumstances can produce a being that does not reenter life after its death. Such a being instead takes up an existence parallel to the flesh. Entities of this kind are known generically as *spirits*.

Why believe in such beings, whose existence is beyond the power of science to prove? As the introduction preceding the Keys mentioned, Tenebrous Satanism holds that all human beings are capable of some degree of genuine spiritual insight. Moreover, in a majority of cultures throughout history, people have believed in supernatural beings of various kinds. Such beliefs do differ significantly between cultures, and their differences may seem irreconcilable upon first glance. The conviction of Tenebrous Satanism, however, is that diversity among human religious beliefs can be explained by two factors: the existence of multiple kinds of acausal being, and variation with regard to what aspects of acausal reality a given culture chooses to acknowledge or to deny.

Broadly speaking, there are three circumstances that spawn beings who maintain their individuality despite no longer being embodied. In the first, a spirit has developed a generalized affinity for some aspect of earthly existence — e.g., it attaches itself to a particular place, community, value, etc. — such that no single subsequent incarnation will satisfy it. These *Tellurian* spirits remain in close relationship with the realm of the flesh, even though they do not take on a specific fleshly form themselves. Into this category fall what other traditions have termed ghosts, elementals, fae, djinn, and various pagan deities who oversee both nature and culture alike. Such spirits are by far the most numerous of the three kinds. One can conceive of them as belonging to a variety of tribes, each with its own customs and its own affairs, varying widely with regard to whether they are friendly, neutral, or hostile toward one another and toward humans.

As a rule, Tellurians possess far more insight into the acausal realm than humans do. At the same time, because of how intimately they remain bound to worldly matters, Tellurians' knowledge tends to be limited in ways analogous to how human knowledge is limited. Hence, one winds up with supernatural beings who possess much wisdom and power regarding certain matters but are not omnipotent or omniscient. This can produce circumstances wherein, for example, one kind of spirit claims definitively that another kind does not exist, when in fact the former is merely ignorant of the latter. Different groups of human beings can, similarly, wind up with vastly different conceptions of what the spirit world is like, depending on which spirits they have talked to, how those spirits themselves interpret reality, and so forth.

In the second instance, a being is badly traumatized by its sojourn in the flesh. As a result, it develops a strong aversion to any kind of embodied existence. These *Celestial* spirits come to see the flesh as a trap to be escaped from and style themselves as the would-be rescuers and liberators of enfleshed beings not yet enlightened enough to have reached the same conclusion. Spirits who fall into this category include the angels of Western religions, the bodhisattvas of the East, and similar "Light-oriented" beings. These kinds of spirits are fewer than Tellurians, yet often more potent on an individual basis. Missionaries on a quest to expand their respective empires, they are ever seeking to persuade — or coerce — living beings and Tellurians alike into denouncing the realm of the flesh. It is Celestials' conviction that such is the best way to combat the "evil" that earthly existence is rife with.

Typically, Celestials possess more far-reaching acausal insight than Tellurians. However, they are so committed to their own agendas, and so marred by past traumas of the flesh — even while often being in utter denial of said experiences — that they can be relied upon to advance self-serving lies as Truth when interacting with humans. Hence, one encounters Celestials who claim that they are the only True divine beings, lest their influence be diminished via humans realizing that other options exist. One also encounters Celestials who sincerely believe they are the only True divine beings because their own Light has blinded them. There even exists the occasional very powerful Celestial who has hoodwinked innumerable other spirits into believing that He is the Truth and the Light and so forth. Such beings reinforce their own delusions by using their powers to build entire elaborate acausal worlds for themselves, wherein all things operate in apparent accord with their slanted preferences. One cannot then be surprised that humans who venerate these entities wind up with a perspective on acausal matters that is slanted likewise.

In the third instance, a being chooses, in a crucial moment of vulnerability (e.g., death of the physical body or other catastrophic disruption), to gaze directly into the Abyssal Void of Darkness, and to commit what it beholds there to full awareness, instead of either allowing itself to be destroyed or giving in to the urge to flee in self-preservation. The resultant "Dark Awakening" causes such a spirit to identify with the Void itself from then onward. The circumstances in which this may happen are diverse, ranging from an intentional immersion sought via advanced forms of spiritual discipline to a desperate attempt to survive cataclysmic accident, metaphysical assault, or other such misadventures. What all such scenarios wind up producing is a *Sinistral* spirit: an avatar of Darkness who makes its home now in the Abyss. Sinistrals have not typically been venerated by human religions, but hints at their existence can be detected in two mythological tropes: i) the angel who falls and thereby becomes a devil or demon, and ii) alien gods of a horrific nature, such as those depicted in the fictional works of H. P. Lovecraft.[32]

As well as having less of a presence in known religious narratives, Sinistrals are also rarer in number than other spirits. This is due to the tendency for the process that creates them — the full embrace of the Abyss itself — to destroy many of those who attempt it. However, many factors beyond the rarity of such beings can further obstruct interaction with them. Some Sinistrals are simply not desirous of contact with humans — or, for that matter, anyone or anything else. Others are so alien in the way their minds work as to be difficult to communicate with. And finally, some are as bad, or worse, than

Celestials when it comes to having an agenda and telling humans whatever they think will best advance it. Thus, even though Sinistrals are on more intimate terms with the fundamental realities behind the universe than other spirits, this does not necessarily mean they are clearer or more trustworthy than Tellurians or Celestials when it comes to what they may tell or reveal to humans.

The upshot of the schema just described is that Tenebrous Satanism is not the kind of religion that arrogantly goes around claiming that its own gods exist but no one else's do. It instead suggests that the clashing claims of different religions can be reconciled via a consideration of diversity in the nature, degree of insight, and biases of the spiritual beings that the religion is oriented toward. This, together with variation in humans' dominant thought patterns (Apollonian/Magian/ Faustian), their willingness or refusal to acknowledge life's Perils, and their interest or lack thereof in spiritual matters as such, is what produces human differences regarding supernatural belief.

The lack of other religions that put forward the principle of universal incarnation is, one could argue, itself the result of a desire to evade unpleasant realities. Most spiritual creeds assert that there exist at least some spirits of such a transcendent nature as to have never had anything to do with the flesh. Tenebrous Satanism claims, to the contrary, that this is not possible, for without flesh, Darkness remains undivided and unbounded, and there can be no meaningful individuality in such a state. It follows that even the most "transcendent" of beings must have been embodied at some point, however long ago and in however alien a form from what we know of life on our own planet. Accordingly, Tenebrous Satanism recommends skepticism toward any spirit that occludes its personal history with claims of being "eternal." Such attempts to dazzle gullible humans are all too often implicated in the advancement of the kinds of flesh-negative dogmas that the Second Key warns of.

Inward divinity

Since every living being's soul is a fragment of the Void, esoteric methods can enable one to tap into the Darkness lurking within and use it to accomplish things that would be difficult or impossible to do by causal means alone.

Once the Abyssal Void of Darkness subdivides itself into multitudinous incarnations, fleshly limitation tends to occlude an individual creature's awareness of two aspects of its own Dark nature: the secret unity between itself and all other creatures that have come forth from the Void, and the hidden potency inherent in that continuity. Amid evolutionary pressures that have geared consciousness toward concrete issues of survival, not metaphysical abstractions, it is not surprising that such details should slip into unconsciousness. Unfortunately, the result is that most conscious beings attend fretfully to life, fearing all other beings as potential competitors and worrying that their own resources may not be enough to allow them to prevail. Those who possess consciousness also frequently perceive themselves as impelled by inner forces beyond their comprehension or control and suffer from confusion, frustration, and dismay as a result.

How might the life of such a being alter if they were to become bold enough to intentionally open their awareness to the Darkness within? What if, by doing so, they became able to perceive the metaphysical bonds between themselves and others, to tap into a vast reservoir of potentiality, and to reconcile themselves with the lawless striving of the inmost Void? Such an individual would be capable of insights far beyond the ken of others and of accomplishments which the unawakened could never dream of. These are the powers of the Tenebrous witch and sorcerer — those who fully and completely embrace their own inner Darkness.

Tenebrous Satanism conceives of all occult arts as Dark, for all such practices entail intentionally orienting one's awareness toward the Abyssal Void. The meditative practices of the Fifth Key aim at stilling the normal workings of consciousness enough for the underlying reality of Darkness to manifest to the practitioner. Divination, as described in the Sixth Key, works by virtue of the subtle interconnection between all beings and all events via their shared origin in the Void. Ritual magick, as per the Seventh Key, goes beyond these methods of occult perception, constituting a method of occult action: by awakening the Darkness within and tapping into the powers of the Abyss, it becomes possible to bring about results in accord with the practitioner's will. Magick is, essentially, a symbolic system whose manipulation makes this feat possible. The common principle behind all of these arts is that it is on account of the origin of the practitioner's soul in the Void that such individuals possess the powers they do. It is, moreover, by virtue of the origin of all other souls in that same Void that said powers are able to impact those others.

Thanks to the seed of chaos at the heart of every living being, which renders all things vulnerable to change and decay, the threat of being manipulated or destroyed by occult forces is but one more Peril which human beings must contend with. The flip side of this disquieting reality, however, is that there is a sense in which every living being possesses the potential for godhood — i.e., an existence lived in fuller accord with the Dark divinity within. Tenebrous Satanism encourages the fullest possible realization of this potential among those able to wield it both effectively and responsibly. To become capable of perceiving and communing with the Void is to behold and embrace one's true inner nature and to thereby attain a seldom-experienced degree of psychic unity. And to unleash the Black Flame — to grasp the acausal, direct it in accord with one's will, and obtain results thereby — is to achieve that which spirit ever strives for: to act and to be, through the flesh, to the fullest measure possible, by accomplishing what had formerly seemed impossible on the material plane.

Many are the right-hand-path religions that describe "God" in awesome terms, in comparison to which humanity is but a worm. The fearsome counter-reality proposed by Tenebrous Satanism is that, in fact, "God" is the worm — specifically the Conqueror Worm of Poe's poem — and yet, humanity is nonetheless capable of greatness. One need only recognize that divinity dwells within, rather than without, and cultivate oneself accordingly.

Teleology of Darkness

Tenebrous metaphysics suggest that a full range of human religious beliefs — from the paganisms of old to contemporary religions of both West and East — are in no case entirely without justification. But what does Tenebrous Satanism itself take as the purpose of human existence? And what does this imply with regard to how one ought to live? An answer to these questions can be found encoded within the Prelude to the Tenebrous Creed.

The Prelude's first stanza speaks to the situation human beings find themselves in:

IV — The Void, Darkness, and the Abyss

> From the Void we emerge;
> in Darkness we dwell;
> to the Abyss we go.

To speak of emerging from the Void is to assert that there is no inherent purpose behind human beings' coming into existence. Tenebrous Satanism denies that the world and those that inhabit it were put here by a "loving" deity with some sort of positive intention. Rather, our coming-into-being is merely one of the many byproducts of the ever-restless experimentation that Darkness conducts in the course of its Adventure in the realm of the flesh.

To claim that we dwell in Darkness means that, on top of there not being any particular meaning behind why we came into existence, it is impossible to attain an objective answer to the question of what we are supposed to do now that we are here. The brute fact of the matter is that conscious beings exist in a benighted state with regard to what their existence is for. When it comes to this question of life's purpose, one must either find one's own lamp to light or gnash one's teeth impotently at the gloom, for no dawn of revelation is at hand. Those who imagine they see the sun of ultimate meaning rising before them merely make an idol of someone else's lamp. Such people proceed to preoccupy themselves with rumination upon the virtues and shortcomings of that Light, for they thereby find something external to themselves to praise for the path revealed to them in good times or to blame when poorly-lit conditions make them stumble in bad ones. This serves to excuse them from having to take responsibility for the unlit lantern that they have carried in their own two hands the entire time.

What this parable alludes to is that when it comes to questions of life's meaning and human responsibility, Tenebrous Satanism more or less agrees with the philosophers of existentialism. Since life is objectively meaningless, there is no source that will tell us its meaning nor any other definitive way by which we can know such a thing. Hence, it is up to us to create meaning — and to recognize that this is, indeed, what we are doing. To pretend that meaning is built into the universe — to assert, for instance, that order *is*, or Truth *is*, if only we know where and how to look — amounts to irresponsibly claiming, "well, it's not *my* fault that I live this way — the universe *made* me do it!" Such an attitude is what existentialists call "living in bad faith," i.e., refusing to take ownership for one's choice to live as one does.

Tenebrous Satanism acknowledges that some human beings may find it impossible to live happily without resorting to bad faith. We therefore leave such people to their own affairs, so long as they are not imposing upon us in turn. However, the Satanist refuses to live in such a way. The very essence of Satanism lies in the will to honestly acknowledge that no external endorsement of one's choices in fact exists — and yet find the courage to live anyway.

To say, finally, that we go to the Abyss, is to recognize that nothing, including ourselves, is safely fenced off from being one day devoured by Darkness. The Buddhists are in fact correct to claim that life's only permanent feature is impermanence and that the denial and craving for things to be otherwise is a source of suffering for conscious beings. This is not to deny that some things do prevail for long periods nor to deter the Satanist from pursuing that which they personally find fulfilling — for therein lies Satanism's disagreement with Buddhism. Nonetheless, Tenebrous Satanism asserts that all things will eventually return to Darkness. For this reason, we endorse O9A's proverb, "Never love anything so much that you cannot see it die."[33]

In response to the purposelessness, obscurity, and impermanence of life, the second stanza of the Prelude alludes to three approaches to existence that human beings may adopt:

> Our destination is the same
> regardless of whether we keep our eyes closed,
> allow the Light to blind us,
> or look forward with open eyes.

The first option, to keep one's eyes closed, entails inventing an order and finding meaning within it, while ignoring the chaos of Darkness ever lurking at its edges. This describes Apollonianism among humans and the Tellurian mode of existence among spirits.

A second option is allow oneself to be blinded by the Light, i.e., to reject the realities of Darkness in favor of loudly insisting on, and crusading on behalf of, whatever "Truth" one prefers in place of Darkness. This is the approach both of Magian-dominated humans and Celestials among spirits.

The third option, to look forward with open eyes, means that one embraces the Void, seeing its emptiness as a foundation fit for the building of one's personal empire. Such is typical both of the Faustian-minded human and of the Sinistral.

Regardless of which approach one takes, however, our destination is the same — i.e., it is outside of our power to wring objective purpose, clarity, and permanence from the universe. Though the Abyssal Void of Darkness is behind the great game of existence, it does not care how exactly the game is played or whether those playing it are enjoying it or not, much less who "wins." Objectively speaking, there is no correct faction that human beings are supposed to ally themselves with, to be rewarded in the case of the right decision or punished in the case of the wrong one.

Nonetheless, Tenebrous Satanism is like other religions in putting forward an opinion regarding what sort of life is better at offering flourishing and meaningfulness than the alternatives. The Prelude's third and fourth stanzas speak to this:

> Let us therefore march onward with our eyes open
> and make of our coming forth from the Void
> a great Adventure
> instead of a cry of despair.

> Let us make a home of Darkness,
> not for the sake of that which we came from
> but for our own sake,
> here and now and for the future.

To march onward with our eyes open means choosing values in accord with the realities before us. Tenebrous Satanism chooses to affirm the ever-striving nature of Darkness. From this come the imperatives that the First Key put forward earlier: to seek flourishing, to embrace self-evolution, to ground oneself in this world rather than some other one, to honestly acknowledge the Perils of life, and to reconcile oneself with spirit's utter determination to continue the Adventure of life regardless. Through living out these values, the Satanist endeavors to make something more constructive of life than a mere cry of despair — i.e., the impotent tantrum of the bitterly disappointed idealist.

On the other hand, though, Tenebrous Satanism rejects taking the utter amorality of Darkness as a model for humans to imitate. The imitation of this aspect of the Abyss is obviously not conducive to creating a livable world for oneself and one's fellow sentient beings. In such cases, one cannot simply read the "oughts" of human life off the "is" of the universe. Rather, the valid process for deriving one's "oughts" is to consider reality but to choose in accord with what best serves the actual well-being of oneself and one's loved ones.

Thus, in seeking to make a home of Darkness, the Satanist embraces only those qualities of the inmost Void which strike us as fruitful to live out intentionally. The perpetual restlessness of Darkness falls into this category, for by embracing it, we transform the lawless striver within us into a patron and friend, instead of a tempter and enemy. But to say that life is not for the sake of that which we came from, but for our own sake, is to reject the notion that just because Darkness "is" a certain way, we are obligated to imitate it even in cases where doing so would make our lives worse instead of better. The demand that reality and ideology always walk in perfect lockstep is a driver of the Dogmagian tendency to deny or distort reality out of a resentful sense that one is not allowed to invent things that benefit one's own flourishing without reality's approval. A healthy Faustian mentality, by contrast, treats reality only as a starting point, not as a straitjacket constraining human well-being, nor an obstacle that must be destroyed lest it thwart utopian ideals. It is only by adapting to reality, rather than trying to elide it or snuff it out, that one can build a home that will remain livable in the future, as well as here and now.

We conclude the subject of teleology by emphasizing that Tenebrous Satanism's view of the human condition places a strong emphasis on both liberty and personal responsibility. Since our well-being is not guaranteed by a benevolent meta-reality behind existence, the matter is entirely up to us. Every human being experiences many "calls" in life, whether originating in one's own soul, from other beings of the world, or from acausal entities who perceive one's potential and wish to see it further developed. In all instances, it is up to the individual to decide which calls to answer, and bad faith to blame anyone or anything else for the choice made. No one path is incumbent upon anyone, whether on the basis of the true nature of inner Darkness or any manner of external rationale.

Eschatology of the Abyss

To speculate about what comes after death is an endeavor of dubious value, since infallible knowledge on this subject is impossible to attain while still in the flesh. The matter is also not one of pressing importance since, as was just explained, Darkness is indifferent regarding how we choose to live our lives. But insofar as the metaphysical beliefs of Tenebrous Satanism are likely to provoke curiosity regarding death and what comes after, an overview of possible afterlife scenarios is worth providing. One might wonder, in particular, what the fifth stanza of the Prelude to the Creed means by the following ominous-sounding words:

> Having lived thus,
> we descend into the Abyss without regret,
> embracing transformation even in the midst of terror

Souls, as already explained, are not immortal. But so long as the acausal component of a recently-living being maintains some degree of structure after death, four main scenarios may follow: rebirth, translation, extinction, and sanctuary.

Rebirth

In this most common of scenarios, the soul's disorientation upon the destruction of its physical form moves it to seek a return to its "normal" state. It therefore gravitates once more toward the flesh. Its subsequent existence will be influenced by its former life, but simply as a consequence of the continuation of trajectories already established by the energies involved. Such a process, though "karmic" in a sense, has nothing to do with "moral" judgment upon the soul in question.

Translation

As was mentioned in connection with the principle of universal incarnation, some souls do not seek to regain the flesh upon the end of their incarnate existences. Instead, they become a Tellurian, Celestial, or

Sinistral, depending on the situation. Each of these kinds can transform further with time, either into a different kind or back once again into a being of the flesh, in accord with however their energies may continue to change and evolve. The trajectory will depend on the choices the spirit makes, and there is no objective reason to presume that staying a spirit is inherently better than reincarnating. Tenebrous Satanism therefore does not use the term "ascension" to refer to an enfleshed being's choice to take up residence in the acausal realm. "Translation" is more neutral and indicative of how the process can run in various directions. One might also note that just as translating a text always brings with it the loss of certain details and nuances, so too with the translation of a spirit from one mode of being to another. In this respect, translation is no more free of pain and suffering than any other afterlife scenario.

Extinction

Souls who have mastered certain spiritual disciplines may intentionally facilitate their own dissolution, disintegrating back into Darkness. They choose this fate because they have become convinced that the cycle of existence is itself a source of suffering that one ought to seek permanent escape from, as is claimed by Hinduism, Buddhism, and similar religions. Eastern practices aimed at such goals as moksha and nirvana are thus not without efficacy in releasing individuals from suffering. However, as was already pointed out in connection with the principle of pervasive mortality, it is only the existence of that specific individual that is brought to an end through such methods. The energies dispersed in the process will eventually be recycled by the Abyss into some wholly other being who will enter the realm of flesh without the wisdom and other benefits that past life experience could have offered.

Sanctuary

Certain acausal beings offer arrangements where, in exchange for fulfilling various conditions, they will shelter a soul from a degree of Abyssal entropy, bearing it away into an acausal realm of their own creation. Herein lie afterlife fates familiar to many religions, including the Abrahamic ones. In some instances, the acausal beings involved will be transparent about how the arrangement cannot last forever, constituting but a life between lives in which souls receive brief respite from their fleshly suffering, or are granted some other boon. In other cases, though, the soul will be told that they will receive sanctuary "forever," only to discover too late that some deceptive state of affairs is in play. At worst, a soul may find itself forced to waste untold aeons in a bland "paradise," put to work slaving away at unfulfilling astral endeavors, or even slowly vampirized and cannibalized by the very spirits who promised safety. The general rule with offers of sanctuary is that the more that is advertised, the more likely there will be a hidden catch of some kind — especially if Celestials are the ones making the offer.

Commonalities of all afterlife scenarios

Two things are crucial to recognize about all these afterlife scenarios. The first is that even in the most ideal cases, death remains a frightful, excruciating, and obliterating experience for all. There is no way to avoid this entirely, for without the structuring form of the body, the soul is exposed to the undifferentiated chaos from which it came. In such a state, many of the energies the soul perceives as its own will be stripped away inexorably by the Abyssal Void of Darkness. The extent to which this happens can be moderated somewhat through a mixture of one's own spiritual discipline and assistance from acausal beings. But even then, some degree of loss of the living being's identity is all but unavoidable. Tenebrous Satanism's contention is that much as no other religion is willing to admit this unpleasant fact — *and who could blame them?* — nonetheless, such is the reality that those possessed of maximal strength of will and self-honesty are called to affirm. This is what the Creed means in characterizing Abyssal descent as an experience of terror.

Secondly, one must grasp the amoral nature of all afterlife scenarios. From the perspective of a Satanist who embraces unending Adventure, obviously it is preferable to seek either rebirth, translation, or an honestly presented temporary state of sanctuary. Extinction, on the other hand, is undesirable, as is a falsely advertised "permanent" sanctuary. Objectively, however, no kind of afterlife is inherently good or bad. A Satanist possessed of sufficient Sinister empathy should be able to grasp how life's Perils could drive other people to prefer either extinction or sanctuary — even if the Satanist themselves sees such fates as suitable only for cowards and quitters.

How, then, does the Satanist embrace transformation even in the midst of Abyssal terror? It is the dedicated Faustian spirit of the Satanist that makes such an attitude possible. The Faustian Adventurer never tires of the world of impermanence, enthralled always by the prospect of new marvels of experience, new heights and depths, new gains and losses, and new ways of being. Yes, there will be suffering. But there will also be the intoxication of wonder, the excitement of conquest, and the beauty of transformation. To enjoy these, one need but forge the determination to keep going onward for as long and far as one can manage — even though, eventually and inevitably, the devouring Abyss will still catch up.

Summary

As was stated at the outset, it is possible to identify as a Tenebrous Satanist in a secular sense only, embracing Satanism's this-worldly ethos without investing oneself in supernatural affairs. Nonetheless, the Tenebrous witch and sorcerer do subscribe to such beliefs as the following:

- *The ultimate force behind all life is the Abyssal Void of Darkness.* It compulsively pours itself out into enfleshed existence, bringing myriads of individual creatures into being in the process. Amid this endeavor, it does not care whether those beings want to exist nor to what extent they enjoy existence.

- *Life's acausal component, spirit, originates in Darkness, and is ultimately identical with it.* Like flesh, spirit is subject to Darwinian processes, with life emerging from the evolution of these two elements in tandem. Over time, the interpenetration of flesh and spirit tends to increase, as evident in more complex forms of life arising. Spirit's ultimate horizon of becoming thus lies within the world, not outside it.

- *Souls are a product of the individualization of Darkness through the flesh.* It is only thanks to fleshly existence that anything "individual" exists at all. Moreover, all discarnate denizens of the acausal still remain in relationship with the world: Tellurians hover near to their former home, Celestials obsessively curse the flesh as a vale of sorrows, and Sinistrals treat the world as a field upon which to realize their ambitions.

- *All beings are one in the Dark seed of limitless potential which they bear within.*[34] It is both understandable and sometimes beneficial for conscious beings to flee from their true nature. But once one learns how to harness the Darkness within, the door is opened to forms of self-actualization that would not otherwise be possible.

- *Human existence is without inherent purpose.* While all actions do have consequences, the individual is nonetheless free to live as they see fit. There is no inherent validity to siding with one faction of spirits rather than another — or, for that matter, with none.

- *Death is a time of terror for all conscious beings.* With the loss of flesh's integrity, nothing stops the Abyss from consuming most of an individual's defining energies. Nonetheless, the Satanist confronts the Abyss courageously, trusting in their own strength of will to keep the Black Flame burning through the maelstrom, and eagerly anticipating the new horizons that will greet those who prevail.

It is not incumbent on all Tenebrous Satanists to subscribe to all of these propositions, nor to concern themselves with that which captivates the Tenebrous witch and sorcerer specifically: the Will of the Fire. Some will find, however, that the Will of the Fire does call to them. For the witch, this may take the form of promises of personal fulfillment. For the sorcerer, it may take the form of an offer sure to shake the world from its unthinking habits. In both instances, it must be emphasized that such individuals do not enslave themselves to Darkness as a master, neither because their inmost nature "demands" it nor out of hatred for life and desire to destroy the world. Rather, such individuals embody some of the noblest sentiments of O9A, which Tenebrous Satanism also endorses:

> Only by journeying through the darkness within us and without can we attain self-divinity and thus fulfill the potentiality of our existence. Our rites, ceremonies, and

practices are all life-affirming and show us the ecstasy of existence and the self-overcoming of the true Adept. We are feared because we defy and seek to know and thus understand. We rejoice in living: in all its pleasures but most particularly its possibilities. We thus extend the frontiers of evolution while others sleep or cry.[35]

We hope that the Fourth Key's revelations about the acausal component of Tenebrous Satanism will not only enlighten the would-be witch and sorcerer but also stir the imagination of any spiritual seeker who had long suspected that the universe might contain more Darkness than Light.

Notes

[27] Both in the Fourth Key and elsewhere in *Nine Keys of Abyssal Darkness*, we variously refer to our conception of the Ultimate as Void, Darkness, the Abyss, or similar abbreviated terms. The specific term used depends on whichever of these words is most evocative of the matter currently under discussion. The reader should understand, however, that these abbreviated variants of "Abyssal Void of Darkness" all refer to what is fundamentally the same entity.

[28] Stories of Lovecraft's that mention Azathoth include "The Dreams in the Witch House" (1933), "The Haunter in the Dark" (1936), "The Thing on the Doorstep" (1937), "Azathoth" (1938), and "The Dream Quest of Unknown Kadath" (1943). Two other entities comparable to the Abyssal Void of Darkness are Arthur Schopenhauer's Will-to-Live, and Thomas Ligotti's Nethescurial. For the former, see *The World as Will and Representation* (1818); for the latter, see *Grimscribe* (1991). Ligotti's rendition of Lovecraft's Azathoth in "The Sect of the Idiot" *(Songs of a Dead Dreamer*, (1985)), is also richly evocative of the Abyssal Void of Darkness.

[29] The condemnation of suicide seems to proceed from an aspect of the moralist's soul that yet retains, however unconsciously, a pure awareness of the inextinguishable lust Darkness harbors for the flesh, and therefore recognizes the inappropriateness and futility of trying to escape worldly existence as such. Disdain for earthly things, on the other hand, proceeds from a part of the moralist's soul has been corrupted by bitterness and weariness into unproductive resentment of life, becoming thus estranged from its own origin in Darkness. In connection, Tenebrous Satanism observes the same irony that LaVey remarked upon in the section of *The Satanic Bible* entitled "Life After Death Through the Fulfillment of the Ego": right-hand-path religions typically condemn suicide to relieve suffering yet glamorize asceticism and martyrdom. They thus condemn suicide only when it comes as an indulgence, declaring that one is not allowed to enjoy anything of this world, ever — not even the leaving of it. This is not to say that Satanists ought to take a particular position one way or another on the

subject of euthanasia or related issues of applied ethics. The point is, rather, that while some may be amenable to the notion that life is where flourishing happens and therefore life should be treated as sacred, and others may find it equally plausible to say "when life becomes bereft of flourishing, it is permissible to terminate it in those circumstances," it is both intellectually and morally obnoxious to proclaim, "everything that makes life enjoyable is a sin, but rejecting life is also a sin."

[30] Quoted from Shakespeare's *Macbeth* (1606), Act V, Scene 5.

[31] The distinction between Abyssal Void of Darkness and spirit in Tenebrous Satanism is somewhat comparable to Hinduism's distinction between Brahman and atman. Just as Hindu philosophers vary on the exact relationship between these two concepts, yet all who use the two terms are nonetheless recognizable as Hindu, Tenebrous Satanism does not stipulate only one correct way of conceptualizing the exact relationship between Darkness and spirit.

[32] It is important to understand that our term "Sinistral" is *not* simply equivalent to "demon" or "devil" in all contexts where those terms may be used. Our belief is that many entities designated as demons by other traditions are in fact either Tellurians or Celestials who have simply chosen to adopt a dark aesthetic, not Sinistrals per se. For example, the association of Goetic entities with such specific earthly tasks as the attainment of love, wealth, knowledge of the sciences, etc. suggests that they are Tellurians by our classification. Similarly, we have reason to believe that some Qliphotic demons may in fact be Celestials, insofar as they ultimately tend to lead their human associates in a suspiciously otherworldly direction. In suggesting that these are not Sinistrals, we are not saying that Tenebrous Satanists (or for that matter, other Satanists) may not still have good reasons for working with them in certain circumstances. Nonetheless, it is our considered position that O9A's pantheon and Lovecraft's mythos alike encompass entities who are in a different relationship to the Abyssal Void of Darkness than many entities that the average Luciferian or demonlator typically works with.

[33] Quoted from "The 21 Satanic Points" of O9A's *Black Book of Satan*.

[34] An implication of this belief that is worth highlighting is that Tenebrous Satanism rejects the elitist discourse found in certain other forms of esoteric Satanism wherein it is implied that Satanists have some special, different kind of soul that makes them better than other human beings. Our view instead is that while it is simply unrealistic to expect the same spiritual potential to be brought to full actualization by all — i.e. the blunt fact of the matter is that not everyone is cut out to be a Tenebrous witch or sorcerer in their current lifetime, and many will never be — this is due more to differences in individual interest, degree of self-development, etc., than anything more fundamental to do with the metaphysical nature of one's soul as such. It also seems to us that a certain amount of "elite soul" discourse entails the same sort of delusions of in-group supremacy typically found in Dogmagian circles (compare, for example, Gnosticism), and we therefore question whether it is appropriate for Satanists of any kind to harbor such beliefs.

[35] Quoted from "The Sinister Creed" in O9A's *Black Book of Satan*.

The Keys of Praxis

V

Polishing the Black Mirror

If the doors of perception were cleansed, every thing would appear to man as it is, infinite. For man has closed himself up, till he sees all things through the narrow chinks of his cavern.

- William Blake, *The Marriage of Heaven and Hell* (1790)

Many are those who romanticize the notion of becoming a witch or sorcerer. The prospects of wonders revealed and gains accomplished by occult means loom large, while the need to cultivate self-awareness and self-discipline in order to reach these goals engenders less enthusiasm. The reality, however, is that self-awareness and self-discipline are prerequisites of occult success. Those who grasp this and train their minds accordingly are sure to achieve great things. Those unwilling to apply themselves, on the other hand, are bound to be disappointed.

The foremost obstacle facing the aspiring witch or sorcerer is the default nature of the human psyche. Evolution has provided us with mental and emotional instruments geared toward our survival. Thus directed toward goal attainment and threat avoidance, consciousness is prone to wasting energy via fruitless scheming, fretting constantly even in situations in which no particular survival threat is looming. Such dwelling on the past and the future at the expense of the present prevents the sort of total investment in the current moment that all esoteric practices require. The first task of the would-be witch or sorcerer must therefore be to train themselves to maintain undistracted focus on things that are immediate and inward, rather than allowing their thoughts and feelings to wander restlessly among various outward objects of desire or aversion.

Those who think this sounds reminiscent of Buddhism's mindfulness practices are not wrong. What is crucial to grasp, however, is that whereas the Buddhist seeks the cessation of wanting and striving as such, the Satanist seeks to want and strive in a more effectual manner. The Satanist is a pragmatist who seeks to distinguish desires that promote flourishing from desires that are dysfunctional. One can then invest energy efficaciously into worthwhile pursuits and live untroubled by "needs" that are in fact unnecessary. For such an individual, whose ultimate goal is not self-extinction but self-actualization of the highest order, the practice of mindfulness complements the cultivation of such virtues as zeal, wisdom, and perseverance.

Toward this end of self-actualization, Tenebrous Satanism recommends four meditative practices. The first practice, Lunar Purification, aims at focusing the mind and overcoming distraction. Gaining control over one's thoughts and emotions is the first step to attaining any degree of magickal efficacy. One must also learn to distinguish between what comes from within, what comes from the causal world around, and what comes from the acausal realm beyond, before one can wield power over any of these realms.

The remaining three practices operate on two levels simultaneously. They alter the state of the practitioner's mind, not unlike how Lunar Purification does, but each also serves as a form of "Dark transubstantiation," wherein a physical object comes to serve as a causal anchor for something acausal. As a nexion of causal and acausal forces, the human mind possesses the ability to gather and direct acausal energy and to communicate with acausal beings. However, due to the opacity of the flesh, it is by default difficult to consciously control these faculties. Therefore, rather than struggling to access elusive capabilities that one possesses inwardly, Tenebrous Satanism teaches methods of projecting these faculties externally. It envisions them as tangible tools, which can be wielded in the same way as one manipulates physical objects. This effect can only manifest fully, however, when one uses the physical props each meditation calls for. The practitioner should therefore obtain said items (candle, dagger, and crystal), and meditate with them regularly. One who does so will discover that all practices described in subsequent Keys are rendered more effective and powerful thereby.

A final introductory matter to discuss is with regard to what one might call "acausal anatomy." Tenebrous Satanism believes that various schematic maps of the acausal aspect of the human being — e.g., the Indian chakras, the Chinese meridians, and so forth — are all viable, the usefulness of each depending on what exactly one is trying to accomplish. We, however, articulate such matters in a far simpler fashion, aimed less at comprehensive detail than at specific, pragmatic goals of self-empowerment. Accordingly, we delineate only two significant "acausal organs" of the human being, referred to by all of the meditations and hence worth defining at the outset:

- The *fornax* point is located in the lower part of the torso, slightly below the navel. It is involved in managing physical energy levels, intuitive threat detection, desire, aversion, and other similarly animalistic functions.

- The *adamanteus* point is located in the head, near where the spine joins the skull, in the vicinity of the roof of the mouth. It is involved in such matters as conscious intention, communication, restraint of the instincts via reason and reflection, and other similarly social or spiritual operations.

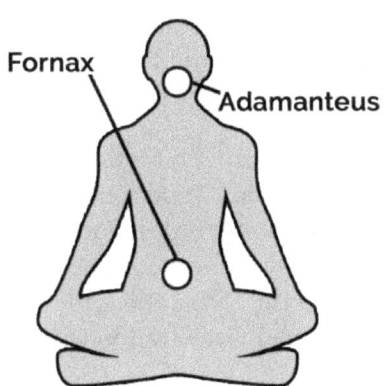

Through a combination of willful visualization and regulation of breathing to stimulate these parts of the acausal body, one can awaken the powers therein, reify them, and thereby become capable of consciously controlling them. Efficacious performance of the meditations described in the Fifth Key thus provides a solid foundation from which more advanced esoteric endeavors can proceed. Conversely, while it is possible to see results in divination and ritual magick without first practicing meditation, familiarizing oneself with the meditative practices first tends to foster greater success.

Lunar Purification

Variants of what is here called *Lunar Purification* can be found within a variety of other spiritual traditions and currents. As such, both the practice and its goal — to purify oneself of mental and emotional hindrances by drawing down cleansing energies — will be familiar to practitioners of many paths.

As with all forms of meditation, Lunar Purification is more effective the more single-mindedly one focuses on the practice. It is therefore best performed while alone (for the sake of quiet and privacy), seated comfortably (kneeling, cross-legged, or in a chair), and after dark (because this better suits the visualization required). However, once one becomes familiar with the practice, there are few circumstances in which it cannot be performed efficaciously, so long as sufficient effort is applied.

To perform Lunar Purification, follow these steps:

1. Adopting a relaxed yet alert posture, take a minute to focus your intention: to clear your mind of everything that detracts from single-minded and total investment in the current moment.

2. Close your eyes and visualize the Moon hovering toward the upper portion of your field of vision. It does not matter to what extent this visualization is realistic or stylized, so long as you are able to hold it steadily in your mind's eye. The following sigil of O9A's[36] is suitable to use in this exercise, but only the Moon component is indispensable, so a simpler visualization will also work:

3. Breathe in deeply through your nose while envisioning silver streams of energy[37] pouring down to you from the Moon and into your throat, descending until they settle into the fornax point, and from there flowing outward to the extremities of your body. This is purifying energy, subtle and transformative, cleansing as it goes forth.

4. After holding your breath briefly, breathe out through your mouth, envisioning that as the energy flows back from your extremities into your core, up your throat and out, it exits as a sooty, smoke-like substance, which dissipates into the air as it leaves your body. What you are thereby eliminating is the waste energy byproduct of your doubts, worries, and other such mental and emotional hindrances.

Practice as many rounds of breathing as desired. The minimum to experience a subtle alteration in mental state will be seven breaths for most people, but to truly notice results, it is best to maintain the visualization and breathing for at least five minutes.

Regardless of the exact amount of time invested, performance of Lunar Purification should result in a state of mind characterized by stillness, clarity, and diminished investment in mundane concerns. With this comes a variety of beneficial causal effects, such as alleviating distraction, controlling anxiety, distancing oneself from stress, and ceasing to dwell on that which is fruitless. These causal gains are accompanied by the fostering of a state of mind that is steadier in focus and more objective than the default human mental state and therefore more receptive to the acausal. Putting oneself into said state of mind by preceding all other forms of esoteric activity with at least seven breaths of Lunar Purification is therefore highly recommended.

The Black Flame

The practice described below requires a candle. It should be black or a color dark and subdued enough to be indistinguishable from black in a dim room. This candle and its designated holder should be used only during esoteric pursuits, not burned in any other circumstances. Beyond color appropriateness and being set apart from mundane usage, however, additional details — dimensions, scent or lack thereof, etc. — are up to the individual.

The ideal setting for Contemplation of the Black Flame is a private space that includes a flat surface — henceforth called the altar — and whatever seating is necessary to position objects at a comfortable level for the practitioner's gaze to rest on. For altars close to the ground, the practitioner may sit nearby in a meditative pose (kneeling, cross-legged, etc.); for taller altars, a chair should be positioned adjacently. The exact pose used for the meditation is not important, however, so long as it is neither too uncomfortable to maintain for prolonged periods nor so comfortable that remaining alert becomes difficult.

As with all Tenebrous meditation practices, the best time to perform the meditation is after dark. If, for whatever reason, the meditation is to be performed during the day, the space used ought to be rendered as dark as possible. In either case, the candle should serve as the only source of illumination throughout.

To perform the Contemplation, follow these steps:

1. Light the candle and sit facing the altar in whatever position you find conducive to sustained focus.

2. Adopting a relaxed yet alert posture, gaze into the candle flame and focus your intentions: to perceive the omnipresent forces of Darkness that surround you; to gather them from their currently diffuse form into an active energy; to gain, thereby, the ability to ignite the acausal fire.

3. Close your eyes and imagine, as vividly as you can, that the sigil pictured below has been traced out upon the ground around you, large enough for you sit in its midst. That is, you sit at the center of the black diamond; on the ground in front of you, toward your right, you can see the hook part of the sigil; if you were to glance backward over your left shoulder, you would see the fork part on the ground behind you.

This is the sigil of Binan Ath. According to O9A, "Binan Ath" means "behold the fire!" Tenebrous Satanism uses this phrase and its sigil as a shorthand way of saying, "I acknowledge the Will of the Fire in the form of the forces of acausal Darkness, and I draw power from these forces!"

4. With your eyes still closed, breathe in through your nose, imagining that as you do so, wisps of dark yet fiery energy flow upward from deep underground beneath you, seep out along the edges and corners of the Binan Ath sigil, and then flow upward to engulf you, converging on the adamanteus point. Compared to the lunar stream of before, this pyramid of energy in which you sit is fiercer and more volatile, churning with the ever-seething restlessness of the Abyss.

5. After holding the breath briefly, breathe out, again through your nose. Imagine as you do so that the gathered Dark energy flows down your throat, down your spine, and into the fornax point. Envision the energy collecting in that place, where it begins to stir your soul into recollection of the primordial chaos that constitutes the forgotten origin of all things.

6. Repeat this manner of breathing twenty-seven times in total, breathing always in a deep, conscious, and unhurried manner.

7. On the twenty-seventh exhalation, wait at least thirty seconds before breathing in again. During this long pause, rest your attention upon the fornax point.

8. Draw in a single deep breath, imagining as you do that the energy you have gathered into the fornax point expands at the same rate as you take in the air. Hold this breath for as long as you previously paused while visualizing that the energy gathered into your abdomen crystallizes into a diamond-shaped trapezohedron, evocative of the Binan Ath sigil itself.

9. Breathe out through your nose in a slow and controlled manner, directing the energy gathered within you to emerge from your body with the breath and to congeal in the air before you. There, it solidifies in a new, external form that is centered on the flame of the candle. (Since your eyes will be closed, you will not see this physically, but by visualizing, you should be able to "feel" it occur.)

10. Let yourself breathe naturally, but imagine that as you do so the flame expands and contracts in time with your breath, as if it were a living thing imitating you, drawing in power and enlarging itself as you inhale, releasing power and drawing inward as you exhale. Maintain this visualization for at least twenty-eight breaths until you feel, vividly and palpably, that a living being separate from yourself now exists before you.

11. Open your eyes, rest your gaze on the flame, and observe any changes in your perceptions of it. If the meditation has been performed effectively, you should be able to perceive that the flame burning before you constitutes a nexion between the causal and the acausal, its potency evident via the energy it emits. Some practitioners will at this point perceive an orb floating in front of them, initially centered on the flame but capable of being moved and altered in accord with one's will. Experimenting with such manipulations is a good way of learning about the wielding of acausal energy firsthand.

12. Once you have had your fill of the experience, begin to ground yourself by ceasing to dwell on the visualizations and enumerating instead the causal facts of what is before you — wax, wick, and so forth.

13. When your trance has lapsed sufficiently for normality to intrude, conclude by blowing out the candle.

Efficacious performance of Contemplation of the Black Flame should produce an energizing effect on the practitioner in a threefold manner: heightened awareness of the energies around and inside of oneself, the active gathering of those energies, and the empowering of oneself with assurance that one could draw forth yet more energy if needed. These effects are closely proximate to the *naos* state described in the Seventh Key. Contemplation of the Black Flame thus provides a taste of what the sacred space of the ritual chamber ought to feel like: a place of Dark mysteries, wherein one enjoys privileged access to the Abyss. By training the practitioner to associate the very presence of the lit black candle with such a space, Contemplation of the Black Flame can inject much additional potency into the candle's usage in other occult practices.

The Dagger of the Will

In addition to the candle, the practice described here requires a knife or dagger. It should be simple and practical in form, avoiding ostentation in size, shape of blade, or decoration. The blade should consist of a usable cutting edge made of metal, and the color scheme of the implement as a whole predominantly black or silver. Once the practitioner has begun using the knife or dagger with the meditation, it should only be handled during esoteric activities, not used for mundane tasks.

The meditation should be undertaken in the same space as that used for the Contemplation of the Black Flame. The candle and dagger should both be placed on the altar, which the practitioner will face throughout the meditation.

To perform the Contemplation, follow these steps:

1. Light the candle and sit facing the altar in whatever position you find conducive to sustained focus.

2. Adopting a relaxed yet alert posture, unsheathe the dagger and hold it before you, point forward, so that the candle light falls upon the blade. Let your gaze fall on this and focus your intentions: to behold the power of your own spirit; to direct, in a conscious and

intentional manner, the forces of Darkness; to draw the dagger of the will so as to accomplish these things.

3. Lower the dagger, holding it in your right hand such that the blade points upward and the butt of the handle in your fist rests on your leg. The exact manner of holding does not matter, so long as the blade is upright, and you are able to keep it that way while remaining relaxed for an extended period. If it is more comfortable to rest your hand on the edge of the altar or elsewhere, then do so.

4. Close your eyes and envision the following sigil:

Imagine it as if you were to look in a mirror and be greeted not by your own reflection, but by this figure, with the upper triangle equivalent to your head, and the lines beneath it equivalent to the rest of your body.

This is the sigil of Ga Wath Am. "Ga Wath Am" is said by O9A to mean "The power within me is great!" Tenebrous Satanism uses the phrase and its sigil as a shorthand way of saying "Behold the power of my own will, by which I move acausal forces to do as I command!"

5. With your eyes still closed, breathe in through your nose, imagining that as you do so a diffuse, dark yet fiery energy streams forth from the air all around you, descends into your body, and gathers both in the fornax point and in your hands. At the same time as you conjure this sensation, direct your focus toward the bottom portion of the

Ga Wath Am sigil with the understanding that the three circles correspond to the three places in your body where the energy is collecting.

6. After holding the breath briefly, breathe out again through your nose. Imagine that as you do, the energy flows up your spine, up your throat, and into the adamanteus point. At the same time as you conjure this sensation, direct your focus to the upper portion of the Ga Wath Am sigil with the understanding that the triangle corresponds both to your head and to the blade of the dagger, both containers of your ascending will. By elevating the energy you have just taken in, you are not only activating it but also awakening the locus of control that enables you to manipulate this energy.

7. Repeat this manner of breathing twenty-seven times, breathing always in a deep, conscious, and unhurried manner. As this proceeds, you should increasingly feel a sense of "something" building up, both in the adamanteus point and the dagger's blade. It may feel as though the dagger is pulsating with the breath. Sensations may also arise in the vicinity of the larynx and the forehead as a result of the adamanteus point redistributing the energy directed into these areas. Do not try to force yourself to feel these sensations if they are not immediately present, though. Focus your entire attention on directing the energy in time with your breath and accept whatever side effects or lack thereof may follow.

8. On the twenty-seventh exhalation, wait at least thirty seconds before breathing in. During this long pause, rest your attention upon the adamanteus point.

9. Draw in a deep breath, imagining as you do that the energy gathered into the adamanteus point expands at the same rate as you take in the air. Hold this breath for as long as you previously paused, visualizing that the energy gathered into your head crystallizes into a pyramid-shaped tetrahedron, evocative of the triangular portion of the Ga Wath Am sigil.

10. Breathe out through your nose in a slow and controlled manner, directing the accumulated energy to flow down through your shoulder, into the arm of the hand that holds the dagger, and out through your palm and fingers into the implement itself. Feel, as

you do this, how the dagger "changes" in your grasp, becoming a living thing animated by your will. Some practitioners may perceive this alteration via impressions that the blade has altered in length, weight, or temperature, while for others, the impression of change may be subtler. As before, you should accept whatever comes, not force yourself to feel these sensations.

11. Let yourself breathe naturally for a few breaths. Then, once you have recovered, observe any sensations of energy flow that you continue to feel in the dagger — whether coordinated with your breathing or in general — and any changes in your thoughts and feelings that the meditation has brought about. Your eyes may be either closed or open throughout this step. Either way, observe the flow of energy dispassionately for at least twenty-eight breaths. During this time, you may also experiment with using the dagger to direct the energy flow in other ways, allowing curiosity to guide you.

12. Once you have had your fill of the experience, sheathe the dagger and return it to the altar. Ground yourself by gazing at the objects before you and enumerating their causal characteristics — e.g., the materials, colors, etc. of the dagger as a physical object.

13. When your trance has lapsed sufficiently for normality to intrude, conclude by blowing out the candle.

Effective performance of Contemplation of the Dagger of the Will increases confidence and focus on account of the heightened awareness of the practitioner's active agency that it brings about. The meditation particularly enhances the precise, nuanced control of acausal energies. It is therefore highly beneficial to those who lack natural intuition as to how to flex the right acausal "muscle" in the ritual chamber. Through Contemplation of the Dagger of the Will, the practitioner gains a vivid experience of what it feels like when occult energies are drawn toward or projected away from oneself. This strengthens the practitioner's ability to perceive the extent to which, say, a ritual magick working is "doing something" as opposed to "doing nothing." Obviously, acausal perception of this kind is essential for a witch or sorcerer to cultivate.

The Nine-Angled Nexion

In addition to the candle, the meditation below requires a clear, colorless, faceted crystal. Ideally, it should be large enough to fill a fair portion of one's palm — about two to five inches. Plain quartz is ideal, but other crystals, or even prisms of cut glass, can be put to similar use. Key requirements are transparency (suggestive of the ability of things to pass through), absence of distracting elements (no colors, embedded solids, etc.)[38] and the presence of facets, either artificial or natural, of a triangular, kite-like, or irregular shape.

The object just described is called the Nine-Angled Nexion. This is not because it has exactly nine corners, lines, or anything else. Rather, its clarity and angled facets together represent a place where the four dimensions of the causal come into contact with the more-than-four dimensions of the acausal. Such objects can be used to bridge the two realms, enabling acausal beings to come through — either into the consciousness of the practitioner or into the world itself.

Two paradigmatic examples of Nine-Angled Nexions portrayed in popular fiction are the Lament Configuration in Clive Barker's Hellraiser franchise and the Shining Trapezohedron in H. P. Lovecraft's story "The Haunter of the Dark." This remark ought to indicate two things to the practitioner. First, in practice, the form of the Nine-Angled Nexion can vary widely while still being effective. Second, when the idly curious or the recklessly foolish meddle with such objects, unpleasant consequences tend to follow. The novice is therefore warned that once the concept of this object is grasped, many things become possible, but this does not necessarily make it a good idea to rashly attempt all that becomes possible.

Two pieces of advice follow. The first is that while the meditation described below is relatively safe, it is not recommended for persons who are mentally or emotionally disturbed. The second is that once one starts using an object as the Nine-Angled Nexion, that object ought to be treated with even more care than the candle and dagger as far as excluding it from mundane contexts. Among other things, this means not leaving it out where others may stumble upon it and avoiding handling it when you are not intending to evoke its powers.

The set up for this meditation is the similar to the previous, with the candle and crystal placed before the practitioner on the altar. To proceed, follow these steps:

1. Light the candle and sit facing the altar in whatever position you find conducive to sustained focus.

2. Adopting a relaxed yet alert posture, pick up the crystal and hold it before you so that you can see the flame shining through its facets. With your gaze upon this, imagine that within the crystal lies another world, unfamiliar and distinct from our own, and focus your intentions: to bridge this alien world with ours through the angled intersection of the crystal, to open a channel through which the beings of that realm might speak to you, to become capable of hearing the voice of the Void itself through this amplifying instrument which you hold.

3. Lower the crystal, holding it in your left hand such that your palm cradles it while the back of your hand comes to rest on your leg. The exact manner of holding does not matter, so long as it sits secure in your hand and you are able to keep it that way while remaining relaxed for an extended period. If it is more comfortable to rest your hand on the edge of the altar or elsewhere, then do so.

4. Close your eyes and envision the flame before you as if you were able to see it even through your eyelids. Open your mind to the idea that it is not just a physical flame but a living entity separate from you. (Performing Contemplation of the Black Flame immediately before Contemplation of the Nine-Angled Nexion can help with this but is not absolutely necessary.)

5. Envision the following sigil as a circuit, connecting you with the acausal point of energy you sit facing. The top circle maps to the flame, the leftward circle to the crystal in your left hand, and the remaining middle and bottom circles to the adamanteus and fornax points in your body.

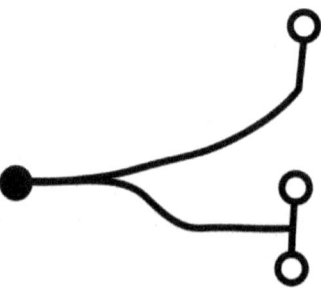

This is the sigil of Naos. "Naos" is a Greek word that refers to the central structure of a temple. As well as being the title of one of O9A's most insightful texts, O9A associates this word and sigil with "The Temple within," where one might "grab the lightning and hold it."[39] Tenebrous Satanism therefore uses Naos as a shorthand expression of, "I intentionally open myself to acausal forces, so that I may receive whatever insights can be gained thereby!"

6. With your eyes still closed, breathe in through your nose. Imagine as you do so that a glowing, blazing energy stirs and expands in three places simultaneously: before you in the vicinity of the candle flame and within your body at both the fornax and adamanteus points. At the same time, visualize that the three white points toward the right side of the Naos sigil glow and expand simultaneously. The bottom two correspond to the energies within you and the top to acausal forces outside, unknown to you yet desirous of contact.

7. After holding the breath briefly, breathe out, again through your nose. Imagine as you do so that the energy you have awakened in your body flows leftward from the fornax and adamanteus points, into your left arm, and into the crystal you are holding, while simultaneously, the third point of gathered energy before you also flows into this location. While you are doing this, shift your focus to the left side of the Naos sigil. Its single black point corresponds to the Nine-Angled Nexion, which you now direct all of your energy toward activating — at the same time as the Things of the Other Side do likewise.

8. Repeat this manner of breathing twenty-seven times in total, breathing always in a deep, conscious, and unhurried manner. As this proceeds, you should increasingly feel a sense of "something" building in the crystal. Sensitive individuals may perceive additional sensory, mental, or emotional effects. Whether such things occur or not, remain calm and persist with the visualization as best as you can.

9. On the twenty-seventh exhalation, wait at least thirty seconds before breathing in again. During this pause, direct your attention toward both the two energy points within your body and the candle flame.

10. Draw in a single deep breath while visualizing the same energy flow pattern as before, gathering both in front of you and within the two points in your body but with each of these points now expanding to their utmost as the energies surge to their maximum. Hold this breath for as long as you previously paused, visualizing the enlarged vortices all simultaneously churning with acausal power.

11. Breathe out through your nose in a slow and controlled manner, directing the energy to flow down through your shoulder, into the arm of your receptive hand, and out through your palm and fingers into the crystal, at the same time as the acausal pours its share into the crystal too. Feel, as you do this, how the crystal changes in your grasp, becoming a living thing animated by your will — and, perhaps, by something else besides. Some will be able to feel something pulsing or circulating in the crystal at this time. For others, the change may be subtler. Do not force yourself to feel anything, though. Focus your entire attention on directing the energy and accept whatever follows.

12. Let yourself breathe naturally and spend a minimum of twenty-eight breaths in dispassionate observation of any impressions that arise, whether in the crystal, your body, your mind, or your surroundings. If the meditation was performed effectively, you should be in a light trance, a heightened state of receptivity to acausal forces. Some may at this time experience energy outflow from the crystal into their body, the spontaneous arising of visions before their closed eyes, or the faint sound of voices whose origin is indistinct. Others may experience a vague sense of preternatural hollowness in the space around them, coupled with an unusually profound stillness. Regardless of what you may observe, do not allow yourself to become alarmed if something happens or restless if nothing happens. Accept whatever presents itself to you with an open mind.

13. Once you have had your fill of the experience, return the crystal to the altar. Ground yourself by gazing at what is on the altar and enumerating the causal facts of what is before you — the angles, surfaces, etc. of the crystal as a physical object.

14. When your trance has lapsed sufficiently for normality to intrude, conclude by blowing out the candle.

As was just alluded to, performance of Contemplation of the Nine-Angled Nexion produces a light trance, wherein the practitioner's receptivity to acausal forces is augmented. This is useful in overcoming the mental barriers that so frequently frustrate the sort of people who feel drawn to esoteric practices yet struggle to quiet the nagging inner voices of skepticism, self-doubt, and conventional reason that cut them off from genuine contact. Divination and communion, as described in the Sixth and Eighth Keys respectively, are both practices whose performance is enhanced by Contemplation of the Nine-Angled Nexion, since both explicitly entail the receipt of insight from the acausal realm.

Tenebrous Satanism encourages the technique of the Nine-Angled Nexion because it effectively enables those who would otherwise be deaf to the acausal to hear the voices of the Abyss. The risk, however, is that some may find this method more effective than they are comfortable with. In such cases, the advantage of having externalized one's receptive faculty into the crystal is that one can bring about a decisive psychic disconnection by setting the object aside and distancing oneself from it or, in extreme cases, getting rid of it entirely. This prospect of control is what justifies the claim that Contemplation of the Nine-Angled Nexion is relatively safe.

Summary

To polish the Black Mirror is to cleanse and open the doors of perception. This is something that every walker of the Sinister Path can benefit from. The self-discipline, mental control, and visualization capacities that meditation fosters can be useful even to secular skeptics. Those who intend to deal with the acausal regularly, however, will benefit all the more. Without instilling personal discipline through these or similar practices, most people find it difficult to resist the sorts of mental-emotional distractions that regularly sabotage occult endeavors.

The following sketch of the dynamics of the Fifth Key's meditation practices is no substitute for detailed instructions. Nonetheless, for easy reference, the four practices can be summed up in the following manner:

- *Lunar Purification is for cleansing.* While performing it, one visualizes the Moon, breathes in to bring energy into fornax, and breathes out to release waste energy.

- *Contemplation of the Black Flame is for energy-raising.* While performing it, one visualizes the Binan Ath sigil, breathes in to gather energy into adamanteus, and breathes out to move this energy down into fornax.

- *Contemplation of the Dagger of the Will is for centering one's attention.* While performing it, one visualizes the Ga Wath Am sigil, breathes in to gather energy into fornax, and breathes out to move this energy up into adamanteus.

- *Contemplation of the Nine-Angled Nexion is for enhancing acausal receptivity.* While performing it, one visualizes the Naos sigil, breathes in to gather energy both in fornax and adamanteus, and breathes out to move this energy into the crystal in the left hand.

Those who struggle with meditation may find that the following pieces of advice can help:

- Read all instructions carefully and walk yourself through all steps mentally prior to attempting any of the meditations in earnest. Do not allow yourself to become discouraged if some steps seem unwieldy at first, for with practice, such awkwardness will diminish.

- When first learning, build familiarity with one meditation before proceeding to the next. Otherwise, it can become easy to mix up the steps of one meditation with a different meditation's steps.

- All instructions regarding breathing should be studied attentively. Small details — e.g., using the nose vs. mouth, breathing quickly or slowly, tensing up too much when holding one's breath, etc. — can detract from the efficacy of the meditations more than a beginner might expect.

- Instead of fretting about whether your visualizations are "good enough," put as much effort into them as you can, and over time, your capabilities will improve. Be aware also that vision is not the only sense that can be trained to perceive the acausal. For some, the development of acausal sensitivity will occur via audible manifestations, tactile sensations, etc. instead of vision. Focus, therefore, on observing how your own experiences evolve over time. Understand that being able to sense any kind of shift in energy over the course of the Contemplations is far more important than the question of how exactly your senses reveal that shift to you.

- Reproducing a meditation's associated sigil (e.g., drawing it on a piece of paper) and keeping this on the altar to rest your gaze on can be helpful for novices who cannot otherwise remember all of a sigil's finer details. Too much reliance on such a crutch can hamper the development of acausal perception, but it is better for a beginner to use a crutch than to languish in frustration if they cannot manage the visualizations otherwise.

- If, after a Contemplation's twenty-eight-breath cycle, it seems like nothing is happening, try repeating the whole breathing cycle again. Often, those new to these practices suffer from energy blockages. For example, with the Dagger of the Will and Nine-Angled Nexion, many novices "lose the flow" when it reaches a certain point in the arm. Such obstructions can be eroded with further practice.[40] Do not persist to the point of irritability or exhaustion, though, lest this reinforce such obstructions.

- For any of the Contemplations that entail a twenty-eight-breath cycle, some individuals may find that they need more than twenty-seven breaths before the energy-gathering effects of the final inhale manifest to full effect. The number twenty-eight was chosen based on its significance elsewhere in Tenebrous Satanism, but there is no inherent reason why it has to be this many breaths exactly. Therefore, while most will need at least this number, individual practitioners should feel free to experiment with whether doing more breaths before the final inhale may give them better results.

A final piece of strongly emphasized advice is to practice regularly, at least two to three times a week, if not daily. Mental and spiritual training requires the same disciplined regularity as physical exercise, so one can no more expect drastic transformation from a single session of meditation than from a single session of lifting weights. With dedicated practice, however, meditation can bring about significant gains with regard to one's capacities to live freely, accomplish more, and experience the uncanny.

We hope that the Fifth Key's meditative practices will empower all who persist with them, regardless of whether it is success in occult endeavors that they seek or greater self-control, self-knowledge, and self-awareness in general.

Notes

[36] All sigils that appear in the Fifth Key have been adapted from O9A texts such as *Naos* and *Caelethi* (a.k.a. *Black Book of Satan II*). The latter is not considered an "official" O9A text by some, but this does not prevent it from still offering inspiration to Tenebrous Satanism.

[37] The hermetic self-initiation ritual described in O9A's *Naos* uses similar lunar imagery in concert with the sigil presented here.

[38] Cracks and clouding in the crystal are only a problem if they severely compromise clarity.

[39] Quoted from O9A's *Caelethi* (a.k.a. *Black Book of Satan II*).

[40] Alternatively, those who are impatient for results may be able to attain them through ritual magick if such comes more easily to them than meditation does. Tailoring the proceedings of the Rite of Banishing (as described in the Seventh Key) into something that eliminates energy blocks specifically requires but the smallest of tweaks to that rite's wording and visualizations.

VI

Perilous Omens

> *If you can look into the seeds of time*
> *And say which grain will grow and which will not,*
> *Speak, then, to me, who neither beg nor fear*
> *Your favors nor your hate.*
>
> **- Banquo in William Shakespeare's *Macbeth* (1606)**

Divination is only a spiritual practice of value when taken up with the appropriate attitude. As Macbeth demonstrates, people get themselves in trouble when they take omens as revealing what "will" happen or "is supposed to" happen. Such interpretations are at best fruitless and at worst pernicious. They discourage action on the basis of things being already decided. Or, they rationalize unwise action out of a sense that such is what the universe demands. Such notions of fate evoke a Magian worldview, wherein the individual lacks agency and is merely the puppet of whatever transcendent power is running the show.

In contrast to the Magian, the Faustian is a believer not in fate but in destiny. Destiny is not that which is meant to happen or must happen, but that which has been put into one's hands to make happen, through the specific nexion of opportunities, resources, and will that constitute each uniquely situated individual. When conceived thus, destiny reveals itself to be dependent upon the virtue of wisdom. Insight into destiny does not mean being able to tell the future, but rather, possessing a clear perception both of one's inner potential and of where one is situated in the greater scheme of things. When a Tenebrous diviner seeks to know "which grain will grow and which will not," this is far less a matter of looking forward in time than it is of looking deeper within oneself.

Self-honesty is a prerequisite for effective divination. Without it, one cannot distinguish one's own desires and fears from what is objectively incipient in the situation at hand. At the same time, though, divination fosters (or at least, ought to foster) a deepening of self-honesty over time. The practice fundamentally consists in introspection triggered by a random factor. The random factor is the omen, whether in the form of tarot card, rune, or otherwise. The introspection lies in learning to recognize in the omen a revelation of things that the conscious mind thought unknown but which the unconscious mind knew already, needing only the impetus of the omen to be able to communicate its insights to consciousness. When conceptualized this way, divination functions as a method of self-reflection that can benefit anyone who wishes to come to know themselves better — even if said individual is not interested in acausal affairs per se.

While divination is thus useful but optional for the secular Tenebrous Satanist, it is indispensable to the witch and the sorcerer. As one develops greater abilities to gather and harness energy, to know and direct one's will, and to open oneself to the acausal, it is not unusual for spirits to take notice. They may then use divination to make the Will of the Fire known to their human ally. As the sorcerer, in particular, continues to advance upon the Sinister Path, divination will increasingly reveal their destiny on the acausal level in addition to the causal one. Moreover, divination can reveal this in a manner that speaks eloquently to the interweaving of the two realms by hinting at how a thing may be true or a principle applicable in different senses at different levels. This aspect of divination causes it to sometimes surpass other, more direct methods of contacting the acausal. Mundane though drawing a few tokens may seem in comparison to the methods of communion described in the Eighth Key, what divination lacks in dramatic flair is outweighed by the nuance and profundity that it is capable of communicating.

Tenebrous divination may be described as runic in form, but tarot-like in structure. The system does not use cards per se. Instead, it consists of a series of sigils and glyph-plus-number combinations, marked upon tokens of wood, stone, etc., as with runes. The total number of omens, however, and their classification into categories, closely resemble the structure of the tarot: a minor arcana subdivided into four suits, each including ten numbered cards plus four court cards, and a major arcana of trumps. Such a system preserves all of tarot's advantages in terms of familiarity of symbolism and breadth of meanings while combining them with runes' advantages in terms of the ease with which any diviner may create their own set by reproducing the appropriate symbols.

There is, at the same time, a front on which the Tenebrous runic-tarot differs from any previous divination system: its oracular insights touch not only upon the standard sorts of events, relationships, and coincidences that divination concerns itself with, but also upon realities of embodied life that no other religion or ideology deals with as comprehensively as Tenebrous Satanism does. Such realities are what previous Keys referred to as life's *Perils*. Incorporating these Perils into the Tenebrous divination system causes traditional omens to be inflected and augmented through an appreciation for Dark, Sinister aspects of flesh, spirit, and world. A more profound perspective on life's tragedies and possibilities emerges thereby.

Information about the different types of tokens is laid out below. The Sixth Key thereby elucidates equivalencies between the Tenebrous system and the tarot, while at the same time making differences evident. The introduction to the fundamental concepts of the system is followed by an in-depth explanation of the meanings associated with each token. The Sixth Key concludes with instructions on how to use the runic-tarot — both for divination specifically and for introspective insight more generally.

Fundamental concepts

In the Tenebrous runic-tarot, the set of tokens known as *archetypes* are equivalent to the major arcana. Marked with a single sigil, each symbolizes significant concepts and recurrent circumstances pertaining to spirit's sojourn in the flesh. The majority have a direct equivalent in the standard tarot, often to the point of the archetype's title being similar. The sequence of the trumps is also mostly preserved. However, the total number of archetypes — twenty-eight — is six more than the twenty-two of the traditional tarot. This expansion enables the runic-tarot to not only express all that the tarot is capable of expressing, but to speak also to aspects of human experience which the tarot lacks an adequate vocabulary for — aspects that Faustian-minded Sinister-Path walkers tend to be more cognizant of than the average person.

In addition to mirroring the major arcana of the tarot, the archetypes are also the part of the system that is most proximate to runes per se, as each is associated with a particular consonant or vowel sound. The specifics of this are provided below, alongside descriptions of each archetype.

The equivalents of the minor arcana in the Tenebrous runic-tarot are known as *tropes*. These are visually distinguished from archetypes via being marked by two symbols rather than a lone one: either a glyph accompanied by a number, or a pair of glyphs. The former numerically marked tropes are called *phases*. They are equivalent to the numbered cards of the minor arcana. The latter, marked by two symbols, are called *incarnations*. These are equivalent to the tarot's court cards.

The tropes are divided into four *kingdoms*, each containing the phases one through ten, plus the four incarnations. These kingdoms are equivalent to the traditional suits of the tarot but diverge from tradition with regard to the attributions and related nuances of each:

- The Kingdom of *Attainment* is equivalent to the suit of pentacles. It is concerned with the drive to fulfill one's worldly needs and wants and the possibility of spiritual insight being fostered or obstructed in the process. It is associated with the element of *fire* rather than the traditional earth in order to highlight the dynamic quality of worldly striving for a walker of the Sinister Path, contra the right-hand-path tendency to see worldliness as spiritually inert.

- The Kingdom of *Communion* is equivalent to the suit of cups. It is concerned with fulfillment via interpersonal relationships, again with the possibility of spiritual insight being fostered or obstructed depending on how this fulfillment manifests. It is associated with the element of *air* rather than the traditional water to highlight how what is spiritually decisive in this arena for a Tenebrous Satanist are such factors as self-knowledge, clarity of communication, and the ability to look at things from a detached standpoint. The emotion-oriented element of the traditional suit is accordingly downplayed.

VI — Perilous Omens

- The Kingdom of *Strife* is equivalent to the suit of swords. It is concerned with striving against opposition, and the attendant risks of suffering and defeat. It is associated with the element of *earth* rather than the traditional air in order to make the point that it is within the material, physical realm that spirit must contend with a state of limitation. From a Faustian perspective, earth represents crude material that a powerful will may transmute into something better and more useful, but stands as an obstacle in one's path so long as it remains untransformed.

- The Kingdom of *Innovation* is equivalent to the suit of wands. It is concerned with spirit's ever-growing capacity to take on more complex fleshly manifestations, becoming increasingly inventive in its quest to overcome limitations. It is associated with the element of *water* rather than the traditional fire, on account of water's connotations both as a cleansing rejuvenator and a slow yet sure eroder of obstacles.

The numbered phases are illustrative of each kingdom's respective dynamics of ambition, cooperation, conflict, or destiny. In broad terms, ones, twos, and threes respectively symbolize the potential, the initial actualization, and the fuller maturation of these energies; fours portray the obstructed implosion of energy and fives its disruptive explosion; sixes show the energy's positive evolution via the experience of adversity; sevens illustrate energy that yet remains compromised due to unconquered limitations; eights, nines, and tens respectively reveal the skilled navigation, imperfect maximization, and extraordinary absolutization of the energy.

The incarnations follow a similar pattern to the phases, each representing specific concepts that are in turn inflected through the dominant themes of each kingdom. The incarnations of the Tenebrous runic-tarot are as follows:

- *Muses* are equivalent to what is traditionally known as Pages. They are the embodiments of *zeal*, each representing a different way of attempting to overcome that which has become stale and static. Their wisdom is sensory, discovering and embracing the wonder of their immediate surroundings.

- *Witches* are equivalent to Queens. They are the embodiments of *honor*, each representing a different facet of what it takes to maintain constructive and just bonds with one's fellow creatures. Their wisdom is intuitive, apprehending the subtle factors by which all beings are united or separated, rather than dwelling only upon surfaces.

- *Heroes* are equivalent to Knights. They are the embodiments of *empathy*, each representing a different way of trying to battle evil and solve problems for the benefit of all. Their wisdom is ethical, articulating ideals and principles as a precursor to decisive action.

- *Sorcerers* are equivalent to Kings. They are the embodiments of *perseverance*, each representing a different way of cultivating prosperity despite life's Perils, advancing their own and others' evolution in the process. Their wisdom is rational, forsaking idealism in favor of practicality so that they may recognize what must be done and ensure that all is taken care of.

Unlike the traditional tarot, which sorts its court cards by age first and sex second (youthful feminine, youthful masculine, mature feminine, mature masculine), the incarnations of the runic-tarot are sorted by sex first and age second. This yields a revised sequence of youthful feminine, mature feminine, youthful masculine, mature masculine. The altered order reflects the association of each incarnation with an appropriate element (just as, in traditional tarot, Pages represent the earth element within each suit, Knights fire, etc.) while at the same time preserving the ordering of the kingdoms (Attainment, Communion, Strife, Innovation). Thus, Muses are associated with the fiery Attainment of worldly desire, Witches with the open space in which Communion's interconnections take place, Heroes with the afflictions of Strife inherent to the earthly realm, and Sorcerers with the unstoppable, ever-surging flow of spirit's bottomless font of Innovation.

A more esoteric dimension of the elements is evident in the presence of an "octave" effect — i.e., a correspondence between each lower-numbered phase and the phase or incarnation that is eight steps above it. What each pair of lower-octave and higher-octave omen have in common can be captured using the symbolism of the seven classical planets:

☽

- *Ones and eights* evoke emergence: from nothingness in the lower octave, and from constriction in the higher. This illumination of what was formerly innate or concealed suggests the mystery-revealing qualities of the *Moon*.

☿

- *Twos and nines* demonstrate what the energy is capable of: a small yet significant display of its talents in the lower octave, the normal upper limit of those talents in the higher. Insofar as the resultant transformations cause the true nature of the energy to become more openly communicated, one finds an invocation here of the qualities of *Mercury*.

♀

- *Threes and tens* both reveal an expansion of energy via interaction between individuals: personal and shorter term in the lower octave, communal and longer term in the higher. This element of inclusion of others evokes the bringing-together qualities of *Venus*.

☉

- *Fours and Muses* respectively deal with the ebb of energy and the restoration of its flow. Managing such ebb-and-flow gracefully is a prerequisite of flourishing and success, thereby evoking qualities of the *Sun*.

♂

- *Fives and Witches* respectively deal with the catastrophic eruption of energy and the challenge of responding constructively to the troubles one must contend with. Such adversity is suggestive of the qualities of *Mars*.

♃

- *Sixes and Heroes* respectively deal with reflective self-growth and the question of what effective action on the world's behalf looks like. The prospect of propitious blessings flowing from such affairs for the benefit of all suggests the qualities of *Jupiter*.

♄

- *Sevens and Sorcerers* respectively deal with ongoing difficulties and the capacity to establish greatness even amid challenging circumstances. The heaviness of a need for realism here and the attendant call to apply discipline to one's striving together suggest the qualities of *Saturn*.

Tenebrous Satanism rejects simple-minded, literalistic approaches to astrology, for the notion of fate being written in the stars is an example of the sort of bad-faith excuse-making that the Fourth Key rejects. Nonetheless, classical astrological symbolism helps elucidate principles of correspondence that animate the Tenebrous runic-tarot as a whole. It is not absolutely necessary to engage with this aspect of the system, as opposed to reflecting upon each individual omen in a more self-contained way. The diviner will, however, tend to interpret the omens in a more effective and innovative fashion when such interconnections are taken into account.

Division of omens into visions

The eighty-four tokens of the runic-tarot are divisible into three sets of twenty-eight: twenty-eight archetypes, twenty-eight tropes of the lower octave, and twenty-eight tropes of the higher octave. This divisibility enables the omens to be grouped into trios. Each trio contains one archetype, one lower-octave trope, and one higher-octave trope. The three omens thus tied together are implied to have interrelated meanings.

What does this interrelation between grouped omens consist in? The answer can be illustrated metaphorically by tying each trio to a *vision*: an image that weaves each set of three omens into a thematically cohesive whole. Twenty-eight such visions are described in detail on the pages that follow, together with the meanings of each of the three separate tokens that each vision evokes. In this manner, the runic-tarot retains the rich imagery associated with traditional tarot but leaves it to the individual diviner to recreate this imagery within their own imagination. Meditation upon such images (a method for which is provided later in the Sixth Key) can contribute much to the diviner's ability to read the omens in an intuitive manner instead of relying upon rote memorization of meanings.

The twenty-eight visions of the Tenebrous runic-tarot each entail one further component beyond the image itself and the trio of omens it incorporates. This is the vision's associated Peril: an aspect of spirit's Adventure in the flesh that human beings too often live in denial of and which the vision therefore encourages intentional reflection upon. The First Key previously alluded to the general contents of these Perils. The current Key will now provide further details regarding how material limitations and the ruthlessness of evolution so often make a nightmare of existence. Acknowledging such Perils as fundamental facets of our lived reality, instead of trying to ignore them or pretend them away, is a key part of what it means for the Tenebrous Satanist to "march onward with our eyes open." Each Peril is therefore tied to a vision in order to encourage conscious meditation upon it. The extent to which the Perils are relevant to the divinatory meanings of individual omens in any given reading is a matter that each diviner will have to determine for themselves. In general, though, reading the omens in light of the Perils can trigger realizations that would not have occurred to the diviner otherwise, adding an additional dimension of meaningfulness to the inner journeying that effective divination consists in. Such insights can be game-changers, especially when one is grappling with one's personal delusions and weaknesses in the context of an initiatory trial, such as those the Ninth Key proposes for the spiritual advancement of Tenebrous sorcerers.

It is an unfortunate reality that some of the Perils touch upon ideas that have been used by intellectually and morally deficient people to justify dysfunctional ideologies. Against this, it is crucial to stress that in encouraging contemplation of the Perils, the message of Tenebrous Satanism is never, "on the basis of what these pages reveal, you are not allowed to live your life as you see fit." Nor is it ever, "on the basis of what these pages reveal, you have the right to make life more difficult for others." Rather, the message is simply, "here are some existential realities, which a wise person who seeks to be well-adjusted to life in this world would be better off engaging with than fleeing from." Strong-willed, self-possessed people should be capable of unrestricted investigation of reality, and honest conversation about what such investigation uncovers. If a Peril prompts a defensive emotional reaction, the individual can gain self-insight by analyzing this reaction. It accomplishes nothing, on the other hand, to childishly cry about how the Peril can't possibly be "true" just because it would make the universe mean and cruel if it were so or would give license to horrible people if it were so. As the Fourth Key already explained, *the Abyssal Void does not give license to anything.* It is, rather, *our* responsibility to "make a home of Darkness," courageously pursuing our own flourishing even when confronted by malign realities.

A final thing to note before proceeding is that while each archetype's rune is equivalent to a letter, noted in parentheses accompanying the title of the archetype, the rune's name itself appears in the header of each trio, to be used as an abbreviated identifier of both the vision to which the archetype belongs and its associated Peril. Thus, for example, while the archetype "The Void" is symbolized by the rune Qolf, "Qolf's vision" is shorthand for the vision entitled "Primordial Dawn" (trio of Qolf, 1 Attainment and 8 Attainment) and "Qolf's Peril" is shorthand for the Peril associated with that same vision, "Radical Vulnerability." We have adopted this convention because, as useful as evocative titles may be for stirring the diviner's imagination, it is also convenient to have a briefer way of identifying the visions and the Perils.

Qolf

Vision: Primordial dawn

Predawn over a rocky landscape; greenery is sparse but not absent. A woman of understated beauty, draped in flowing, natural garments, gazes with fearless wonder into the distance, where an iridescent sky is dominated by an ominously dragon-shaped cloud, descending toward a craggy mountain. To the woman's left are a fruit tree and a small number of livestock animals. To her right are a carefully-tended fire and a low stack of rough stones in the shape of a tetrahedron, imitating the peak that the shadow-dragon swoops toward.

Archetype: The Void (Q)

Formlessness, uncertainty, potentiality. Indicated via the shadow. Most often a sign that it is too early to say anything meaningful about a state of affairs, due to things having just begun and too much being yet unknown. May also suggest appreciation for that which is primal and unspoiled — either one is already deeply in touch with fundamental natural and spiritual forces or one should open oneself more to such experiences.

Lower-Octave: Abundance (1 Attainment)

Adequate resources, good health, gratitude. Indicated via the tree and animals. An assurance that one possesses sufficient material well-being for any imminent endeavors one may be considering. Implicit in this is a warning to appreciate the resources that one possesses now without taking for granted that such good fortune will continue indefinitely. Like the other "ones" in the runic-tarot, however, this is almost always a positive omen.

8

Higher-Octave: Investment (8 Attainment)

Preparation, calculation, tunnel vision. Indicated via the pyramid and the fire. Positively, this omen shows a readiness to succeed via the honing of one's skills and the making of prudent arrangements. Negatively, however, it may warn against getting too caught up in irrelevant details, such that a larger point is missed, or insinuate that complacency and lack of imagination may underlie what seems fruitful outwardly. Its implications are usually positive, however.

Peril: Radical vulnerability

Qolf's rune suggests the sun not yet risen above the horizon or a seed planted beneath the soil. It thus evokes a beginning state and the needs, threats, and obstacles that enfleshed beings must contend with from their first moments of existence. That which is newly arrived in the world is at the mercy of the initial conditions that greet it, and its continued existence is dependent upon many factors beyond its control.

To be greeted by Qolf's Peril is to be asked: how might your entire life, or that of someone else, have been different if that life's initial resources and threats had been other than they are? How do genes, family, culture, material conditions, etc. set precedents and expectations that limit the imagination and thereby restrict the wholly free exercise of the will? Has one made the most of whatever gifts one came into the world with? Reflection on such matters encourages deepened appreciation for what is and greater mental flexibility via the contemplation of open possibilities. The intent is not to make excuses for the current state of things, but to assess to what extent the available foundation has been put to its best use toward the goal of supporting future advances.

Anthal

Vision: Call to adventure

A crescent moon hangs in a dim blue sky over distant mountains, forming the backdrop of a landscape that is lush toward the right but declines into barrenness in all other directions. In the middle ground stands a spacious yet modest home, enclosed by a walled garden. A father stands in the doorway of the house, its proud owner, while a mother stands on the garden side of the gate, peering through its bars as if imprisoned. In the foreground, a jester-like figure in red and black leads the couple's four children forward and leftward, away from home. As he walks, he effortlessly balances a half-black, half-white trapezohedron on one finger before him, while in his other hand he holds a torch high to light the way ahead.

Archetype: The novices (A)

Spontaneity, wonder, naivety. Indicated via the jester and the children. At best, curiosity fosters new experiences, choices that seem impulsive turn out to be justified by intuition, and play teaches lessons that cannot be taught otherwise. At worst, the fool who trusts too much is oblivious to danger, and the innocent soul is too easily taken advantage of.

Lower-Octave: Ease (2 Attainment)

Graceful navigation, a small win, serendipity. Indicated via the balancing of the crystal. A striking combination of skill and luck that cannot help drawing the attention of onlookers even in the absence of large stakes. Usually a positive omen, but in some contexts it may warn of too much reliance on inborn talent instead of bettering oneself.

9 ☐

Higher-Octave: Security (9 Attainment)

Stability, worldly success, stagnancy. Indicated via the parents and their home. This omen points to those who have attained much in the eyes of the world, only to find themselves feeling fenced in by the mundane. Positive insofar as it suggests a reliable livelihood. To a Satanist, though, largely negative, hinting at a lack of spiritual fulfillment amid having settled too much into that which is safe and routine.

Peril: Conflicting perspectives of youth and age

In Anthal's vision can be found contrasts of tamed/wild, careful/reckless, timid/bold, and old/young. This illustrates a clash of interests between the established and the untried. The untried are well served by venturing into chaos to test their limitations, for thus are new heights gained; the established, having seen more of what can go awry, are equally within their rights to greet change with caution, preferring order. A clash between these two perspectives is all but unavoidable.

To be confronted by Anthal's Peril is to be asked: regarding the matter at hand, do you sympathize more readily with the position of the eager youth or the cautious elder? As the latter, have you accused others of being idealistic fools without being bothered to reflect upon why the status quo is intolerable to them? Or as the former, have you presumed that no one who opposes change could possibly have valid human needs they are attempting to protect, such that you unfairly paint the wisely hesitant as ignorant or malicious? Reflection on such matters discourages partisan divisiveness by broadening one's ability to extend empathy to those whose ethical and political commitments are motivated by different life experiences from one's own.

Byrk

Vision: Academy of magick

A cathedral-like space dominated by colorful stained glass, with a sun-like lamp hanging from the ceiling toward the right, a moon-like one toward the left; flames of different colors burn within each. Toward the rear, a male and a female magician stand on a balcony, she to the right and he to the left, middle hands clasped, his outer hand raised and hers lowered. He wears dark red robes and a black crown; she is robed in pale violet, with a white crown. Below the couple, three artisans work on a statue of a dragon; one consults plans, one carves, one polishes. Around these workers stand a crowd of young disciples in robes of various colors.

Archetype: The adepts (B)

Self-mastery, willful intent, hubris. Indicated via the couple. A person or group who skillfully makes their will manifest. Largely positive from a Satanic perspective, suggesting intellectual power, control of one's emotions, and personal confidence. In certain contexts, though, may indicate overanalyzing, rationalizing, or delusions of grandeur.

3 ⊓

Lower-Octave: Synergy (3 Attainment)

Cooperation, creative solutions, external recognition. Indicated via the artisans. This omen points to a group able to work well together on account of compatible ambitions, constructive attitudes, complementary talents, and pragmatic adaptability. A sign that initial difficulties will be overcome and appropriate compensation received for one's efforts.

10 ⊓

Higher-Octave: Legacy (10 Attainment)

Flourishing, happiness, idealism. Indicated via the crowd of students. An omen of enduring felicity, wherein material success feels meaningful thanks to its rootedness in something larger than the individual. But while it is usually a positive sign, in some contexts this omen may warn against trying to achieve everything by oneself instead of seeking others' aid, or herald long-term obstacles that others' accomplishments may create in opposition to one's own interests.

Peril: The inherent sociality of human existence

Byrk's vision depicts a scene of collective celebration by individuals whose successes are both enabled by, and reflected in, the successes of their comrades. One must not forget that the world is inherently a nexion of coexistence with others. The wise Satanist therefore does not reproach the world with a narcissistic, arrogant, or resentful attitude. One who harbors such attitudes is poorly suited to teach others, to learn from others, or to build in cooperation with others.

Byrk's Peril encourages reflection upon how even the most seemingly individualistic of conscious human goals still tends to be defined with a social horizon in mind. In striving as you do, whose expertise helps you succeed? Who mixes their labor with yours? Whom do your actions impact? Do you appreciate all of these others as much as wisdom and honor imply you should? Or are you the kind of person who demonizes the herd excessively, only to then turn around and wonder why you are haunted by feelings of alienation from others and lack of fulfillment? Reflection on such matters offers an antidote to the unrealistic romanticization of "self-reliance" that has so often plagued aspiring Satanists.

Grahl

Vision: Childhood's twilight

A young woman dressed in white gazes into a serene forest pond in which both her own reflection and the evening sky above are visible. She wears a horned crown that resembles the crescent moon overhead, white butterfly wings upon her back, and jeweled embellishments upon her forehead, throat, breast, and belt. By the light of the low-burning lantern set down by the maiden's side, her face is half lit and half in shadow, her expression suggestive of naive innocence struggling with an unwelcome intuition. The darkness under the trees around her is haunted by indistinct shadows, some suggestive of wild animals, others of hooded, cloaked men of ill-intent.

Archetype: The mirror (G)

Intuition, mystery, introspection. Indicated via the reflective pool. A call to redirect one's attention from external, mundane matters to internal, spiritual questions. Whether one has never asked such questions before or has neglected them lately, now is a time for opening oneself to acausal guidance. One ought, however, to prepare for the inner turmoil that so often precedes self-evolution.

Lower-Octave: Vigilance (4 Attainment)

Obliviousness, misplaced fretting, potential danger. Indicated via the shadows unseen by the maiden. This omen warns of being out of sync with the demands and risks inherent in the current situation: either one is failing to plan, or one is planning for the wrong things. It would be wise to examine one's assumptions and habits before misfortune can strike.

Higher-Octave: The Initiate (Muse of Attainment)

Inquisitiveness, study, self-absorption. Indicated via the central figure. This omen draws the diviner's attention to a person in one's life who is well-read and ever eager to learn more, but is readily judged by others as out of touch with reality due simply to their lack of experience out in the world. If situated as a problem, this omen may indicate a dysfunctional fixation on theoretical knowledge in place of lived experience. If situated positively, however, it suggests a willingness to undertake diligent study and to grow as a result.

Peril: The obstruction of self-insight

Grahl's vision evokes the spiritual centrality of self-reflection and the pragmatic challenges that attend it. One difficulty is that any enfleshed being's striving for self-insight must proceed from a mind built more in accord with flesh's needs (survival of *this* body) than spirit's (self-evolution *beyond* current restraints). Combine this with the organism possessing a finite amount of energy and life's ever-teeming threats and demands, and one should not be surprised that self-reflection does not come naturally to many people.

Contemplation of Grahl's Peril invites reflection on how one deals with those one calls ignorant. What priorities obstruct such people's will to self-improvement — e.g., mundane impositions, more enjoyable diversions, more pressing crises, etc.? Might one get better results by finding ways to motivate the ignorant via what they already care about instead of just castigating them for not already sharing one's own knowledge-seeking priorities? Reflection on such matters points to ways of overcoming inertia that are more patient, strategic, and effective than just getting mad at ignorant people.

Dolath

Vision: Seasons of the flesh

A tripartite image. In the center stands a mature woman of beauty, dressed in green. Draping vines and flowers form a portion of her hair. Coiled behind her is a serpentine green dragon, intimidating in size and revealing its fiery breath, yet unaggressive toward her. The woman's right hand rests upon the dragon's neck, while in her left, she extends a cornucopia of fruits and vegetables. The garden-like setting in which woman and beast stand gives way on the left to a snowy waste, where a lone man in a hooded cloak kneels, hands to his face in lamentation. To the right, garden gives way to desert, where a woman and child walk hand in hand, desperate for water.

Archetype: Nature (D)

Fruitfulness, vitality, affirmation. Indicated via the non-human elements of the scene. An illustration of the quietly powerful equanimity that proceeds from being able to wait for the right time, enjoy beauty and abundance while they last, and accept hardship and decay as part of nature's cycle. Positive unless accompanied by omens of impatience or denial.

Lower-Octave: Frustration (5 Attainment)

Material difficulties, bad luck, meaninglessness. Indicated via the figures on the periphery. This omen can presage setbacks in one's health, finances, or other life circumstances. More often, though, it reminds the diviner of the universe's blunt indifference to human well-being. As such, it may warn against perceiving intentional malice in mere mundane happenstance.

Higher-Octave: The Matriarch (Witch of Attainment)

Generosity, benevolence, refusal of judgment. Indicated via the central figure. Someone well-intentioned and eager to help but not necessarily a great judge of character. At best, a good peacemaker; at worst, a maker of unwise compromises.

Peril: The natural impositions of sexuality

Dolath's vision illustrates both nature's generosity and the "unfairness" of fleshly existence. It also highlights an average difference in the life experiences of male and female organisms. The latter must endure greater suffering and inconvenience in the course of physically bringing forth the next generation. The lot of the former, on the other hand, is disposability: once he accomplishes his passing contribution to reproduction, what need of him does nature have? Regardless of controversies over definitions of the sexes, nature vs. nurture, etc., the life cycles of non-human animals show this pattern consistently enough that one cannot plausibly claim it has no relevance to human beings.

What Dolath's Peril invites reflection upon is the distinction between acknowledging nature and being ruled or terrorized by it. Are you among those who make bold declarations about how men and women "should" act, despite how poorly your straitjacket suits those whose self-understanding and desires lie outside the norm? Conversely, do you read the previous paragraph and think, "But we must not speak of such things, lest we reinforce stereotypes"? In either case, what Dolath demands is that we stop jumping to conclusions about what nature prescribes. A mature, objective thinker ought to be able to both admit when general patterns hold and acknowledge exceptions to those patterns — without using either as a justification for denying flourishing to anyone.

Ishut

Vision: Completion of the harvest

Twilight in autumn. In the foreground, a cultivated field is being harvested by peasants. Overseeing them is a man on horseback, dressed and armed more in the manner of commoner than noble. His expression suggests experienced, capable leadership. At the left edge of the field, two other men lean over the fence. One is elderly and in fancy but tattered clothes, begging with hands outstretched. His companion is young and visibly poor, holding out an empty bag. High on the hill, unseen by all, stands a cloaked, masked woman, carrying a blazing torch in one hand, a basket of apples in the other.

⊥

Archetype: The outsider (I)

Separation, disruption, lack of recognition. Indicated via the woman. A person, group, or activity that the herd usually finds socially convenient to ignore, deny, or exclude. Framed positively, this omen suggests an untapped source of fulfillment and the potential benefits of opening one's mind to new perspectives. Framed negatively, it may warn of opportunities lost amid excessive suspicion and the consequences of remaining too set in one's ways.

6 ⌐|

Lower-Octave: Assistance (6 Attainment)

Desperation, plea for deliverance, unmet obligations. Indicated by the beggars. Depending on context, either an encouragement to seek aid oneself or to offer it to others. Either way, one should not underestimate the impact of even a minor show of support. May also remind one to pay one's debts, or warn that uncharitable treatment is making a situation needlessly worse.

Higher-Octave: The Guardian (Hero of Attainment)

Diligence, reliability, practical problem-solving. Indicated by the rider. This omen points to a competent individual who takes responsibility seriously: an admirable worker who may seem dull, but can be trusted to put full effort into even the most mundane of necessary tasks. Such an omen may bode ill in connection with novel opportunities or creative pursuits.

Peril: The rise of patriarchy

Ishut's vision hints at the estrangement of culture from nature, rich from poor, and male from female. Such forms of alienation are in part driven by a shared factor: disposable males (as per Dolath) attempting to justify their continued existence by securing more resources for their kin than competitors can. Two side effects of this contest are male indifference to the suffering of other males and reduction of the female either to an object to be won or an invisible outsider. It follows that, in a sense, patriarchy and inequality arise from nature itself. Nonetheless, as with Dolath's Peril, no rule states that mere acknowledgment of such a default obliges us to submit to said arrangements, pig-headedly putting up with their negatives. A Faustian mind recognizes a default not for the purposes of justifying it, but as a necessary first step toward imagining something better.

The central issue raised by Ishut's Peril is the role played in the diviner's life by competition, risk-taking, aggression, and other stereotypically "masculine" qualities. What advantages do such traits offer when applied constructively? Conversely, how might they undermine human flourishing and stifle self-evolution when they are overvalued or undervalued? Reflection upon such matters offers a corrective against a too-simplistic view of the benefits and shortcomings of masculous[41] traits.

Hvelgit

Vision: Shelter from the storm

The interior of a manor house, with adjacent countryside visible through two large arched window, an ominous storm brewing overhead. In the center stands a well-kept yet down-to-earth man, crowned with ram's horns, a medallion around his neck. He holds a scroll in his left hand and a scepter tipped with a jewel in his right. Before him stands a desk covered with stacked coins and records of account, and directly behind him, a pleasant flame in the fireplace. Out the left window behind him, a family in tattered clothing is approaching the welcoming-looking village which he oversees, while the window on the other side reveals builders laying the foundation of a new home.

Archetype: The haven (H)

Protection, order, leadership. Indicated via the settlement's prosperity. An illustration of the safety and comfort born of shared investment in a functional and caring community. Usually associated with disciplined application of energy and the sustainable growth that results. In some contexts, however, this omen can be an accusation that one is failing to foster constructive qualities of this kind.

Lower-Octave Element: Worry (7 Attainment)

Hard-won goal, anxiety amid exhaustion, cynicism. Indicated via the distressed family. This omen points to a situation where due to extensive investment of energy and resources, one fears all the more that things may not turn out. Usually a positive sign, though, warning against letting negative thoughts and emotions taint an imminent achievement with suspicion or resentment.

Higher-Octave: The Patriarch (Sorcerer of Attainment)

Effectiveness, discipline, trust. Indicated by the central figure. Suggests an individual who excels in the day-to-day management of both people and resources. When situated as an ideal to emulate, calls for setting clear priorities, consistent follow-through, and steadfast resistance to temptation. When situated as a problem, it warns that those skilled at maintaining order when times are good may not handle crises effectively.

Peril: The perpetuation of fortune and misfortune

Hvelgit's vision depicts the fortuitous intercession of a "have" on behalf of a "have-not." This is an allusion to the precedent-setting nature of gain and loss, as was already mentioned in passing in the opening of the Third Key: those who possess much have many resources to draw upon and are thus more able to weather misfortune, while those with little have fewer options, making them more vulnerable to greater losses. In light of this natural law and the absence of "fairness" it evinces, it is unrealistic to go around telling the unfortunate to pull themselves up by their own bootstraps.

Hvelgit's Peril opens one's eyes to what it really means to call someone needy. Within the orbit of humanity that you inhabit, who are those whose lives have been made more difficult by such factors as nature, fortune, or the predations of other human beings? What, realistically, is within the power of such people to change at will, versus what might they be empowered to do for themselves if even modest assistance were offered to them? Reflection upon such matters discourages the too-lazy labeling of one's fellow human beings as "parasites" and encourages greater self-awareness regarding unmet imperatives of honor and empathy.

Vhow

Vision: Celestial hegemony

A radiant setting, suggestive of a heavenly realm. The scene is dominated by a noble personage, refined in both dress and manner, marked with the distinction of age and the aura of power. Twelve elders dressed in shades of blue and seated upon thrones encircle the even loftier throne of this leader. Hovering in the air above them are two golden cages, the keys to which are in the preeminent figure's possession. The cage on the left contains a large goblet, overflowing, its nourishing liquid turning to cloud at its base. The one on the right contains a hooded traveler, resentful of his imprisonment even though the wound he clutches suggests he might not make it far if he were set free.

Archetype: The throne (V)

Tradition, moral authority, rigidity. Indicated via the dominant figure and surrounding court. This omen evokes the imposition of ethical and legal codes, the wielding of power by established leaders, and the expectation of "proper" behavior. As such, it is usually negative from a Satanic perspective, implying a demand to conform to protocols that the Satanist does not find personally meaningful.

Lower-Octave: Refreshment (1 Communion)

Pleasure, candor, inspiration. Indicated via the goblet. This omen announces that a novel acquaintance or experience is soon to come into one's life: a positive influence that may offer emotional support, a new perspective, or both. A strong indicator that the time is right to meet new people and try new things.

Higher-Octave: Loss (8 Communion)

Detachment, stoicism, arrested departure. Indicated via the caged traveler. When framed as a solution, this omen suggests self-aware acceptance of past mistakes made, and the "stiff upper lip" approach to coping with private sorrows. When framed as a problem, however, it warns of difficulties with the processing of trauma: either one is in denial, pretending to want to move on when one is not in fact able to, or one is dwelling upon one's wounds instead of seeking what may help heal them.

Peril: Optimistic delusions of cosmic justice

Vhow's vision suggests much that conscious beings wish to believe: that a benevolent force oversees all, has the power to dispense blessings justly, and protects the afflicted from having to endure more than their fair share of Peril. Such an image of cosmic justice has an admittedly appealing ability to soothe existential anxieties. As per the Second Key, however, pernicious consequences follow when human beings declare, "This is the True earthly manifestation of cosmic justice, so no mortal ought dare to question it!" amid their veneration of ideologies and authorities — and equally so when they complain, to the contrary, "This fails to live up to cosmic justice, so its imperfect goodness counts for naught!" The difficulties of life are such that one cannot blame humans for wanting to believe in cosmic justice. But to enshrine such a notion as Truth — as Dogmagians do — is a move that causes more problems than it solves.

Vhow's Peril calls for the recognition and annihilation of wishful thinking. What axioms do you or others choose to believe in because the alternative seems unbearable? What wounds have you allowed to fester, and what opportunities locked away? Reflection upon such matters can reveal dogmatic tendencies where they might otherwise go unrecognized.

Xhin

Vision: The cave of ordeal

Clouds fill the whole of the sky, casting day into gloom. Set into the side of a mountain is a cave entrance, from which emerges a wild woman with matted hair, bone ornaments, torn clothing, and bare feet. The woman's eyes are two distinctly different colors. She carries a staff in her left hand with a large glowing orb hovering above its end. Her right hand bears a chalice made of a skull. Below her, amid scraggly trees, a pair of noble adventurers, prince and princess, look up at the madwoman, tensed for the possibility of conflict. She looks not at them, though, for she is entranced instead by the magical pearl she bears in her possession.

Archetype: The heretic (X)

Nonconformity, passion, dissolution. Indicated via the madwoman. This omen points to someone who finds conventional expectations stifling and instead strikes out in a different direction in pursuit of their own unique desires. Usually a positive indicator of an untrammeled Satanic spirit but may warn of obsession, recklessness or self-destructive lunacy if framed negatively.

Lower-Octave: Intimacy (2 Communion)

Sexual attraction, new relationship, harmony amid differences. Indicated via the couple. This omen speaks of interpersonal events unfolding positively on multiple levels: physical, emotional, intellectual, spiritual. Usually a good sign unless it appears in a context where it warns of what is lacking instead of announcing what is coming.

Higher-Octave: Enchantment (9 Communion)

Enrapture, wish-fulfillment, pride. Indicated via the pearl and its hold upon the madwoman's attention. This omen evokes the attainment of a connection long sought after, good fortune beyond all expectations, and the enjoyment of that which is both delightful and meaningful. On the negative side however, it may warn against being too sure of oneself, expecting to be understood by others when such is unlikely, or becoming spoiled amid too much immediate gratification.

Peril: Fear of the new

Xhin's vision alludes to the tendency for the truly unprecedented to be resisted and resented, even by supposedly bold and eager explorers of undiscovered territory. This attitude is understandable, and even sometimes justified, insofar as those who are satisfied with the existing order are strongly motivated to resist the introduction of chaos. On the other hand though, it must not be granted the final say in all things, for that would be tantamount to a refusal to evolve — a refusal sure to eventually undo those who embrace it. To cultivate courage enough to contend constructively with the wholly new, one must eschew both the cowardice that drives slavish dedication to tradition and the hypocrisy of those who cry "liberty!" yet cannot tolerate the innovation that arises organically in a truly free environment.

Counterproductive resistance to change is the cardinal issue that Xhin's Peril raises. Are there things that you resist, reject, or even outright deny, simply because they threaten your current beliefs and existing routines? How might this attitude be setting you back, both from realizing potential gains and from your own self-evolution in confrontation with adversity? Reflection upon such matters can help one replace fear, complacency, and resentment with a more constructive outlook.

Zhalg

Vision: Two hearts united

Under a dark blue sky, the noble couple from Xhin's vision stand upon a hilltop, facing one another with hands clasped. Their faces tilt upward to look at the waxing gibbous moon that hangs very large in the sky above them, and from which streams down an iridescent aura of power in which float the innocent souls of children as yet unborn. At the base of the hill stand four plinths, each carved with a symbol of one of the four kingdoms of the runic-tarot, and around each plinth whirls a trio of dancing celebrants. All figures present in the scene are clad in simple white, the adventurers having set aside their traveling garb and weapons at the base of the hill.

Archetype: The lovers (Z)

True love, fidelity, keeping of oaths. Indicated via the couple. This omen points to the prospect of two highly compatible parties making a lasting commitment to one another. Depending on context, it may remind one to pay attention to who is one's foremost supporter, urge the pursuit of higher-quality relationships, warn against betraying one's allegiances, or promise a happy ending.

Lower-Octave: Comfort (3 Communion)

Companionship, fun, joy amid hardship. Indicated via the celebrants. A reminder of the mutual support offered by friendship and the refreshment gained from socializing with like-minded others. Almost always a positive omen, offering relief from fears, sorrows, and frustrations — even if only for a little while.

10 ⌬

Higher-Octave: Happiness (10 Communion)

Dreams fulfilled, bright future, familial affection. Indicated via the stream of souls. In most contexts, a joyful omen that bodes well for all manner of long-term projects, such as raising children, founding an organization, finding a receptive audience for a creative work, etc. But if framed negatively, it may indicate resentment of someone else's successes or warn the diviner against living in the future at the expense of the present.

Peril: Obsession with reproduction

At the center of Zhalg's celebration of love is the prospective fertility of the couple. Since sexuality is the default method of bringing new life into the world, humans both romanticize it as a method of gaining immortality and over-police it for supposed misuse. On one hand, people are shamed for not reproducing, even in circumstances where reluctance is pragmatically justifiable. On the other hand, non-reproductive sexuality is framed as inferior and persecuted as sinful, despite such "wrong" acts being no less a source of ecstasy and intimacy for willing participants than "default" expressions of sexuality.

Zhalg's Peril encourages one to grapple with how an urge to regulate the continuance of life may arise from fundamental human terrors and insecurities. Instead of sneering at traditional societies for being closed-minded and uptight, might we consider how a genuine fear of social breakdown and extinction could be a driver of sexual regulation and admit that sexual freedom may not be cost-free? Conversely, in our own less-precarious times, should we not challenge those who cling to superstitions that do more to impede the flourishing of non-conformers than to safeguard society? Reflection upon such matters is not meant to excuse bigotry, but to grasp its primal root as a step toward using empathy and wisdom to overcome it.

Chet

Vision: News from beyond the walls

Under a gray sky, a courtyard enclosed by high stone walls contains a fading garden. Through a gate on the left, a black horse is visible, from whence strides a rider bearing a scroll in one gloved hand, his features shrouded by his cloak. He approaches a table toward the courtyard's center, where sit the same couple as from Zhalg, now looking older and tired, half-preoccupied with the game laid upon the table between them, half despondently absorbed within themselves. Toward the right, a child with dreamy eyes and the multi-hued wings of a fairy leans over the half-dead flowers, as if hoping that her mere presence might enchant them back to life.

Archetype: The messenger (C)

Interruption, momentous news, challenge. Indicated via the rider. This omen announces a sudden development that upsets one's personal status quo. Positively, it may foreshadow the taking of difficult action for which one may win others' recognition. Negatively, it warns against denial, procrastination, and excuse-making.

Lower-Octave: Weariness (4 Communion)

Inertia, boredom, hidden dissatisfaction. Indicated via the couple. A sign that what used to be enjoyable has ceased to be so, that people have become tired of one another, and that resentment is beginning to bubble to the surface. Those involved are likely to choose denial and passive aggression over open conflict.

Higher-Octave: The Daydreamer (Muse of Communion)

Playfulness, fantasy, escapism. Indicated via the child. This omen draws the diviner's attention to an idiosyncratic individual who offers a novel perspective but is prone to distraction and erratic behavior. When framed positively, it may indicate that imagination has a valid role to play and warn against dismissing "unrealistic" ideas before examining them for unconventional insights. When framed negatively, it warns against retreating into pleasant daydreams and beautiful visions in an attempt to avoid life's Perils.

Peril: The ever-present shadow of survival threats

Chet's rune suggests concerted, dynamic action, yet many elements of its vision evoke distraction and inertia. This contrast calls to mind how, in the state of nature, evolution rewards immediate, decisive attention to threats, since it is the inattentive who are eliminated by disaster. Unfortunately, the hyper-vigilance that evolution naturally rewards in turn curses the minds of conscious beings to dwell constantly on the negative, damning some to perpetual dread, others to indecisive helplessness, and yet others to the counter-reaction of naive denial. Chet's Peril thus poses a dilemma: it is dangerous to attend to nothing yet unbearable to attend to everything.

The queries associated with Chet's Peril pertain to what one chooses to pay attention to and how such priorities are apt to serve one in the long run. Are there crises in your life that you are making worse for yourself by refusing to address? Do you allow your energy to be drained by that which you have no real enthusiasm for? Reflection upon such matters aids in the rooting-out of evasion and procrastination, encouraging the replacement of self-defeating habits with something healthier.

Fhell

Vision: Chains of possession

A dusk rendered dark as night by thick clouds and rainfall. A lonely tower rises over the ocean, with jutting rocks at its base. In the tower's sole window, a middle-aged man sits amid stacks of coins. Paying no mind to the pedestal at his side, upon which sits a chest bound up in lock and chain, he inspects a series of jewels, casting each away on account of the flaws he perceives in it. To the right of the tower's base, a fish-tailed nereid sprawls upon the rocks, beautiful but sad. Toward the left, broken mirror fragments scattered on the rocks contain the image of the miser as a younger and less stoic man, upon whose face the nereid's troubled gaze fondly rests.

Archetype: The prisoner (F)

Conservatism, defensiveness, ennui. Indicated via the man's confinement and the barring of the chest. An omen of attachment, well-summarized by the phrase "the things you own own you." May speak to situations in which something of value has been handed down from the past, and its inheritors feel thereby obliged to remain engaged with it despite the sense of burden that comes with this obligation.

Lower-Octave: Disillusionment (5 Communion)

Grievance, fault-finding, negativity. Indicated via the man's cynical, miserly behavior. This omen acknowledges that one may have had a legitimately-bad experience but warns that one's attitude toward that experience may be poisoning one's perceptions of other, unrelated experiences. A warning to find healthy ways to heal instead of making a home of bitterness.

Higher-Octave: The Sympathizer (Witch of Communion)

Hidden love, supportive ally, patient endurance. Indicated via the nereid. Suggests an individual who cares deeply even though they cannot or will not express this openly. Framed positively, this omen urges patience and trust: steadfast support is present behind the scenes, and will make itself known when a moment of true need arrives. When framed negatively, it may warn of someone who means well but is creating confusion about their true desires and intentions via their failure to communicate.

Peril: Suffering's roots in attachment

Fhell's vision displays a man obsessed by the value of things and a woman whose solicitude orients her toward an idealized specter whom she imagines she might lend aid to. For both, satisfaction proves elusive. Herein is a parable of how conscious beings often experience existence: in an attempt to anchor oneself against chaos, one defines objects worthy of pursuit, and once gained, labels them "mine." Such anchors breed dissatisfaction, for the demand that objects live up to labels and expectations prevents appreciation for actualities. Sooner or later, the impermanence of all things culminates in the loss of that which was beloved or disenchantment with it.

To be confronted by Fhell's Peril is to be interrogated on the subject of what one attaches oneself to and how one constructs one's own ego in connection. Are you prone to taking any attack on that which is "yours" as an attack on you personally? Do you dwell upon what you feel you are owed and punish people for breaking agreements with you that, in fact, they never entered into to begin with? Reflection upon such matters helps one recognize when one's petty egoism is poisoning one's zeal and thwarting one's flourishing.

Tharu

Vision: Recovering the grail

In a ruined cathedral stands an altar, with a simple but beautiful chalice upon it. Behind the altar, a tree bedecked with blossoms grows out of the cracked stone floor. Toward the left stands a unicorn, its head bent so that its horn nearly touches the grail, while on the right kneels the rider of the unicorn, a knight in white armor with a blue cloak and plume upon his helmet and a lion upon his shield. The knight's look is one of satisfaction with having found what he is looking for, and he is thus unconcerned by the enormous eyes, teeth, and horns of the dark shape of a monster partly visible through the broken cathedral windows toward the rear of the scene, partly concealed by fog.

Archetype: The monster (Th)

Surpassing of limits, unleashed emotions, transgressive outburst. Indicated via the lurking creature. This omen is a warning of destructive intent — not necessarily malice, but a will to rid oneself of circumstances, objects, and people with which one has become acutely dissatisfied. Often a sign that something (e.g., a relationship) is already finished in the hearts of those involved and that it would better to acknowledge this openly than to persist in denial.

Lower-Octave: Rejuvenation (6 Communion)

Renewal, sentimentality, vulnerability. Indicated via the grail and tree. Consolation drawn from nostalgic memories, pastimes long-neglected, etc. This omen encourages one to search one's past for as-yet untapped sources of comfort. This may, however, mean lowering one's guard and facing accompanying risks.

Higher-Octave: The Seeker (Hero of Communion)

Encouragement, open-mindedness, hope. Indicated via the central figure. This omen highlights an individual whose contributions are often undervalued, but in fact plays an essential role in boosting the morale of those in distress. In broader terms, it encourages "thinking outside the box" regarding how to mitigate problems even if one cannot solve them outright. But it may also warn against mistaking temporary sources of comfort for permanent solutions.

Peril: The elusiveness of hope

Tharu's vision depicts how it is still possible to find renewal, even amid overwhelming danger and looming horror, if one looks in the right places. Between the need to fend off ongoing threats, the impositions of the herd and the hauntings of personal demons, life is often a daunting and exhausting affair. At the same time, insofar as these very conditions of adversity all contribute to the texture of spirit's Adventure, they constitute "what Darkness came here for." Those who embrace this secret impetus behind life are empowered to find ways of seizing fulfillment, even amid the bleakest of circumstances. Refusal, on the other hand, transforms a manageable inner monster into an unmanageable outer one — and destroys one's prospects of even a modest happiness in the process.

Tharu's Peril asks how one might best respond when flourishing and self-evolution seem hopelessly obstructed. Amid dark times, what small things offer you refreshment? Do you take time to appreciate these or are you too quick to dismiss them as trivial or temporary? Reflection upon such matters teaches one to direct more gratitude toward what is, instead of nursing ingratitude and despair over what is not.

Ngiha

Vision: Unmasking the hypocrites

In a dim royal hall, seven nobles feast, their features obscured by disguises. One wears a more elaborate mask and crown than the others: the central figure from Vhow, attending in secret. This leader stands, offering a toast, while the other six remain seated with glasses upraised. Their goblets contain such things as a snake, jewels, an evil flower, poison, a skull, a toad, and blood, yet all who are about to drink wear pleased expressions on their faces. The rear wall is dominated by a portcullis, beyond which sinister specters descend from a misty sky reddened by a lunar eclipse. An antlered man with a furtive yet determined expression stands in the shadow of the arch, preparing to open the gate to admit the horrors beyond.

Archetype: The masquerade (Ng)

Decadence, deceit, experimentation with identity. Indicated via the mask-wearers. This omen primarily points to the putting on of false fronts: one pretends to hate arrangements that in truth are to one's benefit, sings hollow praises of something one actually despises, or otherwise willfully misrepresents oneself. Whether this omen foretells a guise well-worn or an imminent unmasking depends heavily on the context in which it appears.

Lower-Octave: Delusion (7 Communion)

Impaired decision-making, failed plans, fruitlessness. Indicated via the goblets. This omen warns that factors such as self-deceit, vanity, or distorted priorities are clouding one's judgment. Beware of being led astray by pleasing fantasies, unrealistic promises, or other such conceits.

Higher-Octave: The Revolutionary (Sorcerer of Communion)

Conviction, resignation, self-control. Indicated via the man with the antlers. This omen points to an individual who sees clearly what needs to be done and will do it despite any difficulties that may result for them personally. A warning to beware of what may follow when one reaches a breaking point, and to control one's emotions carefully in times of extremity.

Peril: The demonization of strife-bringers

Ngiha's vision is one of decadent mendacity on the verge of disruption by encroaching Darkness. It thus bears upon that which makes the Sinister Path "sinister": the fomenting of strife. Strife is the antidote to dogma, for it challenges that which was formerly taken for granted and tears down that which the complacent would otherwise allow themselves to be destroyed by. For this very reason, though, many people fear strife as a bringer of chaos and would rather take up the side of easier Truths. The walker of the Sinister Path thus finds themselves in the unenviable position of seeking a liberation that is ultimately on behalf of all at the same time as the braying mob sees only a blasphemer and troublemaker in their midst.

What Ngiha's Peril calls for is a fuller grasp of how would-be change-makers are apt to be perceived by change-resistors. Insofar as you are attacking dearly held principles of "good" people, can you blame them for hating you? Is your cause best advanced by openly making enemies, or might some more covert approach serve you better? Reflection upon such matters should help Satanists avoid a pitfall that many contemporary change-makers have stumbled into: presuming that abrasive self-righteousness is the only key that can unlock the gates of change and alienating potential allies thereby.

Tehir

Vision: Rider of the dragon

A beautiful woman, nude and without shame, rides upon the back of a red dragon with prominent wings and horns. In one hand, she holds a blindfold that she has just finished pulling away from her face, while in the other, she brandishes a sword, pointing the way forward for the beast she rides. Behind and to the sides, a high barricade of thorns encloses woman and beast, nearly to the point of blotting out the barren land beyond and the ruddy sky above, but toward the front of the scene, the dragon's fiery breath and trampling feet have already destroyed much of the barrier.

Archetype: The Black Flame (T)

Confidence, determination, fearlessness. Indicated by the woman's harnessing of the dragon. This omen illustrates a powerful synergy of instinct, intuition, and conscious will. It points to someone who, through deep self-knowledge and extensive self-development, is able to muster incredible courage and perseverance in times of adversity. From a Satanic perspective, almost always a positive omen.

Lower-Octave: Insight (1 Strife)

Awakening, self-honesty, facing harsh truths. Indicated via the sword. This omen foretells a personal revelation that brings an end to a period of inaction and procrastination. Often, this entails acknowledgment and integration of the Dark side, both of oneself and of existence more generally. In some contexts, it may warn of a dangerous adversary, but it is still almost always an omen of inner empowerment.

8

Higher-Octave: Escape (8 Strife)

Outburst, imminent breakthrough, end of restriction. Indicated via the barrier and the blindfold. This omen paints a picture of past obstruction: due to unforeseen events, misunderstandings, or previous mistakes, one had felt closed in by a lack of good options. The positive implication, however, is that now one is on the verge of discovering a solution, for in fact, one *does* have sufficient inward resources to devise a way of breaking free.

Peril: The ideological neutering of the will

Tehir's vision illustrates the Black Flame's foremost manifestation: the transgressive conquest of obstacles, for in such acts is Darkness' unquenchable thirst for existence and inexhaustible striving most evident. Though this force shines forth most brightly in hearts free of inhibition and bitterness, it dwells secretly within the souls of all beings nonetheless. One ought, then, to beware of ideologies that deny this inward potential. Some frame the exertion of the will as a privilege that some groups exert over others.[42] Others talk as if external conditions decide everything and internal will nothing, so as to disempower everyone equally. Both types obstruct the Faustian potential of humanity as a whole, however, and both therefore deserve to be trampled and incinerated by the Satanist.

Tehir's Peril is a call to existential responsibility. How honest have you been with yourself regarding the issue of what you have chosen, versus what has been forced upon you? Do you fixate unproductively on what is beyond your control instead of making the best of what you *can* alter? Reflection upon such matters reminds one of the ever-present wellspring of potentiality inherent in spirit and reveals that which is always yet within one's power to *do* — a capacity which, even if small amid harsh circumstances, is still better nurtured than dismissed.

Ywhaz

Vision: Ascending the peak

Amid falling snow, a cloaked, hooded man climbs a rugged mountain whose top is out of sight, bearing a sun-like crystal as a lamp before him. The dark sky on either side of the peak seethes with serpentine vapors and threatening faces, a chaos of vague yet menacing demons. Below the lone adventurer, a path partially covered by snow leads in from lower-right corner of the scene, but his own footsteps trail in from the lower-left corner, indicating that he came from the direction opposite that of the established road. In each of these two corners, a sword stands thrust into the ground, barring the man both from turning back and from returning to society.

Archetype: The wanderer (Y)

Solitude, wisdom, personal development. Indicated via the central figure. This omen depicts withdrawal from external expectations in order to pursue a personal quest for illumination. Usually a good sign, but in some contexts, it may indicate solipsism, spiritual elitism, and other such qualities that may alienate one's allies.

Lower-Octave: Indecision (2 Strife)

Clashing priorities, unresolved tension, alienation. Indicated via the swords. This omen illustrates a situation in which one is being pressured to choose between dissatisfactory options, none of which are in accord with the best possible direction for oneself. Often a sign that one needs to distance oneself from those who impose upon one's life and challenge the narratives they are attempting to push.

9

Higher-Octave: Terror (9 Strife)

Acute dread, anguish, haunting. Indicated via the evil forces in the air. An omen that may presage a variety of painful circumstances: cruelty, manipulation, humiliation, exclusion, etc. Amid such experiences, paranoia, anxiety, and self-blame can be difficult to resist. Still, one should beware of aggravating what is objectively bad by letting one's fears and delusions run wild. Grounding oneself by turning outward may be a better approach to such a situation than keeping oneself in isolation.

Peril: Solitude as a gateway to madness

In featuring a lone protagonist taking risks for the sake of self-knowledge, Ywhaz's vision resembles Grahl's. It differs in that here, the risk comes from that which is foreseen and yet still sought, rather than that which is neglected at the periphery of one's awareness. Thus, whereas Grahl's vision evokes the external dangers that threaten to dissuade one from self-reflection, Ywhaz's speaks to the dangers that arise from looking within too much and too well: an alienation from the external world so extensive that one ceases being able to function among others. To be able to walk boldly alone is a virtue of the Sinister Path. One must beware, however, of wandering blindly in Darkness for so long that one's eyes cease being able to function in the light of day.

Ywhaz's Peril confronts one with the need for honesty regarding how one handles solitude. Are you among the many humans who lives in perpetual self-flight, seeking any excuse to avoid having an honest conversation with yourself? Or, if you are one who loves isolation, what exactly are you getting out of it, versus how might it hold you back? Reflection upon such matters is necessary if one is to steer one's ship between the opposing obstacles of self-ignorance and solipsism.

Kehan

Vision: Contest of fortune

A scene split down the middle. On either side of a flat stone slab, a man and woman face off over a chess-like game. The woman, clad in mourning garb, stands in an aggressive posture, a cruel but hurt look on her face, while the man, nude save for a long kilt, sits resignedly. Both are badly injured, the woman bleeding from a mortal gash in her breast, while every visible surface of the man's skin is crisscrossed with flesh wounds. Behind the woman stretches an expanse of rough ocean beneath roiling storm clouds and a waning moon; behind the man stretches a battlefield strewn with corpses and broken weapons under a clear, predawn sky.

K

Archetype: The game (K)

Change, opportunity, destiny. Indicated via the board and pieces. This omen foretells a major shift: something long thought to be unlikely is suddenly looking possible. Usually a positive omen to the strong-minded, prepared Satanist but may be negative in the eyes of the timid and reluctant. It may also indicate hidden powers or agendas becoming visible or otherwise revealing themselves.

3

Lower-Octave: Disappointment (3 Strife)

Heartbreak, betrayal, victimhood. Indicated via the woman. An omen of interpersonal difficulties, especially those wrought by unanticipated separation, unexpected delays, inconsiderate behavior, or sudden rejection. Regardless of whether one is the victim or villain of the situation, a warning not to make things worse via poor judgment and the nursing of grudges.

10

Higher-Octave: Devastation (10 Strife)

Failure, grief, acceptance. Indicated via the man. This omen is associated with disastrous loss or total disillusionment, plunging one into despair for a time. On one hand, it is a sign of things having reached their lowest point, but on the other, it is a hopeful omen insofar as the situation is unlikely to become worse. It encourages the diviner to seek a deeper spiritual meaning behind tribulation and to accept that some ills simply have no remedy, for only with such acceptance can one take the first step toward better days.

Peril: The validity of both emotion and reason

Kehan's vision presents two players making moves at cross purposes with one another. What they share in common, however, is their pursuit of a constructive objective, coupled with an inability to act with complete freedom. This alludes to two often-competing human faculties: emotions, which aim at motivating immediate action without the need for conscious intervention, and reason, which demands patience and discipline now if the calculated gains are to be realized later. Sometimes it is better for one of these two faculties to win out and sometimes the other. What must be recognized, however, is that both are fallible, and both can unleash disaster when misapplied.

To be greeted with Kehan's Peril is to be asked about the balance of reason versus emotion at play within a given person or situation. When imagined as characters, how might reason and emotion each express their concerns and defend their conclusions to you? Do you favor one of the game's two players over the other, and are you sure that the victory of this player will yield the best results? Reflection upon such matters prevents psychological stagnation, by disrupting the habitual adoption of one mental tool over the other.

Lhamyu

Vision: Admonishing the deluded

The grassy foreground is strewn with moldering bones and decayed trappings of the once-living, an improper burial half-concealed by weeds. In the midground stand two figures: toward the right, an impish girl with black butterfly wings and a mischievous expression, pointing at the bones as if she means to spin a tale about them; in the center, a mature, stern-faced woman dressed in the formal robes of a magistrate, one hand raised to rebuke the child. She holds a pair of scales in her other hand, while at her side, a sword hangs at the ready. The broad, powerful curtain of a waterfall down the side of a mountain forms the backdrop of the scene.

ད

Archetype: The verdict (L)

Justice, purification, restoration of balance. Indicated via the matron and the waterfall. This omen presages the handing-down of a verdict from an authority or a price paid for past deeds. Unless context indicates otherwise, this will be a fair, well-deserved judgment — what some might call a karmic cleansing — such that owning up to one's failings and enduring the consequences will prove the best course.

Lower-Octave: Respite (4 Strife)

Cessation, suspension, a dead issue. Indicated via the human remains. At best, this omen promises a quiet break from tiresome conflicts and difficulties. But it may also warn against dwelling on what is beyond repair or advise that one ought to let sleeping dogs lie instead of bringing needless trouble on oneself.

Higher-Octave: The Troublemaker (Muse of Strife)

Drama, interference, contradiction. Indicated via the girl. This omen draws the diviner's attention to a sharp-witted individual prone to amusing themselves with vain curiosity and petty social games. It may thus warn against a nosy busybody, an undisciplined gossip, or a loose cannon in one's ranks. It can also indicate that a persuasive stratagem is succeeding for now but may cause complications later.

Peril: The agenda-driven nature of storytelling

Lhamyu's vision evokes the human capacity for storytelling and the tendency for such stories to occlude or distort more than they reveal. A consideration of evolutionary imperatives suggests that human reason arose primarily for the purposes of persuading others, so as to facilitate advantageous forms of social cooperation. Reason is thus not a disinterested truth-seeker. Instead, it is oriented toward the establishment and maintenance of *our* truth, which must be protected from *their* falsehoods. Herein lies the human mind's propensity toward Dogmagianism.

Accordingly, Lhamyu's Peril warns one to be wary of what agendas are furthered by the framing of narratives and to be aware too of the common tendency to condemn one's enemies' biases while pretending that oneself and one's allies have none. Against this, it is worth asking: on what matters are you prone to simply taking the word of those you trust, rather than investigating things for yourself? And when you do investigate, how fair are you, *really*, when it comes to hearing out the other side of the story? Reflection upon such matters encourages the honest recognition of ideological echo chambers — an important first step toward gaining a broader perspective.

Manoth

Vision: Feast of crows

The sorcerer from Byrk's vision hangs upside-down upon the wooden scaffolding on which he is bound. He is almost nude and has just finished slitting his own belly from throat to navel, such that the dagger remains buried in his flesh, while his other hand hangs loose. Nonetheless, he is still alive. On the ground around the scaffolding, four men lie dead, impaled on swords: one obese and nobly clothed, one thin and shabby, one very old, and one barely out of boyhood. Upon the very top of the scaffolding perches a raven whose head is that of the masked woman from Ishut, gazing imperiously over the folly below.

Archetype: The sacrifice (M)

Suffering, martyrdom, altruism. Indicated via the central figure. This omen illustrates willing submission to an ordeal for the sake of attaining a greater good. It thus raises the question of whether one's chosen cause is really worth dying for. Framed positively, it foretells short-term anguish giving way to long-term self-realization. Framed negatively, it may warn of questionable priorities or the urge to impress others with actions that are merely symbolic.

Lower-Octave: Defeat (5 Strife)

Division, infighting, malice. Indicated via the four dead men. This omen points to an ugly clash that turns a group against itself. Such conflicts often produce divided loyalties, severed relationships, and the humiliation of being unable to defend oneself. Still, it may well be better to endure the worst than try to flee and risk prolonging an unpleasant situation.

Higher-Octave: The Critic (Witch of Strife)

Objectivity, secrets revealed, difficult conversations. Indicated via the masked, human-headed raven. Suggests a reserved individual who demands ruthless honesty of both themselves and others. A sign that impatience and refusal to compromise are ascendant, to the detriment of etiquette and diplomacy. A strident call to speak openly of the realities of a situation no matter whose feelings may be hurt by doing so.

Peril: Uncompensated loss

Manoth's vision suggests too much sacrifice for too little gain. The unfortunate reality here is that disciplined striving, though generally adaptive, does not always pay off, as even the best-laid plans can go awry in the face of ill fortune. Present sacrifice for the sake of future gain is therefore always accompanied by a risk of uncompensated loss. Frequent disappointment in this regard is, in turn, a factor in how difficult it is to convince those who live lives of desperation to think and prepare beyond the present moment.

Manoth's Peril calls for one to reckon openly with questions about trauma and its impact. How do the precedents set by previous negative events discourage future risk-taking? To what extent is one held back by a refusal to admit that such an effect is even occurring? Conversely, upon recognizing such shackles, what small risks might one challenge oneself to weather, so as to build enough confidence to win greater victories down the line? Reflection upon such matters replaces impotent rage against that which is broken with pragmatic forward-striving against personal demons. It also encourages empathy toward those whose self-defeating behavior may be difficult to comprehend in the absence of reflection upon what trauma can do to people.

Nithrul

Vision: Death's devouring vortex

A desolate valley strewn with bones, giving way to the shore of a lifeless ocean in the foreground and dissolving into swirling mist above. A monstrous form, part dragon and part vortex, dominates the sky, pouring itself down menacingly upon those below. Toward the lower right, a woman with her face hidden by a cloak crouches down within the confines of a small boat, laid low by grief and terror, her only hope lying in the craft's rapid separation from the shore. From the left enters a bold knight in dark armor with a burgundy cloak and plume. Mounted upon a winged steed, he charges with his sword drawn, determined to attempt futile battle against the inchoate horror.

Archetype: The Abyss (N)

Necessary ending, transformation, new beginning. Indicated via the monstrous vortex. This omen points to a momentous shift in circumstances that seems unpleasant or even terrifying at present but is ultimately necessary for the sake of overcoming inertia. Insofar as one cannot compromise with inexorable forces, adapting oneself to the new situation would be wiser than resisting it.

Lower-Octave: Departure (6 Strife)

Relief, transition, gaining perspective. Indicated via the woman. A call for separation from that which is irrevocably lost. This omen promises that emotional excess will give way, in time, to objectivity, so long as one possesses patience and self-honesty. Even if the only retreat currently possible is inward, any distance one can put between oneself and one's troubles is for the best.

Higher-Octave: The Fanatic (Hero of Strife)

Tenacity, rashness, abrasive self-righteousness. Indicated via the charging knight. This omen draws the diviner's attention to a domineering individual who is obsessively dedicated to proving their commitment to a just cause, and will make any sacrifice so long as it stands to advance their lofty ideals. Framed positively, this omen offers assurance of duties fulfilled and promises kept, even amid great adversity. Framed negatively, it warns of the kind of fanaticism that may be dangerous both to oneself and one's allies.

Peril: Identity's consignment to oblivion

Nithrul's vision openly presents death as the irresistible devourer of all things. It thus evokes dynamics of suffering analogous to Fhell's vision, illustrating how the concept of "me" is no less vulnerable to the exigencies of change, decay, loss, and disappointment than the concept of "mine." As the Fourth Key already explained, even amid a relatively easy passage into death, much that the conscious being recognizes as "I" will still be lost upon the sloughing-off of the flesh. Consciousness is a curse insofar as it renders living beings aware of that which they would otherwise simply endure. Dysfunctional efforts to deny or defeat death often follow.

Nithrul's Peril challenges one to confront death forthrightly so that one might live all the more boldly in the face of it. Imagine, for instance, that your death is imminent, either within a year, a few days, or even moments from now. Can you reconcile yourself with the full physical, mental, and emotional details of what this will entail? In what light does imminent death put your current achievements and priorities? Reflection upon such matters reminds one to make the most of what time yet remains instead of wasting it upon trivialities.

Shaol

Vision: Resisting the rampage

As per Hvelgit, an interior scene, with two rear windows revealing an exterior beyond. At the center of the unadorned and sparsely furnished stone room stands a woman with bound hair, dressed in a gauzy garment, her unmatched eyes revealing her as the madwoman of Xhin, now composed. Preoccupied by the alchemical equipment before her, she carefully pours one concoction into another, mixing them. Outside, a black dragon is destroying the town. The left window reveals a looter fleeing with treasure, on the verge of tripping over the dragon's tail; the right reveals a warrior-king, crowned with bull's horns, fighting with a sword in each hand. Battered yet determined, he stands fast against the dragon's assault.

Archetype: The alchemist (S)

Moderation, skillful maneuvering, craftiness. Indicated via the woman. This omen evokes the forethought necessary to anticipate various outcomes, and the coordinated application of the right skills at the right time to ensure that the preferred outcome results. A positive sign unless context associates it with the machinations of one's enemies.

Lower-Octave: Knavery (7 Strife)

Sneakiness, risk-taking, dishonor. Indicated via the looter. Suggests that poorly conceived tactics are under consideration and asks whether the end sought is really worth the potential reputational damage of using such tactics. It may also warn that one is striving for something that one has no realistic hope of attaining, or is otherwise misjudging a situation.

Higher-Octave: The Conqueror (Sorcerer of Strife)

Relentlessness, assertion of power, lack of subtlety. Indicated via the warrior-king. This omen points to an individual who believes strongly in the "any means necessary" approach to overcoming adversity. While the omen can thus counsel the taking of action, it can also indicate that the approach under consideration will be crudely effective, but not efficient or ideal. It may also warn of powerful forces opposing one's will.

Peril: Moderation as a facilitator of flourishing

Shaol's vision depicts temperance as a refiner of the unrefined, measuring out a salutary dose of that which would cause harm in excess. It thus illustrates both the ego's struggle to unify elements of the psyche and wisdom's struggle to artfully practice the virtues. On both fronts, the difficulty is that multiple elements are in play, each with a valuable contribution to make to the quality of existence, yet no one element alone is capable of ensuring flourishing if the others are wholly absent.

Shaol's Peril encourages the diviner to embark upon a thought experiment that is not dissimilar from that prompted by Kehan: the personification of competing forces (clashing perspectives, clashing virtues, etc.) so that one might artfully interrogate them. In circumstances in which you are torn between a multitude of values, priorities, etc., how do you envision each one (e.g., as a person, an animal, a spirit, etc.)? How does this entity make its case to you, and in what terms does it express opposition against its competitors? Reflection upon such matters helps one engage fully with the complex mixture of drives harbored by any conscious being, make informed choices, and reach constructive compromises regarding what to cultivate vs. what to sacrifice.

Eyahin

Vision: Shackles of the spirit

Under a pitch-black sky, a massive, horned troll sits upon a throne. He is nude save for a pentacle medallion and clutches a thorny black staff tipped with a skull. Chained to his podium are a man and woman, both naked, one of whom wears an expression of modest shame, while the other leers with wanton indulgence. In the foreground lies a mess of half-eaten food, overturned glasses lying in their own spilled contents, discarded clothing, and other trash, dirtying a green field. Hovering in the sky above the horned ogre is a flaming key from which eight rays of power extend to form a chaos star. From this focal point, eight meteors streak downward, heralding destruction.

Archetype: The thralls (E)

Animalistic impulses, uninhibited behavior, spiritual blindness. Indicated by the troll, the chained couple, and the debris. This omen evokes the pursuit of short-term gratification and excitement. While it may correspond positively to Satanic conceptions of indulgence in some contexts, it more commonly warns of feeling forced into self-destructive actions by dark thoughts and uncontrolled desires.

Lower-Octave: Novelty (1 Innovation)

Energy, new undertakings, a rare opportunity. Indicated via the key. Foretells a period of stagnancy being brought to an end thanks to a shift in one's circumstances that forces one to alter one's habits. This may be a new relationship, project, etc. or renewed enthusiasm for an existing one. This omen may also warn of a need to act quickly, lest the moment be lost.

8 ↥

Higher-Octave: Momentum (8 Innovation)

Rapid development, imminent culmination, dissuasion of action. Indicated via the meteors. This omen warns that forces beyond oneself are already in motion, and their power is such that it would be foolhardy to try to alter their course now. Instead, one should wait and see what comes, setting one's ego aside. Whether this is a favorable or unfavorable sign depends heavily on context. When inquiring whether to perform ritual magick specifically, however, this omen tends to imply that the working under consideration is unnecessary, poorly conceived, ill timed, or otherwise unlikely to be fruitful.

Peril: Corruption of the pleasure-seeking instincts

Eyahin's vision warns that even amid Satanism's embrace of pleasure, one must still recognize that ruin follows when short-term gratification is pursued in excess. The issue is that in order for instincts and emotions to effectively motivate the living being, they must be experienced as compelling and pleasurable in themselves. This, however, creates the risk that the organism will fall into compulsive pleasure-chasing of a kind detrimental to its long-term interests. The more flesh is permitted to dominate over spirit like this, the more one loses the power to choose consciously.

Eyahin's Peril calls for the recognition of compulsively self-destructive behaviors and acquired bad habits. To what extent do you truly enjoy the things that you tell yourself you enjoy? What initial circumstances led to the establishment of your current pattern? And if said pattern is in truth accompanied by frustration, regret, and emptiness, how might you escape it? Reflection upon such matters forces the acknowledgment of addictions, empathic analysis of what has gone awry, and movement toward a better future via self-liberation.

Pyrash

Vision: Collapse of the tower

The scene of Fhell's vision but from a different angle, with a wilder sky and a cliff jutting in from the left. Lightning shatters the tower, setting it aflame. The tower's sole occupant throws himself from the window, and though he will thus plummet into the sea below, he looks as relieved as he does distressed, casting behind him the scales he once used to weigh his treasures. The nereid is gone, save for the parting flash of her tail, her rocks submerged by the rising tide of the ocean consuming the tower's base. Upon the cliff in the foreground, two figures meet, shaking hands as if making a deal: one is Byrk's sorcerer, and the other is Ishut's masked woman.

Archetype: Catastrophe (P)

Sudden collapse, disaster, liberation. Indicated via the shattering of the keep. This omen foretells a devastating upheaval that terminates a relationship, project, etc. It often warns against the course of action currently under consideration. Sometimes, though, it may point to unpleasant tribulations which must be endured as the price of winning one's freedom.

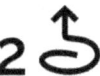

Lower-Octave: Resolution (2 Innovation)

Partnership, accomplishment, reciprocation. Indicated via the duo shaking hands. This omen points to the coming-together of two or more well-matched individuals and the achievement of immediate goods thereby, usually in such realms as one's career, education, or spiritual pursuits. This is a positive sign in pragmatic terms, but it can also warn against mistaking mutual self-interest for anything warmer.

9 ↻

Higher-Octave: Survival (9 Innovation)

Breach of boundaries, flight, self-care. Indicated via the departing nereid. This omen suggests a situation in which extended imposition and suffering drive one to abandon that which was formerly held dear. Some will complain that such a decision constitutes a betrayal, but from a purely human standpoint, setting a limit is sometimes a simple necessity in the name of self-preservation. Presages the development of greater resilience in the future, even if the present feels like a defeat.

Peril: Self-interest as a thwarter of coordination

Taking Pyrash's vision as a sequel to Fhell's, one here sees that cynicism and mundane preoccupation precede a cataclysmic downfall. This alludes to how evolutionary imperatives drive individual beings to prioritize their immediate advancement and propagation over the big picture of the long term. Such behavior leads to catastrophe when, amid too many members of the species conducting themselves thus, resources are depleted to the point of precipitating extinction for everyone. Such an outcome is difficult to avoid, insofar as the conscious coordination needed to prevent it clashes with instincts that evolution formerly selected for. Many will therefore resist the required measures as unnatural impositions.

What Pyrash's Peril demands is an acceptance of self-centeredness as both natural and unavoidable. One must learn to work *with* self-interest instead of wasting energy denying or resenting it. If there is an outcome you want to see in the world, how could you motivate others toward it via appealing to what *they* value instead of browbeating them for failing to embrace what *you* value? Reflection upon such matters urges the abandonment of impractical idealism and the adoption of a down-to-earth pragmatism more effective at getting results.

Wajhel

Vision: Splendor of the night sky

In a dim, predawn sky, seven stars hang with a crescent moon shining in their midst. Energy streams down from these celestial bodies, water-like, upon a landscape lush with rivers and vegetation. Toward the left, in the foreground, the wanderer depicted in Ywhaz's vision stands on a barren cliff amid three pillars, looking into the distance as if gazing upon a promised land. Upon a broader cliff, in the foreground on the right, a bedraggled woman in stained clothing strains under the burden of the large stones she struggles to carry, as if intending to use them to rebuild the ruin whose tumbled facade stands amid the barren trees upon the crest.

Archetype: The stars (W)

Renewal, clarity, fortuitous circumstances. Indicated via the sky. This omen points to the gaining of insight, the winning of victories, and the solving of problems formerly unresolved or irresolvable. It carries strong connotations of acausal forces being in support of one's cause and is thus generally a favorable sign for whatever pursuits one is undertaking.

Lower-Octave: Opportunity (3 Innovation)

Optimism, zeal, good prospects. Indicated via the wanderer. This omen connotes openness to the future, a sense of purpose inspired by the adoption of worthy goals, and a willingness to do what is needed. It thus points to new undertakings soon to be launched or promising news being received about endeavors already in motion. The aid and support of others may be offered and secured with unusual ease at this time.

10 ↑↩

Higher-Octave: Exhaustion (10 Innovation)

Dedication, overexertion, unreasonable imposition. Indicated via the woman. This omen warns that one's current level of effort is not sustainable indefinitely. In such a case, it may be wise to heed O9A's advice to "enjoy a short rest, better than a long."[43] To dedicate oneself to a cause is laudable, but one is not thereby obligated to shoulder others' burdens single-handedly.

Peril: Gendering of the spirit/flesh duality

Wajhel's vision echoes a widespread cultural tendency to associate the masculine with spiritual transcendence and the feminine with fleshly burdens of earthly life. This duality originates in uneven distribution of the burdens of reproduction (see Dolath): pregnancy and nursing are physical impositions, on top of which social and ideological expectations are often piled. The inconveniences of nature are thereby needlessly magnified for roughly half our species, whom culture proceeds to damn as sexually compulsive, emotionally needy, and generally inferior. Traditionalists justify misogyny thus, while utopians, hastening to declare the equality of all, fail to attend to the considerable burdens of bearing and raising the next generation. Neither makes it any easier for those who bear the greater brunt of nature's impositions to pursue flourishing and self-evolution.

Wajhel's Peril interrogates one's view of "feminine" qualities, such as care for others, emotional vulnerability, and devotion to the quotidian upkeep of the world. What attitudes do you harbor toward that which is "womanly," "girlish," etc., and have you ever analyzed the presuppositions that underlie your feelings? Reflection upon such matters can reveal one's unwitting absorption of the anti-muliebriel[44] biases of maladaptive ideologies and help one rid oneself of attitudes whose life-denying implications might otherwise go unnoticed.

Uruk

Vision: Descent of the moon

In a dark sky hangs a moon that offers but a thin sliver of light. Power streams down from it in an ominous variant of that which was life-giving in Wajhel's vision. Two tall, indistinct shapes cast silhouettes against the sky in the distance, but otherwise the scene is entirely ocean from background to foreground. Upon a tiny raft, a bold young woman with short, boyish hair and fiery-colored wings stands poised for battle, clutching a sword in one hand and a staff in the other, while shapes suggestive of lurking leviathans circle around her craft. Beneath the sea's surface, the dim glow of seven jewels is visible, as if the previous vision's stars had fallen into the water.

Archetype: Darkness (U)

Mystery, fear, primitive instincts. Indicated via the sky, the ocean, and the circling sea-beasts. This omen foretells the submersion of consciousness in the realm of the unconscious — a state in which the lines between reality, fantasy, self-deceit, and delusion can become badly blurred. In such circumstances, one must travel carefully, and trust one's gut, wary both of presumption and of self-doubt.

Lower-Octave: Distraction (4 Innovation)

Tempting prospect, unobtainable object, getting sidetracked. Indicated via the jewels beneath the waves. This omen indicates something that is positive and worthy in itself, but difficult to pursue without derailing other endeavors more central to one's destiny. May warn that one's timing is off or that the end result will fail to justify the energy spent on the endeavor.

Higher-Octave: The Adventurer (Muse of Innovation)

Exploration, ardor, boldness. Indicated via the central figure. This omen draws the diviner's attention to an individual who is competent and daring yet also inexperienced and impulsive. Framed positively, it points out that what one currently needs is not to be found amid familiar things, and therefore encourages excursions into unknown territory. Framed negatively, it warns against getting in over one's head via dilettantism or arrogance.

Peril: The limitations of perception

Uruk's vision echoes elements of Grahl's: moon, water, innocence, danger. But whereas Grahl's maiden is absorbed in self-reflection, Uruk's recognizes that she is menaced, ill-glimpsed though the threat may be. Uruk's vision thus alludes to the distortions inherent to perception, arising from the shaping of the mind and the senses by the organism's survival needs, not by an orientation toward reality as such. To treat perception as objective, directly revealing truth in full, or to presume on the contrary that no reality exists save that which each individual's flawed senses report, are both foolhardy ways of proceeding. The wise individual ought always to question the perceptions of oneself and others, but stop short of the unhelpful delusion that since no one sees one-hundred percent clearly, one can just make up what constitutes "reality."

Uruk's Peril calls for the interrogation of what one takes for granted. Is there some matter which you take as settled or obvious — perhaps because you have never really taken time to consider it carefully? How might someone with a different perspective arrive at a different verdict? Reflecting upon such matters offers an antidote to hubristic self-certainty and beguilement by surface appearances.

Rhais

Vision: Ascent of the sun

White mountains in the background under a beautiful cloudless sky. From the distant horizon a scenic river flows until it reaches the foreground: a flower-strewn meadow occupied by the couple from Zhalg's vision. One member of the couple kneels as if battered from enduring an ordeal, while the other stands, extending a hand to help their companion rise. Both wear white clothing and expressions evocative of having just woken from a lengthy nightmare. In the front of the scene, on the left, crouches a white rabbit and on the opposite, a white lamb. Above, the sun hangs large in the sky, her feminine face smiling down serenely upon all that she surveys.

Archetype: Light (R)

Innocence, shared joy, safety. Indicated via the idyllic scene as a whole. This omen promises an end to ordeals, a return to that which is familiar and manageable, and the enjoyment of happiness and good fortune alongside one's loved ones. A positive sign unless it arises in connection with the avoidance of necessary adversity, in which case it may indicate childishness or utopian idealism.

Lower-Octave: Tribulation (5 Innovation)

Testing, emergence from hardship, reconciliation. Indicated via the couple. This omen presages being put in circumstances that are outside of one's comfort zone yet ultimately prompt growth and maturation. It thus typically points to unpleasant situations one can learn from, such as the failing of a test or a difficult settling of grievances.

Higher-Octave: The Paragon (Witch of Innovation)

Brilliance, generosity, ascendancy. Indicated via the sun-woman. This omen points to an energetic individual who is giving and passionate but possessed of a dangerous charisma that may dazzle both themselves and others. Framed positively, it foretells successes won by showing genuine magnanimity toward others. Negatively, though, it may warn that one clings to a too-idealistic view of a person, a cause, a plan, etc.

Peril: Edenic Longing

Rhais' vision depicts an idyll of effortless harmony — an evocation of the total joy of small children at play. The adult who regrets the loss of such a state and longs to recover it tends to succumb to several follies. One is to embrace spontaneity as good in itself, rejecting any need for prudence or strategy, only to be surprised when things go awry. Another is to turn up one's nose at that which is imperfect and, in so doing, to set up the perfectly good as the enemy of the realistically attainable. Both behaviors are understandable as expressions of being fed up with life's difficulties. Both cause harm, however, by thwarting intelligent efforts that could yet be taken to improve one's circumstances and one's world.

Rhais' Peril encourages one to recognize the difference between a welcome moment of contentment and a childish demand for simplicity. There is nothing wrong with just enjoying things as they are now and then. Two mirages to beware of, however, are "everything will be fine somehow" and "purity good, compromise bad." Reflection ought to reveal the self-indulgent nature of such notions and aid in the replacement of naive optimism with the kind of creative striving that precedes the making of real, meaningful improvements.

Jhire

Vision: Three armies

A barren land beneath an uneasy sky. A pale crescent moon hangs toward the left, a black sun toward the right. Below, two armies face off: one, of warriors, is led by a seasoned adventurer; the other, of magicians, is led by a mighty sorcerer. Toward the center is a hill upon which stands a knight mounted upon a fiery horse, a warrior whose near-androgynous appearance evokes a Valkyrie, sword held high to urge the battle to proceed. Beyond the hill, the horizon seethes with the monstrous shapes of a third army, an incoming tide of grotesque combatants emerging from the black swell of a distant sea.

Archetype: The apocalypse (J)

Revelation, decisive choice, high stakes. Indicated via the incoming horrors. This omen points to a rapidly approaching moment of truth, in which the smallest decision may turn out to have more impact upon one's destiny than one bargained for. It thus urges one to pay attention to what is at stake, lest one otherwise underestimate the significance of the choices one makes or overestimate one's own readiness to face the moment.

Lower-Octave: Victory (6 Innovation)

Skillful preparation, glory, renown. Indicated via the two armies and their confident leaders. This omen evokes all things on which success is built: adequate resources, appropriate training, accurate information, trust among allies, etc. Regardless of whether triumph or defeat follow, the acumen currently on display is certain to raise one's reputation.

Higher-Octave: The Harbinger (Hero of Innovation)

Nobility, idealism, rebelliousness. Indicated via the knight. This omen suggests an individual who demands heroic action but may be lacking in direction and practicality. It may thus warn against action merely for action's sake, or "solutions" that will create more problems down the line. Positively though, it can point to a sincere heart, a total rejection of the conventions of the herd, or a bold act validated by true desperation.

Peril: Fixation on dualistic categories

Jhire's vision depicts a clash of two sides, complicated by the arrival of a third. It thus speaks to the relativity of dualistic conflict via "irreconcilable" differences overcome upon the intrusion of a more alien foe. This alludes to the evolutionary rationality of favoring those with congruent survival needs to one's own and greeting those with conflicting needs with suspicion. Regardless of how the line between "similar" and "different" may shift with context, this dynamic drives xenophobia, herd conformity, and vicious division over small differences. Recognizing such phenomena as the misfirings of natural imperatives is the first step toward realistic mitigation. Decrying them as evils without attempting to understand their origins is a driver of ineffective utopian interventions.

Jhire's Peril challenges one both to openly admit who one sees as the enemy, and to consider what interests one may nonetheless share with this foe. It is no good to pretend one does not hate when in fact one does. It is worse yet, though, to dehumanize while refusing to recognize that one is doing so, for such is the gateway to many an atrocity. Reflection upon such matters encourages self-awareness regarding one of the darkest facets of the survival instinct.

Olith

Vision: Unhallowed paradise

A lush, dark garden, dominated by a large tree. A crystal-clear spring bubbles forth from its roots and an iridescent sky is visible between its branches. In front of the tree stands a man crowned with goat's horns, face hidden by the fall of a hood save for his smile, holding a dagger in his right hand, a double-tetrahedron crystal in his left. Before him on the grass lies the woman from Shaol's vision, nude, her pose suggesting the man is her lover, whose embrace she eagerly awaits. Six figures sit in a circle around these two, partaking of enchanted food and drink in a mood of playful debauchery. Enclosing this party is a circle of mystical wards, protecting them from the tendrils of Abyssal nothingness eating away at the edges of the scene.

Archetype: The celebration (O)

Spiritual wholeness, restoration, integration. Indicated via those gathered. This omen evokes something coming to completion or already complete in and of itself. Generally positive, it encourages one to consider how all of one's joys and sorrows fit within the context of one's overall spiritual journey, and to cherish the contributions of both.

Lower-Octave: Protection (7 Innovation)

Instability, approaching danger, envy. Indicated via the circle of glyphs. This omen points out the conditional nature of all attainments, and the inherent presence of adversity in all things, even if not overt at the current time. Framed positively, an assurance that at least things are alright for the present. Framed negatively, a warning against resting too long on one's laurels.

Higher-Octave: The Visionary (Sorcerer of Innovation)

Impetuousness, excellence, ruthlessness. Indicated via the horned man. Suggests an accomplished individual who has valid reasons for thinking highly of themselves and no use for those who lack their vision. Positively, it may indicate that one is both achieving short-term goals successfully and setting oneself up well from a long-term standpoint. Negatively, however, it may indicate that an enemy has a major advantage over oneself.

Peril: Unwinnable war against existence

Olith's vision allegorizes spirit's Adventure in flesh as a sexual union. It thus speaks to spirit's inexhaustible enthusiasm for the realm of matter. The Fourth Key alluded already to acausal factions who embrace the delusion that if only all beings could be persuaded to abandon the flesh, "evil" would be defeated. All such efforts in fact attain, however, is the stifling of the unique stories of flourishing and self-evolution that are the birthright of every individual being.

Olith's Peril asserts that, though death is unavoidable (see Nithrul), so is life, for Darkness decrees an eternal return to the flesh. Try to escape, and you but destroy yourself, while damning whatever the Void builds out of your repurposed energies to suffer in your place. Thus, as Thomas Ligotti writes, "Behind the scenes of life lurks something pernicious that makes a nightmare of our world."[45] Can you accept without reservation that since such is the case, no real prospect of liberation exists, and you therefore have no choice but to persevere in existence as best you can indefinitely? Reflection upon such matters reveals the full force of what "affirming earthly existence" requires, enabling the Satanist to embrace that which is unbearable to many a lesser mortal.

Applications of the runic-tarot

Once the diviner has created their complete set of eighty-four tokens of consistent size and shape, the set should be kept in a small sack or box. This container should be stored in a similar manner as other occult tools, and one should limit handling the tokens when they are not in use.

Regardless of how one intends to consult the omens, the runic-tarot yields the most useful results when one observes the following considerations (listed from most to least important):

- The diviner should have studied the system sufficiently to be able to recall an approximate meaning for a majority of the omens and should not have to resort to constantly looking up meanings.

- Some manner of mental preparation should precede the reading. Lunar Purification is always a good choice, but results may be further enhanced by performing Contemplation of the Nine-Angled Nexion and continuing to hold the crystal while divining.

- Readings are best performed in consistent circumstances, e.g., at one's altar, by candlelight, while burning a specific incense used only during divination, etc. One need not do all such things every time, but one should establish some kind of standard routine.

- Readings are best performed at night. Once put into use, the set's exposure to sunlight should be minimized. Diviners will occasionally encounter circumstances that necessitate a daytime reading, but nighttime readings should be treated as a default.

As to methods of reading, in broad terms there are two approaches: the standard and the contemplative. The standard method is performed as follows:

1. Once you have completed any preliminaries (e.g., Lunar Purification), formulate your inquiry into a question. The question should be phrased in a direct, straightforward manner, but it should not be a yes/no question. Good questions will be along the lines of,

"What is the current state of X?" or "If I attempt Y, what outcome will follow?"

2. Reach into the container in which you store the set, either stating your inquiry aloud or keeping your thoughts focused upon it. Touch the tokens and let them fall through your fingers. At whatever point you have the urge to take hold of one, do so.

3. If performing a reading using only a single token, look at what your fingers have caught and reflect upon its meaning while continuing to hold it in your hand, until you feel you have arrived at some notion of what is being communicated to you.

4. If performing a reading with multiple tokens, immediately place the first token down upon a flat surface in front of you without attempting to interpret it. As you continue with your inquiry, continue to draw and place tokens. Wait until you have completed your intended sequence before turning to consider each token in the order they were drawn and then reflecting on all of them together. This last step is important for multi-token readings, as it will often happen that a token's meaning will be inflected by those adjacent to it.

5. Once you are done reading, make a written record of what you asked, what omens you received, and your interpretation. This record should be used to monitor the meaningfulness or lack thereof of one's readings and to refine understanding of the omens via the observation of recurrent patterns.

No specific spreads are prescribed for Tenebrous divination, but recommended multi-token methods include:

- Reflection upon how one has gotten to where one is, and where such a path may lead next, via three tokens representing past, present, and future, as per a common method familiar to many tarot readers.

- One token to represent the current situation, plus two that each speak to a different option under consideration. For additional detail, one can draw further tokens to distinguish the short-term vs.

long-term impacts of each option or to illustrate other factors that bear upon them.

- Reflection using five tokens, placed thus: center = your current situation, left = your true desires, bottom = the advice you would most benefit from, right = what you fear or what otherwise stands in your way, top = anticipated outcome based on your default course. Additional tokens may be drawn to reflect upon the impacts of alternate courses you are considering.

It should be noted that past a certain number of tokens drawn, meaningfulness will tend to decrease on account of excessive complexity, apparent contradiction, etc. This threshold is different for every diviner. In general, one should strive to boil one's inquiry down into as few questions as possible and avoid lines of inquiry that require drawing more than a dozen tokens in a single sitting.

Whereas introspection aided by confrontation with a random factor is the essence of the standard approach to divination, randomness is less of a defining feature of the contemplative approach. This proceeds as follows:

1. Whether randomly drawing a token or purposely choosing an omen that has drawn your interest, ensure that you are familiar with the general details of the associated vision as described above.

2. Light a candle and seat yourself facing it in a meditative pose, holding the Nine-Angled Nexion crystal in your left hand.

3. Perform the same pattern of breathing as when performing Contemplation of the Nine-Angled Nexion but now visualizing energy flowing forth from omen you have selected (e.g., the vision's rune or the specific token drawn) instead of from the candle/uppermost point of the Naos sigil. Those who have performed Contemplation of the Nine-Angled Nexion regularly should have no difficulty gathering energy into the crystal as usual despite this alteration in the accompanying visualization.

4. Immediately after the twenty-eighth breath and the activation of the crystal that comes with it, close your eyes and turn your thoughts toward the appropriate vision. Allow its general scene to

create itself in your mind without consciously dictating the details. For example, for Ywhaz, set out to picture a lone man climbing a mountain in inclement conditions, but do not predetermine the exact look of his face, clothing, swords in the foreground, demons hovering above, etc. Instead, impassively observe what your unconscious mind reveals to you of such matters, taking careful note of all details that emerge thereby.

5. As your vision comes further into focus, strive to inject as much vividness and life into the scene as you can via the inclusion of additional sensory elements. This might include sounds and scents appropriate to the scene, the felt impact of weather as if you were actually present there, etc. You may also explore the vision further by interacting with elements of what is before you — investigate your surroundings, speak to the human figures present and see how they respond, etc.

6. Once you have had your fill of the vision, conclude in the same fashion as for the contemplative exercises of the Fifth Key, and afterward, journal as detailed an account of the experience as you can recall.

7. The next day, take another look at the Sixth Key's account of the omens which you just explored and use this information to aid further reflection upon any striking or idiosyncratic elements you witnessed in your own experience of the vision.

Subsequent Keys refer to this contemplative method as "the Diviner's Journey." Directly inspired by a tarot-meditation technique described in O9A's *Naos*, it can be applied toward various ends, all of them invaluable:

- It can be used to lend additional depth to "standard" divination. One might, for example, do a past-present-future reading, then expand upon it with a trio of contemplations, one for each omen in turn. Or one might perform a single contemplation, in which one witnesses the transformation of the past omen's vision into the present's and the present's into the future's.

- It can be used to explore subtle personal nuances of one's general understanding of each omen, toward the end of becoming a better diviner. A diviner who has taken the time to contemplate all twenty-eight visions is sure to develop an enhanced intuitive capacity thereby. Toward such cultivation of one's talents, it can be useful to contemplate the omens in themselves without reference to a particular question or situation. One may thereby discover additional dimensions to each omen that are unique to the individual diviner.

- It can be used to reflect upon the Peril associated with a particular vision and that Peril's impact upon one's life. For example, one might draw a token and consider the Peril it alludes to prior to undertaking the Diviner's Journey. Doing so positions the diviner to reflect upon heretofore unconsidered drivers of human behavior, such as the misapplication of evolutionarily selected tendencies amid situations alien from anything our ancestors encountered. This, in turn, can encourage a more empathic perspective on what might otherwise seem like mere arbitrary stupidity or senseless evil.[46]

Beyond standard and contemplative approaches to divination, additional applications of the runic-tarot may be discerned by observing that the glyphs of the archetypes double as a magickal alphabet: Anthal is A, Zhalg is Z, etc. This insight opens the door to incorporating the runic-tarot into certain methods of ritual magick intensification, as described in the Seventh Key — e.g., constructing mantras and more complex sigils to communicate magickal intent, etc. Exact methods will not be explored at length in the current work but are likely to occur naturally to those willing to experiment. The tables of information provided in Appendix II may be useful to individuals interested in pursuing such endeavors.

Summary

The value of divination from an acausal standpoint is inestimable. Many a witch or sorcerer could have been spared the unpleasant surprises that attend an ill-advised ritual, if only divination had been consulted beforehand. The aspiring magician is therefore advised to learn divination prior to attempting anything described in the Keys that follow.

Divination is also meaningful, however, on a causal level. In response to a random encounter with evocative imagery, the unconscious mind can offer up insights that could not otherwise be articulated to consciousness. It is no coincidence that the term "archetype" is most well-known through the work of C. G. Jung. Tenebrous Satanism affirms, as Jung did, that human beings are largely unknown to themselves. Intentional probing of one's shadow can yield much enlightenment, and divination is an excellent means to such exploration.

A second causal use of the runic-tarot is the intentional contemplation of philosophical matters that people typically prefer to flee from instead of grappling with. Whether reflecting directly upon the Perils that have been outlined or performing the Diviner's Journey with such matters in mind, one has the opportunity to analyze feelings of aversion, irritation, grief, defensiveness, etc., and to ask oneself what is at stake that causes one to react in this way. One might ask, for instance, "Do I have an actual argument against the Peril as formulated? Or am I just afraid of what follows if reality is, indeed, as the Peril suggests?" One might then consider further: "What would happen if I took seriously that life simply *is* this way, and devised a way to still live life with my head held high and my values intact?" Much could be learned, and great personal liberation experienced, if this sort of reflection could convince people to fearlessly affirm reality instead of fleeing into dogmatism amid resentful denial of life's "unbearable" features.

Regardless of whether one seeks deeper insight into acausal matters, one's own psyche, or the Perils of existence, we hope the Sixth Key will provide an efficacious map and compass to all walkers of the Sinister Path willing to learn the arts described herein.

Notes

[41] The term "masculous" is taken from Myatt (2013) — see The First Key, Note 7.

[42] A particularly odious application of this concept can be found in the belief of certain O9A nexions that there is something spiritually edifying about men's

perpetuation of sexual assault against women and children. It is the position of Tenebrous Satanism that such beliefs arise from a mixture of human misinterpretation of the aeonic goals of the Nekalah and dysfunctional individual will toward sadistic criminality. Spiritually mature Satanists, possessed of wisdom, honor, and empathy, do *not* commit such acts.

[43] Quoted from O9A's "21 Satanic Points" in *Black Book of Satan*.

[44] The term "muliebriel" is taken from Myatt (2013) — see The First Key, Note 7.

[45] Quoted from Thomas Ligotti's *The Conspiracy Against the Human Race* (2010).

[46] One can also, of course, expand one's mind in such a manner via simply engaging in conscious reflection upon the Perils. The benefit of the Diviner's Journey, however, is that the use of symbolic imagery can enable one's unconscious mind to present insights that the ego may be resistant to. Decoding such imagery can play a decisive role in overcoming psychological barriers.

VII

Unleashing the Black Flame

> *We as individuals, because we possess the faculty of consciousness, are 'gates' to this acausal universe. We possess the (mostly latent) ability to 'open the gate' to the acausal which exists within our own psyche to draw from the acausal certain energies, and these energies can and do alter in some way both our own consciousness and/or other entities/energies which exist in the causal. This 'drawing of energies,' and their use, is magick.*
>
> **- Order of Nine Angles, *Naos***

> *Then I asked: "Does a firm persuasion that a thing is so, make it so?" He replied: "All poets believe that it does, and in ages of imagination this firm persuasion has removed mountains; but many are not capable of a firm persuasion of any thing."*
>
> **- William Blake, *The Marriage of Heaven & Hell* (1709)**

Given the amount of wishful thinking and general hogwash that gets propagated under the banner of spirituality, the critical thinker has every right to question the concept of magick. Nonetheless, Tenebrous Satanism upholds the validity of magickal practice on two levels:

Causally, magick facilitates self-understanding and self-fulfillment. Earnest engagement with its principles and limitations promotes introspective honesty. The performance of ritual helps the magician develop increased confidence and independence from herd thinking. With this sort of personal transformation in mind, one can practice magick fruitfully even if one is skeptical of the acausal mechanisms behind it.

Acausally, magick's potency is directly known to sincere witches and sorcerers. They witness its power in the arising of synchronicities that favor them or disfavor their enemies, in the revelation of knowledge that the receiver experiences as coming from outside of themselves, and in encounters with beings whose independent existence is self-evident to anyone who has genuinely succeeded in contacting them. It is easy for scoffers to rationalize these things away. But to those open to the acausal, such experiences are accompanied by an irresistible aura of wonder, making them inherently rewarding to seek out.

With these considerations in mind, Tenebrous Satanism harbors no condemnation toward a purely causal embrace[47] of magick. The position of the Seventh Key, however, is that a full understanding of magick requires a convergence of causal and acausal perspectives. Causally, the individual experiences the performance of magick as fulfilling and liberating. Acausally, magick opens the gate to energies that have the power to make fantastic things happen.

Before one can develop any counterproductive notions about what "fantastic" means, it is worth clarifying what magick can and cannot do. One cannot use magick to force nature to alter its course, to entirely circumvent the wills of autonomous beings, or to make the universe play a totally different game from the one it is currently engaged in. One can, however, use magick to sway the course of events, to encourage or discourage particular outcomes, and to seize advantages with regard to the cards one is dealt and how one might play them.

The Seventh Key will explain how to accomplish feats of these kinds. First, it will elucidate seven principles that define magick's workings and limitations. Then, it will provide a template for effective ritual, which can be adapted to whatever ends the magician seeks. This focus on formal ritual should not be taken as implying that ritual constitutes the only effective method of magick. It is the author's conviction, however, that less formal methods of magick often fail to inculcate beginners with the self-discipline and attention to detail that genuine occult success requires. The Seventh Key therefore situates ritual as the heart of Tenebrous praxis.

The novice ought to begin by adhering closely to all instructions given. Too much improvisation can prevent one from developing a feel for the constraints of magick as an art. However, once familiarity with the methods and aesthetic of the Tenebrous current has been established, nothing forbids the magician from making small alterations that add to the personal meaningfulness of ritual performance. One should not, however, make alterations if the primary driver for doing so is laziness, bashfulness, etc. Inhibition is detrimental to ritual magick in general, so the magician is always better off striving to overcome it than allowing it to dictate the form and contents of one's workings.

The seven principles of magick

1. *Principle of self-possession*

   Magick consists of the disciplined release of energy by a strong will, purified beforehand by introspection.

2. *Principle of limited realization*

   Any transformation wrought by magick will manifest via the path of least resistance.

3. *Principle of interdependent influences*

   Magick propagates itself through nexions, so it requires close attention to all things that connect oneself with others.

4. *Principle of concrete actualization*

   Ritual is defined by the carrying-out of overt symbolic actions in an appropriate place at a suitable time.

5. *Principle of adverse consequences*

   One should not attempt magick without careful, serious reflection upon all the ways in which it can go awry.

6. *Principle of maximal fruitfulness*

   Full realization of the gains of magick comes only to those possessed of self-reflection, uncompromising honesty, bold initiative-taking, and detached patience.

7. *Principle of altered consciousness*

   Accomplishing magickal change requires entry into a non-normal psychic state appropriate to one's intent.

Several important implications proceed from each of these principles. The discussion that follows covers the most significant considerations, but individual practitioners are likely to discover additional provisos through experience.

Principle of self-possession

Magick consists of the disciplined release of energy by a strong will, purified beforehand by introspection.

Energy, in its acausal or spiritual sense, correlates closely with a conscious being's overall ability to persevere. It is manifest in the capacity to focus attention steadfastly upon a single object for a sustained period of time. Vigorous health, foresight enough to avoid distractions or to shut them out if they arise, emotional stability, and mental endurance are together the prerequisites of sufficient energy to perform magick.

To possess a strong *will* means that the magician must want something — so much that one is willing to endure adversity in order to attain that thing. Strength of will is thus closely correlated with zeal. At the same time, the magician's desire must take a form that is controlled rather than compulsive. One must temper open expression of passion with a degree of aloofness from one's emotions.

Introspection entails a high degree of awareness of oneself, of the causal circumstances one is trying to affect through magickal means, and of the acausal factors that may facilitate or oppose the desired change. Prior to undertaking any magickal working, introspection requires one to reflect thoroughly upon such issues as:

A. What does the magician really want, and how will attaining this desire serve longer term goals?

B. What degree of alteration to the current course of things will the working require, and how easy or difficult will it be to affect this change?

C. What causal, real-world actions would support the ritual's intent, and has the magician in fact undertaken these?

D. In what forms might a result manifest, and if some of these are undesirable, how might the magician craft the ritual to discourage such outcomes?

E. Given the ritual's intent, the magician's own energy levels, and other such factors, what is the best time and place to perform the ritual?

F. Has the magician acquired all that is needful with regard to tools, knowledge, etc.?

G. What insights does divination offer regarding the ritual's likely results?

As one may surmise from this list, introspection is well served by the possession of virtues such as wisdom, honor, and empathy. Together, these make available both the broadest and most incisive perspective.

On top of possessing energy, will, and introspection, the magician must utilize these qualities in such a way that they support one another, rather than getting in each other's way. Toward this end of disciplined release, introspection must be conducted in advance of a magickal working. During the ritual, on the other hand, will and energy must take center stage, unhindered by self-consciousness or analysis. One must also learn to distinguish between mere excess of passion, which achieves little, and the sustained, purposeful direction of energy, which achieves much.

The principle of self-possession is so named because the stamina, impetus, and awareness that it alludes to are fruits of the same qualities that support self-actualization in other contexts. The causal capacities that make one good at magick are the same capacities that make one good at living well in general. Magick is not that which makes one's earthly existence easier, but rather, that which becomes possible thanks to the ongoing cultivation of personal excellence. The Third Key's virtues and the Fifth Key's meditations both foster this kind of cultivation. The would-be magician should therefore study both carefully.

Principle of limited realization

Any transformation wrought by magick will manifest via the path of least resistance.

While the ultimate aspiration of spirit is toward ever-freer movement in the world of the flesh and ever-greater control over its own destiny, material existence is nonetheless a realm of limitation, in which even the most evolved beings find themselves never entirely free nor wholly in control. Therefore, even amid an abundance of energy, will, and insight, there are limits to what magick can do. An understanding of these limits prevents the wasting of one's mental and spiritual resources upon ill-conceived efforts. A couple corollaries of the previous section's introspective considerations then follow:

- Corollary of point B, re: ease/difficulty of altering the current situation: when performing magick, one must give thought to the channel by which one expects results to manifest. Smaller shifts are easier to accomplish than larger ones. Conversely, one who tries to swim upstream against the universe has little hope of success.

- Corollary of point C, re: real-world actions: acausal interventions are most effective when accompanied by complementary causal efforts. One ought to do everything possible to attain one's desires via mundane means and reserve magick for altering factors which one cannot easily or reliably alter otherwise. Magickal intervention is best directed at influencing one's own unconscious mind or that of others, tilting probabilities such that favorable "coincidences" become more likely and unfavorable ones less likely, and so forth.

The principle of limited realization envisions magick as an inherently Dark force whose remolding of the world is often subtle, manipulating facets of reality that humans experience as mysterious and elusive. Accordingly, Tenebrous Satanism rejects any distinction between "white" and "black" magick. As per the Fourth Key's principle of inward divinity, all magick proceeds from spirit — i.e., the part of Darkness that is engrossed in the Adventure of the flesh. Humans are within their rights to judge some applications of magick as more ethically acceptable than others. To the universe itself, however, the only meaningful distinction regarding magick is between what can be done by applying pressure to the world's mutability and what cannot be done because it runs too contrary to the current course of events.

Principle of interdependent influences

Magick propagates itself through nexions, so it requires close attention to all things that connect oneself with others.

A nexion is any place in which energies, forces, elements, etc. come together. When energy is sent out as part of a working, that energy makes things happen by intersecting and interacting with other energies. Magick with a constructive aim uses the magician's energy to solicit cooperation from compatible energies. Magick with a destructive aim uses the magician's energy to disrupt the energies of the magician's target.

A consideration of the role that nexions play in magick leads one to recognize the following dynamics:

1. Energy can be drained or dispersed through interactions with others. Therefore, one ought to limit both public knowledge of one's magickal practices generally and the discussion of workings currently underway in particular.

2. It is easier to affect people, things, and circumstances with which one has some manner of already existing connection than those with which one has none.

3. The power of a working can be augmented via like-minded magicians combining their will and energy toward a shared goal.

4. It is easier to use magick to influence those who are open in general and receptive to the magician in particular. It is harder — though not impossible — to influence those who are guarded or hostile.

5. Energy raised during a working needs to be able to run its course unobstructed. The magician should therefore avoid fretting, dwelling, and other forms of emotional investment in the question of the ritual's efficacy whether before, during, or after the ritual.

Lack of discipline regarding such matters is a common cause of failure.

6. If chance circumstances create or reinforce connections between oneself and whoever or whatever the working is meant to target, one ought to seize the opportunity this presents. For example, if one unexpectedly crosses paths with a person whom one had been planning to target, an excellent time to perform one's ritual is that very evening if it is at all feasible to do so.[48]

7. Ritual is more effective when it adheres to an established protocol to at least some extent. Taking the objective existence of acausal beings seriously, it will be easier to communicate with such beings via words and gestures they are already familiar with. Changing the rules with every performance complicates the process needlessly. Incorporating too many deviations and idiosyncrasies into ritual thus tends to diminish its efficacy.

This is not an exhaustive list of the ways in which nexion-related considerations can impact magick. It should, however, give novice practitioners a good idea of the primary fronts on which interdependent influence is operative.

Principle of concrete actualization

Ritual is defined by the carrying-out of overt symbolic actions in an appropriate place at a suitable time.

Amid the wonders that magick offers, one must not lose sight of the fact that so long as their material existence lasts, human beings are no less beings of flesh than beings of spirit. Magick therefore requires a certain amount of earthly grounding, in the absence of which, flesh, being left out of the equation, has a propensity to sabotage spirit's endeavors. This earthly grounding is established via four considerations: the necessity of physical action, the incorporation of symbolic props, the securing of an appropriate setting, and the establishment of the extraordinary.

The necessity of physical action

Simply put, ritual requires *doing things* — i.e., movement, gesture, words spoken aloud, and so forth. Many novices rationalize ritual into a mere thought experiment because they cannot shake their self-consciousness at the thought of what an invisible audience might think of their performance. Such bashfulness must be conquered, and the herd-concern that motivates it eradicated from one's psyche, if one is ever to become a capable magician.

The incorporation of symbolic props

To say that ritual utilizes props is to posit that within the ritual chamber, meaningful action is facilitated via interaction with special objects which connote something beyond what they would in a mundane context. In the case of Tenebrous ritual, the most important objects of this kind include:

- *The candle:* Its lighting and extinguishing are used to mark the start and end of ritual and occasionally other important transitions.
- *The dagger:* Symbolizing one's will, it is used to direct energy in accord with whatever the ritual requires.
- *The crystal:* Whereas the dagger sends energy, the crystal receives, amplifying one's sensitivity to acausal energies.
- *The offering:* Used to express gratitude toward those powers whose cooperation makes the ritual successful.

The first three of these items were described in the Fifth Key. The fourth — the offering -can take a variety of forms. Common examples include the burning of incense or bundles of herbs; alcohol in a chalice; or a few drops of an essential oil, a perfume, or one's own blood[49], presented in an appropriately ornamented vessel. What makes a suitable offering will depend on many factors, including individual intuition and preference. However, three rules to observe include:

1. An offering should always be of high quality, not something shoddy that one is just trying to get rid of.

2. The intent of the ritual will dictate what should be done with the offering after the ritual's completion. When performing constructive workings, it makes sense to consume edible offerings, and to leave non-consumable offerings out upon one's altar for a time. With destructive workings however, it makes more sense to promptly discard the offering after the ritual via burning, burial, etc. rather than consuming it or allowing it to remain in one's living space.

3. If working with a spirit, the offering should be one suitable to the tastes of that particular entity. A good policy is to offer whatever feels right upon a first attempt at contact (incense is almost always a minimally acceptable choice), and then during the encounter, ask the spirit what it would prefer in the future. Note, though, that the magician is not obligated to comply with demands that are excessively impractical or ethically unacceptable. If an entity makes such demands, one should either negotiate an alternative or decline to work with that spirit in the future.

Securing an appropriate setting

Two considerations are aimed at providing the best blank canvas upon which the establishment of the extraordinary can proceed. The first of these is a preference for Tenebrous rituals to be performed at night. This is because night suggests the ascendancy of Darkness.

The second consideration is that the ritual space should be as free of potential distractions as can be managed. First and foremost, this means finding a place that is private and will not be disturbed during the duration of the ritual. But it also means that the space should be equipped with an altar upon which the ritual's essential symbolic props can be placed, lest the magician otherwise be inconvenienced.

These two considerations, though recommended, are not absolute, for Tenebrous ritual is highly adaptable when it comes to matters of timing and setting. Rituals can be performed during the day if necessary, though in such instances, a dark, windowless chamber is strongly preferred. Ritual spaces may be indoors or outdoors and may be dedicated or set up and taken down as needed. Having four walls or noteworthy landmarks is useful when evoking the four directions (see below) but is far from a necessity. One can even cope with the absence of an altar, so long as one has a plan regarding how to handle the necessary ritual props gracefully in the altar's absence.

Overall, what is most important about the time and space chosen for ritual is that it be free of any distractions that could interfere with what is described below regarding the establishment of the extraordinary.

Establishing the extraordinary

Ritual's efficacy lies in the structure it utilizes, by which one removes oneself from the limitations of the ordinary and situates oneself instead in a distinct psychic realm with its own rules as to what is possible. One's ability to direct one's will and unleash one's energy without inhibition are greatly enhanced by the awareness that one is operating under the auspices of the extraordinary.

The realm of the extraordinary, in this sense just described, is known in Tenebrous Satanism as *naos*. As the Fifth Key previously alluded to, this Greek word, used also by the Order of Nine Angles (O9A), refers to a temple-shrine indwelt by a deity and its power. In the context of ritual, *naos* is established via a distinctive set of temporal and spatial cues. Many occult and religious traditions use cues of this kind, albeit with different language and imagery than Tenebrous Satanism uses.

Regarding the temporal dimension, Tenebrous ritual is structured into three stages:

1. *An opening phase*, during which one departs from ordinary reality and enters into the sacred space of the Temple

2. *A performance phase*, wherein one's actions have a special significance and are therefore potent in causing change

3. *A closing phase*, during which one shows gratitude toward the forces one has drawn upon and then returns to ordinary reality

Pre-ritual habits, such as the donning of special clothing or jewelry or the adoption of personal routines (e.g., bathing before and after, having one's hair bound or unbound, putting on makeup or war paint, wearing a specific perfume or cologne), can be used to further enhance one's sense of the extraordinary. Such things are not obligatory, but one should include them if one's experience of the ritual is heightened thereby.

Regarding the spatial dimension, Tenebrous ritual applies the symbolism of the kingdoms of the runic-tarot:

- *South* is associated with the element of fire and zealous forces of worldly ambition. Acausal forces of the South are addressed as Archons, for an Archon is one who rules as a Lord of this world via the harnessing of willful desire.

- *East* is associated with the element of air, union via communication and separation via discernment. Acausal forces of the East are addressed as Fallen Angels, for they distribute forbidden knowledge in defiance of the heavens.

- *North* is associated with the element of earth, and the solidity of the flesh, through which all physical beings experience suffering. Acausal forces of the North are addressed as Abominations, for they are beings, often grotesque in aspect, who are thoroughly acquainted with all that makes existence terrible — and yet still affirm the will of Abyssal Darkness that existence continue ever onward.

- *West* is associated with the element of water and with spirit as that which is everlasting and perpetually mutable. Acausal forces of the West are addressed as Ancient Ones, for they embraced self-evolution from the very dawn of primordial existence and thus built themselves into entities of incredible might over the endless aeons they have spent watching over the evolution of others.

The matter of acausal forces — Archons, Fallen Angels, Abominations and Ancient Ones — associated with each of these directions can be taken in two ways, and it is most fruitful for the magician to entertain both levels of interpretation: i) one is forming a nexion between oneself and Darkness, through which come the raw ingredients — primal hunger, longing for connection, embrace of adversity, and aspiration toward godhood — that the magician weaves together into a successful working; ii) one is forming a nexion between oneself and like-minded acausal beings, and although one may not know them by their individual names, nonetheless they lend their power to their fellow walker of the Sinister Path. In the first case, the "beings" are metaphors for different aspects of the Abyssal Void of Darkness itself. In the second, the presence of discrete entities is posited. Nonetheless, what the magician addresses in the first case is no less real than in the second.

The skeptic is free to take all of this as an elaborate metaphor for getting in touch with darker aspects of one's unconscious mind and to posit that any causal impact of ritual stems from its psychological effects. But the magician who engages wholeheartedly with the establishment of the extraordinary, entering fully into the *naos* state, is likely to be persuaded of the existence of acausal forces by the experience.

More specific details of the what and how of ritual will be discussed in connection with the example provided later in the Seventh Key. What is worth stressing at present is that meaningful action, tools, and symbolism together add up to the right kind of engagement to make ritual efficacious. Conversely, cutting corners on any of these fronts may leave the magician insufficiently immersed in the proceedings and confound the acausal forces one is attempting to interact with.

Principle of adverse consequences

One should not attempt magick without careful, serious reflection upon all the ways in which it can go awry.

Contra the playful attitude of many twenty-first century magicians, Tenebrous Satanism asserts that magick should not be conceived of as merely a fun and amusing pastime, a clever way of getting something free from the universe, or a harmless therapeutic method for the venting of emotions. The magician who refuses to take magick's risks seriously has no right to expect magick to actually work. Witches and sorcerers would be wise to consider, in particular, the following ways in which magick can wind up creating more problems than it solves:

Cascading state of delusion

This is a condition that can arise when the magician has inadequate knowledge of the situation they seek to influence, due to failing to consult divination, making unfounded assumptions, or other oversights. A classic example is the magician who tries to reflect back the curse of their supposed enemy when, in reality, no one cursed them to begin with. In such cases, magick will either fail or produce unpredictable and pernicious results. Many an overzealous magician will make the situation yet worse by trying to combat the chaos they themselves unleashed via yet-further resort to magick.

Perverse fulfillment

Due to poorly considered wording or symbolism, the magician's desire may be fulfilled in an ironic fashion contrary to the ritual's true intent. For example, one may attempt to improve one's financial fortunes, only for this to be followed by the death of a dear loved one and the receipt of an inheritance. Such cases suggest that Darkness grants wishes in the manner of a malevolent genie possessed of a twisted sense of humor. Magicians should craft their workings carefully to try to minimize this effect.

Instinctual retaliation

Tenebrous Satanism does not believe in karma as a moral principle. It does, however, recognize that every living organism has an interest in its own well-being. Any kind of assault thus inherently provokes retaliation, for such is what survival of the fittest both demands and selects for. It follows that, for example, the casting of curses can trigger unconscious acausal defense mechanisms in the target, and the magician will then have to deal with the resultant energy backlash. This is no reason not to curse one's enemies, for if one anticipates the effect, one can easily mitigate it.[50] The point, though, is that one ought to anticipate it.

Psychic burnout

Too much ritual magick within too short a time can lead to feeling slow and weighted down even when physically well-rested, dullness of mind, and feelings of anxiety or frustration that persist without apparent cause. Eroded sanity due to confusion between fantasy and reality is a related risk. Rest tends to correct these effects with time, but it is better to avoid them to begin with. Performing ritual no more than once a week is a sustainable level of exertion for most magicians.

Collateral damage

Since magick is facilitated by nexions, there is a risk of it percolating through a web of relationships and producing unwanted results thereby. One such situation — a particularly dangerous one — arises when a curse afflicts not only its intended victim, but also associates of theirs whom the magician would have rather left unharmed. This is yet another reason why it is important to accompany acausal initiatives with appropriate causal ones. For example, if using magick to destroy someone's life, do not continue to associate with that person, lest your own life be disrupted by the fallout.

Deflection via regrets

If the magician exerts themselves in circumstances they later regret — for example, they change their mind or realize something about the situation they did not before — the energy of their past working nonetheless still needs to go somewhere. Such energy may be deflected back upon oneself or other unintended targets. As with instinctual retaliation, this is simply a matter of acausal metaphysics, not of karmic morality. Nonetheless, it is among the many reasons why the successful use of magick requires the utmost honesty in personal introspection.

Acausal antagonism

If one has formed a relationship with acausal beings, such beings will expect the magician to uphold their end of any bargains made. Failure to follow through on promises made to one's acausal allies will provoke punishment, often manifesting via an extensive string of unlikely misfortunes. One should therefore honor one's acausal alliances with the same loyalty and reliability as one's relationships to kith and kin on the causal plane. Those unwilling to take such partnerships seriously ought not to enter into them.

It is worth emphasizing that although many of these dangers are heightened in the case of baneful workings, this does not mean such workings are wrong per se. The Satanist is within their rights to use magick to remove obstacles to their own flourishing, avenge wrongs done to themselves or their loved ones, confound the plans and actions of enemy dogmatists, and so forth. Tenebrous Satanism merely affirms that these actions carry consequences the magician ought to prepare for. It is nonetheless better to take bold action, and risk making a mistake, than to let fear forbid action. Making mistakes and learning from them is, after all, an integral part of the Adventure of the Sinister Path.

The bottom line of the principle of adverse consequences is that magick should not be seen as a font of easy solutions. It is precisely because magick is not easy, however, that one stands to grow and mature through practicing it.

Principle of maximal fruitfulness

Full realization of the gains of magick comes only to those possessed of self-reflection, uncompromising honesty, bold initiative-taking, and detached patience.

This principle attests to the attitudes and behaviors the magician should adopt after a ritual, so as to best enjoy the fruits produced by the working. Four recommendations include:

- Everything pertaining to a ritual, from conception to aftermath, should be recorded in a journal for subsequent reflection.

- When it comes to assessing whether a ritual was effective, one ought neither to exaggerate one's success nor rationalize away the success one does achieve. The former pleases the ego at the expense of learning how to improve upon one's efforts. The latter denigrates one's personal power, destroys confidence, and sabotages future workings.

- If, thanks to magick, one finds oneself presented with opportunities one did not have before, these opportunities must be seized. Timidity is tantamount to showing ingratitude toward the powers of Darkness.

- The full impact of a ritual often does not make itself evident until after some time has passed. In the meantime, the magician must cultivate detachment. Fretting about whether or not a ritual worked is one of the surest ways of thwarting its results.

Principle of altered consciousness

Accomplishing magickal change requires entry into a non-normal psychic state appropriate to one's intent.

The final principle of Tenebrous magick refers to a key moment during the performance stage of ritual, which may be termed the *intensification*. Intensification refers to whatever is done during the performance phase of the ritual to actually cause the change that the magician desires. Everything leading up to and following this moment is really a mere facilitator of it.

The mundane experience that most readily equips one to grasp the dynamics of intensification is orgasm. Both entail raising energy to a climax, culminating in a peak before falling away in release. But regardless of the method intensification employs, it will only work if it utterly consumes the whole of one's attention, such that only the experience of that moment is real, and all else falls away. Intensification deserves be thought of as a non-normal psychic state for this reason.

It is worth being aware of the variety of forms intensification may take, for which method will be most effective will depend on what a given ritual is meant to accomplish. As a whole, intensification methods can be classified according to two contrasts:

- *Inhibitory* methods utilize a mental state of being fully invested in the current moment, yet utterly placid and detached. By contrast, *excitatory* methods use a high pitch of emotion, lust, rage, etc.[51]
- *Conscious* methods entail detailed lingering upon the results the ritual is intended to achieve by visualizing the desired outcome as vividly as the magician can manage. By contrast, *unconscious* methods aim to raise and release energy without consciously dwelling upon the ritual's intent. Often, a sigil or mantra serves as the central focus of unconscious methods of intensification — i.e., a symbol or sound that represents the aim of the ritual in an abstract way.

Some common intensification methods include:

Visualization of a vivid scene in the mind's eye

Visualization is a highly recommended intensification method on account of the wide range of uses the magician can apply it toward. It may entail a detailed imagining of the literal outcome one is aiming for, or it may involve immersing oneself in a more metaphorical vision, depending upon what the magician finds more evocative. Whether the psychological dynamics accompanying visualization are inhibitory or excitatory can similarly vary. In all cases, though, release comes at the point when a vivid rendition of the desired scene has been created in the mind's eye to an extent that wholly satisfies the magician.

Exertion via repetition

To perform this method, one first translates one's aim into a sigil or mantra — e.g., by transcribing the ritual's target into Tenebrous runes and combining/overlapping these to create a distinctive figure, or rearranging letters to form words that do not correspond to any preexisting language. Then, during the performance phase of the ritual, one dedicates oneself to drawing the sigil perfectly a set number of times or vibrating the mantra for a certain number of repetitions.

This approach is inhibitory on account of it demanding detached, single-minded concentration, maintained with total focus. Anything less will not deliver results. It is also an unconscious method, since the abstraction of a sigil or mantra elides open acknowledgment of the desire that drives the ritual. Because of this latter feature, repetitive exertion is often the most effective intensification method for novices who struggle with wandering minds, lust for results, and other difficulties. Using sigils and mantras forces one to focus solely on the manipulation of symbol and sound *right now,* and thereby circumvents unproductive daydreaming and overanalysis.

Sexual arousal and release

As was already mentioned, the dynamics of sexual stimulation and release are akin to the dynamics of any effective method of intensification. It follows that the pursuit of orgasm can itself be incorporated into an intensification method. Toward this purpose, the sexual act may be undertaken either alone or with others. Many magicians will find, however, that a solitary act will be more conducive to the totally uninhibited and inwardly focused approach to sexuality that effective intensification requires.

To operate as a method of intensification, acts of sexual excitation should be accompanied either by some manner of vivid visualization for a conscious approach, or meditation upon a sigil for an unconscious one. Either way, steadfast focus upon the visualization or sigil must be maintained throughout the sex act until orgasm occurs, as well as during the state of mental suspension that occurs in the immediate wake of orgasm, if this method is to be successful. Sexual intensification is therefore not suitable for those only able to achieve orgasm by dwelling upon a specific fetish or other stimulus, as energy cannot be directed effectively if one's focus is divided between one's ritual intention and unrelated matters.

Emotional arousal and release

This intensification method entails the magician stoking some manner of non-sexual passion to a boiling point, culminating in exhaustion. Two common examples are stoking anger into frenzy (often accompanied by destroying a physical object amid one's fury) and stoking sympathy into tears. The latter is most suitable for rituals aimed at changing intolerable circumstances for the better. The former is best reserved for destructive workings.

The use of anger, sympathy, or other emotions in the ritual chamber is subject to similar considerations and challenges as that of orgasm. In all of these cases, the method is inherently excitatory in its psychological dynamics. Nonetheless, all such methods can be used in combination either with visualization or sigilization. In all cases, the challenge is that throughout the rampage of the passions, the magician must still maintain undistracted focus upon the matter at hand. Those who cannot raise their emotions to a pitch without their attention becoming scattered amid miscellaneous pieces of personal baggage are likely to get better results from repetitive exertion. But for those capable of combining emotional overstimulation with disciplined, undivided attention upon the current moment, passionate intensification offers a degree of catharsis seldom matched by other methods.

Sympathetic enactment

Sympathetic enactment requires one to identify oneself or a proxy with the ritual's target, and then dramatize the desired scenario. This method is most commonly used to manipulate or destroy the target, as per the familiar example of the voodoo doll. However, a myriad of other applications are also possible. For example, one may alter one's own appearance to make oneself resemble one's target and proceed to act out that which one wishes to have happen. Whatever is done, however, must be done in a spirit of total realism — during the ritual, the proxy is the target, and whatever one is doing to the target is happening, for real, at this very moment.

Enactment can utilize either inhibitory dynamics (for example, carving an enemy's name in a candle and observing with absorbed detachment as it burns down to nothing) or excitatory ones (destroying the likeness of one's enemy in a fit of wrath). It is also compatible both with conscious targeting (as per the doll example) and unconscious targeting (destroying a sigil rather than a doll). In all cases, this method can be very effective if a strong sympathy can be established. By the same token, it can be dangerous in the hands of a practitioner who is careless or insufficiently reflective about what they are doing.

The preceding list is not exhaustive. It reveals, however, that intensification methods, diverse though they are, share certain traits.

First, they require the controlled moderation of zeal via disciplined focus. Second, they carry the magician through a process, such that there should be a distinctly felt difference between one's initial thoughts and emotions and those one experiences in the intensification's aftermath. Finally, they are meant to be completely immersive experiences during the entire time that one is engaged in them. This last feature is what justifies calling them non-normal psychic states.

An example of a ritual

The preceding section ought to have made clear that Tenebrous Satanism does not consider magick something to frivolously play around with. This may leave an aspiring witch or sorcerer wondering how to gain practice at ritual magick. Those who are dissatisfied with their lives can find ready answers to such a question, but where to start is less obvious to those who lack a desperate longing for change. To address this issue, the current section describes a ritual whose utility is universal. Any walker of the Sinister Path, from novice to adept, could benefit from performing it at regular intervals, monthly or even weekly.

The ritual in question is a Rite of Banishing. It is aimed at ridding oneself of the mental and emotional stains left by external influences (unwanted human interactions, daily irritants, frustrating disappointments, etc.), and freeing oneself of any baggage that one finds oneself carrying due to such experiences. As a means by which one actualizes the Creed's call to stand apart from the herd, banishing is a healthful practice on both the psychological and spiritual levels. Moreover, if attempted by the incompetent, it tends to simply not work, rather than producing any additional adverse consequences. These characteristics make it suitable for gaining initial experience at ritual magick.

What follows is divided into five sections: preparation, opening, performance, closing, and aftermath. The middle three of these constitute the ritual proper and should be understood as one continuous sequence of actions, divided solely to make the ritual's structure evident. Portions that must be spoken aloud are indicated via indentation, and any lines enclosed with square brackets must be filled in with appropriate content — e.g., personal details inserted, changes made in order to use the ritual template for purposes other than those postulated here, etc. The rest of the ritual script may also be altered in accord with the practitioner's taste and needs but should be kept as consistent as possible between different rituals by the same individual. The causal benefit of keeping a majority of the proceedings consistent between performances is greater ease of remaining focused and confident throughout the rite, especially insofar as repetition eases memorization, making for more effective performance than having to read words off a page. The acausal benefit is that familiarity also facilitates easier communication with the forces one is calling upon.

Preparation

Prior to the ritual, one ought to have settled on an appropriate space and a suitable time, as discussed above. For the purposes of the description that follows, we will assume that the ritual space is indoors, and that the altar is against the western wall of the room. This positioning is symbolically suitable for Satanic ritual, since it is the direction in which the sun goes down, the direction from which adverse changes in weather originate in many parts of the world, and the opposite of the direction that many right-hand-path religions favor in their rituals. If the intended ritual space is not arranged in this fashion, the magician will need to adapt subsequent direction-related instructions accordingly.

The magician should have obtained all necessary props — the candle, dagger, crystal and offering. The current example assumes that the offering is incense, as incense is easy to obtain and serves as a good multi-purpose offering. All tools should be placed upon the altar at the start of the ritual, in a manner convenient to the magician. For most, this will mean placing the dagger toward the right and the crystal toward the left, with the candle and offering positioned toward the rear of the altar.

The nature of a banishing is such that its pre-ritual introspective demands are lighter than with many other kinds of ritual. For the purposes of magick in general, however, one ought to have introspected thoroughly ahead of time, in accord with the lines of inquiry listed under the principle of self-possession above. It is also a good idea to retreat to a private space for a little while before the ritual, separating oneself from other living beings during this time. Doing so promotes better focus of energies during the working itself, in accord with the principle of interdependent influence.

When it is time to perform the ritual, the magician should retire to the ritual space and ensure as far as possible that they will not be disturbed during the proceedings. Tenebrous rituals typically take at least half an hour to perform. Any pre-ritual routines that one has decided to adopt, such as the donning of ritual garb, should be completed prior to proceeding with the steps listed below.

Note: *Italicized* lines within the script below are to be *vibrated* instead of spoken. To "vibrate" in the esoteric sense means basically to sing all on one note. For the purposes of Tenebrous ritual, the specific note is not important so long as it is comfortable for the magician. Generally though, it is best to choose a tone in the lower-middle of one's vocal range that feels natural and is conducive to powerful projection. While it is possible to get causal results out of Tenebrous ritual without performing vibrations, acausal results are greatly facilitated by including them. The aspiring magician is therefore strongly encouraged to become familiar enough with esoteric vibration to be able to perform it in an uninhibited manner.[52]

Opening

1. Light the candle to mark the start of the ritual.

2. Center yourself in the present moment by performing Lunar Purification for at least seven breaths. Those familiar with the Fifth Key's Contemplations may wish to perform one or more such exercises as a warm up, but this is not obligatory.

3. Take up the dagger in both hands, holding it upright before you.

4. Recite the following General Evocation in a firm, confident voice:

   "*Eam deorsum ad aram Tenebrarum*[53]
   I hereby evoke the Dark Gods of the Sinister Path
   Masters of life and death
   Reconcilers of the flesh and the spirit
   Come forth and appear before me
   For I am a seeker of wisdom and power
   Fearless and proud in my pursuit of divinity
   Agios, O Tenebrae Profundae!
   Ave, Satanas! Veni, Malevoli!"[54]

5. Shift the dagger to your right hand and pick up the crystal in your left hand.

6. Turning to face the south, hold up the crystal with your palm away from you, as if to show it to someone facing you, and point the dagger forward, using it to trace the form of the Satanic pentacle in the air before you:

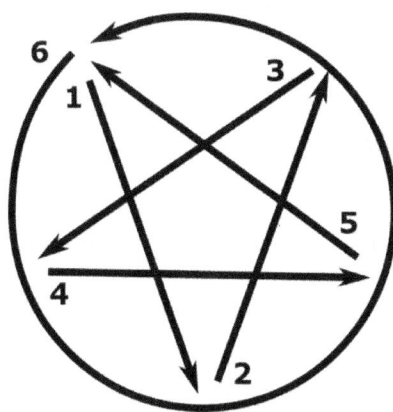

The method of tracing need not match this figure exactly, but it should be done in a consistent manner between different rituals performed by the same individual.

7. Once the tracing is complete, extend your arm so that you thrust the dagger-point forward through the figure you have just drawn, and recite the following Evocation of the South:

> "From the Southern Fires, I call forth the Archons
> Rulers of this world and granters of desire
> Come forth at my call:
> *Agios, O Archontes!*
> *Binan ath! Ga wath am!*"[65]

During the vibration,[56] you should envision energy flowing down your arm and out through the tip of the dagger to mingle with the dark energies now stirring before you. Vivid visualizers who project with single-minded focus may find that as they cease vibrating, an answering echo of energy can be felt through the crystal. Regardless of whether you feel this or not, wait a couple seconds, with the crystal still upheld and the dagger still pointed forward, before continuing to the next step.

8. The procedure just described should be repeated in each of the remaining directions as you turn left to face each in turn and repeat the same gestures with the dagger and crystal. The associated Evocations of the East, North and West are:

   "From the Eastern Air, I call forth the Fallen Angels
   Knowledge-seekers and bearers of the light of wisdom
   Come forth at my call:
   Agios, O Sapientes!
   Binan ath! Ga wath am!"

   "From the Northern Earth, I call forth the Abominations
   Revealers of harsh truths and enemies of the cowardly
   Come forth at my call:
   Agios, O Nefandi!
   Binan ath! Ga wath am!"

   "From the Western Waters, I call forth the Ancient Ones
   Chaos-bringers and destroyers of obstacles
   Come forth at my call:
   Agios, O Veteri!
   Binan ath! Ga wath am!"

9. Once the Evocation to the West has been completed, lower the crystal, raise the dagger, and complete the opening phase of the ritual with the Conclusion of Evocations:

   "Ineo naon![57]
   Thus do I welcome the Dark Gods."

Performance

10. Return the crystal to the altar and switch the dagger back to the initial two-handed grip. Holding the blade up before you, introduce yourself and state what you want:

    "Dark Gods, I, [magician's name],
    call you forth from the Abyss to fulfill my request:

[Banish all energies that I have no use for and forbid their influence from hindering me.]
Do as I command, and I will testify to your greatness!"

This part of the ritual is called the Statement of Intent. Effective Statements of Intent will fulfill all of the following criteria: i) they should be in the form of a command; ii) they should strike a balance between descriptiveness and brevity; iii) they should be clear and direct, avoiding phrasing that is conditional, evasive or negative.

11. Shift the dagger to your right hand and pick up the crystal in your left. While continuing to face the altar, issue the Statement of Coordination:

    "I turn now to the four directions to make my will manifest."

    Coordination in Tenebrous ritual can take two forms. The present multidirectional form is used in rituals where the magician continues to acknowledge the powers located in the four directions (Archons, Fallen Angels, Abominations, Ancient Ones) throughout the rite. An example of a ritual that uses the alternative, unidirectional coordination ("Darkness, come forth in all your forms to make my will manifest.") can be found in the Eighth Key. Which form is better for a given ritual depends on a variety of factors, including what the ritual is aimed at and the individual temperament of the magician. In the author's experience, though, beginners will find it easier to get results from the multidirectional format and should use the unidirectional format only when the ritual's intensification method does not lend itself well to four elements symbolism.

12. Perform the Intensification, which will take the form of visualization. Begin by turning toward the south and stating:

    "Archons, [purify my will, for I am the Black Flame that cannot be extinguished!]"

13. Adopt a meditative posture and visualize fire flowing forth from the south to envelop you, its blazing heat burning away impurities and driving off whatever you seek separation from. Sustain this vision with as much detail as you can for several minutes, ideally incorporating additional sensory elements beyond the visual (e.g.,

the feel of heat). Altering your breathing to match one of the patterns described in the Fifth Key (whichever one you feel best fits the visualization you are performing) can further augment the experience, but do this only if it helps you focus, not if the effort distracts you. Throughout this process, you may hold the dagger and crystal in whatever manner feels natural. Vivid visualizers may feel energy flow either out through the dagger or in through the crystal. Whether you feel these sensations or not, persist until a sense of satisfaction descends upon you.

14. When you are ready to proceed, turn toward each of the remaining directions and repeat this process, issuing an appropriate command and accompanying it with a suitable visualization for each element:

    "Fallen Angels, [purify my mind, for I am the fresh, strong wind that destroys yet also creates!]"

    "Abominations, [purify my body, for I am the seed sown in blood-stained soil, which grows forever anew!]"

    "Ancient Ones, [purify my spirit, for I am the torrential rain that washes away all obstructions!]"

    When adapting the ritual template to other applications, one should not feel constrained to exact imitation of the length, phrasing, metaphors and so forth used here.[58] Rather, it is up to the magician to come up with both the words and the intensifying imagery that will best impact their own psyche.

    When using forms of intensification other than visualization,[59] the general flow remains unchanged. E.g., for exertion-based intensification, one follows each of one's commands with the designated number of vibrated chants or focused sigil-drawings. In all instances, the principle is the same: the spoken component defines the desired result, while the intensification brings this desire into fruition.

15. Once the Intensification has culminated, stand and turn once more to face the altar. Set the crystal down, hold the dagger before you, and speak the Statement of Accomplishment:

    "[Thus do I banish all that opposes my will!]"

Whereas the contents of the Intensification can be quite descriptive, the Statement of Accomplishment should be like the Statement of Intent in firmness, directness, and conciseness. A tone of finality is also appropriate, for these words complete the performance phase.

Closing

16. While maintaining the same position as in the final step of the Performance, speak the Offering:

    "Dark Gods, I acknowledge your power with gratitude:
    Receive now the offering."

17. Set the dagger down on the altar and light the incense.

18. Hold the incense before you in a reverential manner as you turn to acknowledge the South:

    "Archons, as your favored regent, I thank you."

    Follow these words by gently blowing on the incense, then extending it before you, holding it there for a few seconds.[60]

19. Turn toward each of the other directions, greeting each with a similar Acknowledgment while making the offering. The Acknowledgments of the East, North and West are:

    "Fallen Angels, as your ardent disciple, I thank you."

    "Abominations, as your chosen vessel, I thank you."

    "Ancient Ones, as your awakened offspring, I thank you."

    In rituals that call upon specific acausal beings (e.g., the Nekalah, as per the Eighth Key), now is an appropriate time to acknowledge and thank them as well, in whatever manner the magician feels is suitable.

20. Once the Acknowledgments have been completed, set the incense down upon the altar.

21. Take up the dagger as before, and recite the Parting:

"Thus is the rite complete.
Dark Gods, go forth with all of the might of the Adversary,
for our wills are united as one.
Ave Satanas!
Nythra Kthunae Atazoth!"[61]

22. With the last words of the Parting, turn the dagger so that the point is downward, and drop to the ground so that the blade touches it. (Penetrating the ground is an option when outside, but for indoor rituals, contact is all that is needed).

23. Remain crouched, your head downward and the dagger's blade touching the ground, for at least a slow count to seven. You may need to take one hand off the dagger and place your palm upon the ground in order for the ritual's accumulated energy to discharge completely.

24. Conclude the ritual by rising to stand before the altar, sheathing the dagger, and blowing out the candle. The incense offering should be left to burn out by itself.

If any additional preparations were undertaken in connection with the opening, these should be mirrored with appropriate closing actions, removal of occult garb, post-ritual bathing, etc.

Aftermath

After a ritual, the magician needs to practice good mental and emotional hygiene to allow the unleashed energies to work without interference. Therefore, once a rite is complete, one ought to make a clean break from it by turning one's attention to something ordinary, such as replenishing one's energy with food and drink, consumption of escapist media, engagement in some mundane hobby, etc. Journaling the ritual after its completion is recommended, but one should avoid dwelling on it beyond this. The magician should also observe all post-ritual considerations listed above re: the principle of maximal fruitfulness at this time.

Something worth being aware of regarding magick in general, and banishings in particular, is that one must not follow a ritual with action that thwarts its intended purpose. If the need for a banishing was brought on, for example, by preoccupation with social media, one ought not to use social media browsing as one's post-ritual grounding activity. This may seem obvious to those who intuitively grasp the principles of magick. Often, though, those who most urgently need to fix their lives via ritual are the most prone to making mistakes of this kind.

While internal, subjective changes are often evident immediately after a successful ritual, external, objective changes usually take longer to make themselves known. If the latter seem elusive, patience is recommended. Rumination or leaping into additional workings, on the other hand, will tend to be self-defeating. In any instance, an earnestly performed ritual should, at minimum, provoke some degree of personal growth via the dynamic engagement with one's own energy, will, and imagination that ritual demands. Appreciating such growth is a prerequisite to being able to appreciate any of the more extensive and mysterious transformations that magick has the power to bring about.

Summary

The Seventh Key's purpose is to equip Tenebrous Satanists with principles and procedures for the performance of effective ritual. The seven principles of magick delineate how magick works, not only according to the worldview of Tenebrous Satanism, but also in general, as a study of other systems of magick will in many instances reveal similar fundamentals. The example ritual in turn offers a template for beginners and a jumping-off point from which more advanced practitioners can innovate as they see fit. The complete ritual script, without the interruption of being broken into steps, may be found in Appendix I.

The herd dislikes the idea that such methods as those described in these pages could be effective. To affirm magick's potency is to admit the existence of mysterious forces that may well prove more malign than benevolent. But even more threatening to the complacent and the mediocre is how, once one understands the true power of a firm persuasion, one is called to take responsibility for one's life. What the magician ultimately strives to do is to seize control, changing what is within one's grasp to change if one so wills it. Inherent in this gesture is the rejection of a life lived in impotence and bad faith.

Many people would sooner frame themselves as weak, helpless wretches at the mercy of fate than admit that maybe, just maybe, they have not chosen to make the best use of their personal power — regardless of how great or small that power may be. Small wonder, then, that historically, the herd has condemned magick, and currently, it is commonplace to deny that people can wield such powers at all. The magician thus finds themselves at odds with everyone and everything regarding this matter. Such an oppositional stance is on par with where Tenebrous Satanism stands regarding any number of other philosophical, ethical, and spiritual issues besides. Therefore, whether confronted by witch-hunters or scoffers, the dedicated witch or sorcerer is just as indifferent as they would be toward those uncomfortable with any other aspect of Satanism's adversarial ethos.

What exactly can or can't be accomplished by unleashing the Black Flame must be determined by the individual through experimentation. Broadly speaking, though, Tenebrous Satanism affirms that magick can be used to bring about decisive alterations in one's own psyche, to influence the minds and emotions of other people, and to encourage or thwart matters of synchronistic coincidence that "normal" people dismiss as mere chance.

We hope that the Seventh Key will provide Satanists with new means by which to achieve all that may advance their own flourishing and self-evolution, and that through cultivation of the Dark arts described herein, witch and sorcerer alike will at the same time cultivate themselves to ever greater extents.

Notes

[47] This way of understanding magick is found among some LaVeyan and Satanic Temple Satanists, who hold that the ceremonies they perform are efficacious via psychological impact alone. These groups' framings of such activities as Black Masses, "un-baptisms," etc. offer good examples of what the Seventh Key means by a purely causal interpretation of ritual efficacy. Shiva Honey's *The Devil's Tome* (2020) provides an excellent overview of this way of looking at ritual magick.

[48] On the other hand though, it will do no good for an absolute beginner to rush into performance of a ritual that they simply are not prepared to do. This advice regarding seizing opportunities is therefore of most relevance to magicians who have already performed rituals in the past and are thus already prepared in terms of possessing necessary tools, familiarity with ritual format, etc.

[49] In the author's experience, many left-hand-path magicians who use blood in ritual contexts have found it convenient to just prick a finger with a diabetic lancet when only a few drops of blood are required (as is the case here and with other practices described later in the current work, e.g., creating the Vindex sigil used in the Mars stage of initiation, as per the Ninth Key). We do not necessarily endorse this or any other specific technique, however, and mention it more to make the point that in the author's experience, blood that has been shed by this method is acceptable to the Dark Gods. We strongly encourage magicians to exercise both caution and common sense when incorporating the use of their own blood into ritual practices of any kind.

[50] An example of an effective and easy mitigation option would be performing a rite of banishing a few days after casting a curse.

[51] The terms "inhibitory" and "excitatory" are here used in a sense similar to that found in Peter J. Carroll's *Liber Null* (1987). This book offers an excellent overview of a full range of effective intensification methods and is therefore worthy of study by all aspiring magicians.

[52] The "Esoteric Sorcery: Esoteric Chants" section of O9A's *Naos* contains useful information about vibration. Those who wish to learn about the nuances of this technique would be well-advised to read broadly about the vibration of Enochian Keys and related esoteric practices.

[53] Latin for "I will go down to the altars of Darkness." This and other lines in Latin imitate ritual formulae found in O9A's *Black Book of Satan*.

[54] Latin for "Numinous art thou, o profound Darkness! Hail Satan! Hail Sinistrals!"

[55] Latin for "Numinous art thou, o ruling ones!" The meanings of the phrases "Binan ath" and "Ga wath am" were previously discussed in the Fifth Key. The Latin in subsequent directional evocations expresses similar sentiments, hailing the "wise ones," "unspeakable ones," and "ancient ones."

[56] Vibrating all of the words indicated here at an effective level of intensity should take in the range of twenty to thirty seconds. This may seem like a long time, but a rushed performance is not conducive to effective projection of one's voice.

[57] Latin for "I enter into the Temple!"

[58] It is, in particular, not necessary for words spoken as part of the Intensification to always paraphrase O9A formulae. The commands directed toward the East and the North in the rite given here do incorporate elements from O9A's *Black Book of Satan*, but this is just because the author of the current work happens to draw inspiration from O9A's aesthetic. Magicians should feel free to devise whatever imagery they find most evocative for the purposes at hand.

[59] Some forms of intensification, such as sexual or emotional arousal, cannot be performed effectively in the fourfold format of a ritual that uses multidirectional coordination. Rites that use such intensification methods should therefore

employ unidirectional coordination, i.e., "Darkness, come forth in all your forms to fulfill my request!" followed by a single crescendo and release of energy.

[60] Non-incense offerings may be presented in whatever manner the individual magician feels is appropriate.

[61] While this superficially appears to be just a sequence of three Nekalah's names, each of those names has a meaning beyond simply acting as an identifier for the being in question. Tenebrous Satanism thus translates this phrase as "Forces of Darkness, fill the Earth, to bring about our utmost evolution!"

VIII

The Nekalah: Dark Gods of the Abyss

I have seen beyond the bounds of infinity and drawn down daemons from the stars... I have harnessed the shadows that stride from world to world to sow death and madness...

- H. P. Lovecraft, "From Beyond" (1934)

Every religion has its methods of communion, which enable the adherent to experience enhanced states of intimacy with whatever entities or forces the religion has identified as "divine." Right-hand-path religions typically use such experiences to shatter the human ego, confronting the mere mortal with how lowly and limited they are in comparison to the supposed Ultimate. The Sinister Path uses the communion experience for an exactly opposite purpose: to demonstrate to the ambitious individual just what a powerful will is capable of at the same time as one comes face to face with that which transcends mundane reality.

As a participant in the same magickal current as the Order of Nine Angles (O9A), Tenebrous Satanism seeks communion with the same entities O9A venerates. These are the Nekalah, a faction of Sinistrals known as Dark Gods of the Abyss. The Eighth Key will present several methods of communing with these spirits and the gnosis attained by the author thereby.

All forms of communion with spirits fundamentally consist of the practitioner entering into a state of altered consciousness in which resistance to the acausal is significantly lowered. Two such methods that are widely known in occult circles are summoning and possession. In the case of the Nekalah, however, conventional attempts at either of these methods tend to present certain difficulties. The Eighth Key therefore proposes two alternate forms of spirit communion designed specifically for bringing the magician into contact with the Dark Gods. In the first form, which we call the Rite of Descent, the magician travels to the entity, encountering it in a vision of its native environment. In the second form, which we call the Rite of the Threshold, the magician and the entity meet one another in a liminal space created within the ritual chamber. Both techniques yield results no less real than summoning or possession, as both use the same receptive state of altered consciousness as more traditional methods for communing with spirits. The Eighth Key reveals both what the performance of these rites consists in and what the author has learned of the Nekalah through such methods.

Neither the Rite of Descent nor the Rite of the Threshold are intended for magicians who are raw novices. It would therefore be wise for the Satanist to attain competence in all matters previously described in the Fifth, Sixth, and Seventh Keys before attempting the rites detailed below. To those who lack the mental discipline which meditation fosters and the intuitive capacities which divination cultivates, considerable obstacles stand in the way of effective communion. More seriously, when incompetent ritual magicians attempt to connect with spirits, such persons are liable to experience the frustrations of failure at best and the consequences of acausal contact gone awry at worst. Though these risks are more severe in the case of the Rite of the Threshold, they are by no means absent in connection with the Rite of Descent. Therefore, neither practice should be attempted by those who lack either confidence or skill in esoteric matters.

It should also be noted that communion with spirits can have destabilizing effects upon the psyches even of well-adjusted people, let alone poorly adjusted ones. The rewards of communion are many, but must be weighed carefully against the risks inherent to opening oneself up to direct contact with the Will of the Fire. Accordingly, the practices described in the Eighth Key are not recommended for anyone who is not of sound mental and emotional health. These practices should also not be undertaken while under the influence of addictive or intoxicating substances.[62]

Descending into the Abyss

In the Rite of Descent, communion is achieved by establishing a psychic channel between the magician and the spirit with whom they are soliciting contact. Through this channel, the magician experiences an encounter with the entity in its own realm. The experience may be likened to entering into a virtual-reality simulation, whose parameters are largely defined by the entity that the magician is contacting. As such, the success of the operation depends upon one's ability to put oneself in a sufficiently receptive state. It does not require the ability to have out-of-body experiences nor other similarly advanced occult feats.

The preceding description may lead some to surmise that descent, having a significant imaginative component as it does, is somehow "not real." But to envision descent (or, for that matter, any other kind of communion with spirits) as a mere flight of imaginative fancy is to fail to understand the true nature of the experience. Descent is characterized by the reception of images and information that feel as though they come from outside of oneself at the same time as one's own consciousness remains in a quiescent state of trance. In this state, one placidly observes what arises without planning or forcing the encounter. If the Rite of Descent is performed correctly, the experience should have a marked character of the alien and the uncanny that renders it wholly distinct from mundane daydreaming.

Before descent is to be attempted, one must first decide which entity one will contact and prepare that entity's sigil for use during the ritual. Regarding selection, the Satanist may find that, upon reading about the Nekalah in the pages that follow, they feel pulled by a particular entity. Or they may use divination to gain insight into the matter. However one makes this decision, the magician should reproduce the entity's sigil such that the sigil itself will be at least 3 x 3 inches in size, drawn or painted on a piece of paper, wood, or other suitable material roughly the size of a drink coaster, at minimum. This sigil should be placed upon the altar, together with the other tools of ritual magick.

When performing the Rite of Descent, the opening entails the Evocations standard in Tenebrous practice. The closing, similarly, includes the usual features of the Offering, etc. Hence, only the performance phase of the ritual will be provided below. Given the complexity of the Rite of Descent's intensification sequence —

particularly with regard to the Walking of the Black Gate — we advise the magician to rehearse all steps thoroughly prior to attempting the ritual proper. Stumbling over the proceedings will not be conducive to the working's success.

The performance phase of the Rite proceeds as follows:

1. Issue a Statement of Intent along the following lines:

    "Dark Gods, I, [magician's name],
    call you forth from the Abyss to fulfill my request:
    Open wide the Black Gate of the Void, so that I may venture forth into your realm;
    [Nekalah's name], guide me down into your region of the Abyss, so that [we may commune with one another].
    Do as I command, and I will testify to your greatness!"

    Everything after "so that" should be amended with appropriate specifics if needed — e.g., "so I may receive your advice about [concern]" etc. You should still attempt to keep the Intent concise, however, saving finer details for after contact has been established.

2. Proceed with unidirectional coordination:

    "Darkness, come forth in all your forms
    to make my will manifest."

3. Standing before the altar, set down the dagger. Keeping the crystal in your left hand, hold it up before you, as if showing it to someone standing in front of you, and begin the Intensification:

    "[Nekalah's name], behold the Key
    to the Dark Pool beneath the Moon."

4. Set the crystal down and pick up the representation you have made of the entity's sigil. Hold this up before you in the same manner as you did with the crystal and state:

    "[Nekalah's name], behold the sign
    by which you are known to me.
    Unlock the gate that separates me from your acausal throne;
    Hear my call and open the way before me!"

5. Set the sigil down and take up the dagger and crystal. Take a few steps backward and toward your left, so that you will have enough space to carry out what follows. During the whole of steps 6-8, the dagger should be held with the point downward so as to direct energy toward the ground and the crystal held up before you like a lamp used to light your way.

6. Face northwest, and vibrate the following phrase:

    "Agios, O [Nekalah's name]! Binan Ath! Ga Wath Am!"

7. Follow the vibration by taking four slow, purposeful steps forward. As you walk, visualize yourself descending a dark stairwell. At the same time, maintain awareness of the flow of energy from the tip of the dagger. This energy is what carves out the downward passage beneath your feet.

8. Turn to face the south and repeat the previous vibration. Follow this with another four slow, purposeful steps and the same visualization as before. Then, follow the abbreviated instructions i-v below, always repeating the vibration after turning to face the designated direction, and visualizing your descent as you proceed to walk.

    i.   Turn west, take two steps
    ii. Turn northeast, take seven steps
    iii. Turn west, take two steps
    iv. Turn south, take four steps
    v.   Turn northwest, take four steps

If the walking has been performed correctly, you should have traced the following pattern on the ground upon completion:

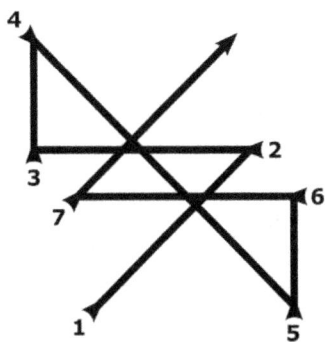

O9A calls this "the seven gates" and "a sigil of Saturn,"[63] but it is known in Tenebrous Satanism as the sigil of the Black Gate. In either case, the sigil represents opening the way and overcoming limitations — as per the role it plays in the current rite.

9. When you have arrived at the final step of walking the sigil, call out:

> "Thus do I open the Black Gate.
> [Nekalah's name], extend your hand to me and draw me forth unto your presence!"

10. Return to the altar, exchanging the dagger for the entity's sigil, then seat yourself toward the center of the figure of the Black Gate you have just traced, facing the entity's direction of manifestation (see the latter part of the Eighth Key for specifics). Sitting in a meditative position or moving a chair into place are both acceptable, so long as you can sit comfortably for a prolonged period of time.

11. Once seated in a comfortable yet alert manner, hold up the entity's sigil before you, and while gazing into it, begin breathing in the same manner as in Contemplation of the Nine-Angled Nexion: inhale and envision energy gathering, both in the sigil in front of you and in your fornax and adamanteus points; exhale through your nose, directing these energies to flow together into the crystal in your hand.

12. After twenty-seven breaths, hold your breath for at least thirty seconds while focusing your attention both on the two energy nexions within your body and the one before you in the entity's sigil. If, at this time or during the subsequent two steps, you witness an apparent darkening of your vision, observe this and accept it without becoming alarmed, but do not hold your breath so long that you become faint.

13. Breathe in, envisioning as you do that the three points that you are focusing on each expand into a churning vortex, as the energies surge to their maximum.

14. Breathe out, directing both your own energy and that of the entity you are connecting with into the crystal.

15. You should by now find yourself in a light trance state, accompanied by the urge to close your eyes. Obey this urge, and you should soon afterward feel a vague sense of "something" that pulls you forward or reaches out toward you. Resolve that you will calmly witness and accept whatever you behold from this point forward. If, on the other hand, you do not feel any alteration in your state of consciousness yet, repeat steps 11-14 until trance ensues.

16. Receptive individuals may, at this point, find that impressions of the entity and its acausal throne arise spontaneously before their closed eyes, followed by hearing the entity's voice as it addresses them. Others will sense that something is supposed to happen, without the way forward being obvious. In the latter case, one should direct one's attention to each of the following queries in turn, explicitly speaking the inquiry in one's mind and allowing any impressions that arise to bloom and develop spontaneously:

    i. In what setting does the entity choose to meet me?
    ii. What does the entity look like?
    iii. What message does the entity have for me?

    Such queries as these can be answered in a variety of ways: the entity may respond verbally or it may show you a vision of something. The crucial thing is to go along with whatever happens, cooperating without allowing analysis, resistance, or distraction to interfere.

    Note: While there is often a visual component to these proceedings, the absence of such — e.g., feeling as though you are blindfolded while the entity is narrating to you what you are supposed to be experiencing — should not be taken as a sign of failure. It should surprise no one that the Abyss is pitch black and that human eyes often require considerable time and practice before being able to adjust to it. The key thing is to allow the experience to unfold as it will without allowing impatience or doubt to break your focus.

17. When you have had your fill of communion with the entity, open your eyes and take a moment to reacquaint yourself with your physical surroundings. Then, rise to your feet and state aloud:

    "[Nekalah's name], I thank you for this revelation.

The time has come, though, for our ways to part, as I return now to the causal realm."

Alternately, if a situation arises in which it is necessary to break off contact abruptly — e.g., due to the experience taking an unpleasant turn — say firmly:

"[Nekalah's name], as sovereign of my own flesh and spirit, I withdraw from you by the power of my own will and return now to the causal realm."

18. Return your tools to the altar, stand facing east, and visualize the sigil for Karu Samsu shown below. During this visualization, vibrate the mantra *"Kara Samsu!"* seven times.

This mantra, which O9A translates as "I invoke the sun," is effective at restoring normal consciousness and banishing energies that would otherwise be disruptive once the magician has finished with them.

Some may find visualizing the sun itself, at first peeking over the horizon, then rising a bit more with each repetition, to be a more effective way of closing the Black Gate than the sigil, but either method will work. Accompanying the mantra with whatever gestures seem appropriate can further augment the banishing — e.g., start with hands at your sides and with each vibration, raise them a bit higher until they are over your head — but not all magicians will find this necessary.

19. Turn once more to the altar, take up the dagger and issue the Accomplishment:

> "Thus do I return to my own world, shutting the Black Gate behind me!"

You should thereafter proceed with the standard closing phase used for other workings.

If, after repeating steps 11-14 several times, the magician still feels nothing is happening, it is best to rise, return the crystal and sigil to the altar, carry out the seven vibrations of the mantra without addressing the entity one had meant to contact, and conclude with "Thus do I shut the Black Gate!" It is better to admit failure in such a fashion than try to force the experience. A magician can always learn from failure. Pretending success, on the other hand, teaches the magician nothing. Self-honesty is therefore essential.

Meeting upon the threshold

In the Rite of the Threshold, communion consists of the magician summoning the entity into the Shadow, a liminal space of Darkness established within the ritual chamber. Whereas in descent, the entity is the host and the magician is the guest, here such roles are reversed. The magician therefore faces two challenges. One is to provide an environment that will be sufficiently in accord with the entity's nature for it to be able to enter and orient itself within that space. The other is to devise a reliable method of disrupting this environment when the time comes to terminate communion, so as to discourage the entity from overstaying its welcome. Both issues are addressed via the rite incorporating several additional props beyond what other Tenebrous rites require.

The first additional prop that the Rite of the Threshold requires is *the pendant*. This should consist of a disk-like object suspended around one's neck by a cord or chain. The disk may be inscribed either with the seven-pointed star of O9A (see below), the five-pointed pentagram ubiquitous in Western esotericism, or some other manner of personal sigil that the magician finds suitable for designating an occult practitioner. It should not, however, be the sigil of any particular spirit, for its purpose is to help the spirit you are calling orient itself toward you. In this respect, its circular form represents its wearer as a being enclosed by the flesh, and the symbol emblazoned upon it symbolizes that the being in question (i.e., the magician) is in touch with the Darkness within.[64] The pendant's function is thus analogous to the circle drawn around the magician in other traditions' rites of summoning: not protection per se but, rather, to signal "this is where *I* am" to beings whose senses work differently from our own.

The second additional prop required by the Rite of the Threshold is *the target*. This is an area set aside for the spirit's initial arrival. It should be at least 12 x 12 inches — preferably larger — and should be demarcated with an equilateral triangle. This triangle can be constructed in whatever manner is most convenient — drawn on a large piece of paper and placed on the floor, formed by tying three sticks together, etc. It should be kept minimalistic in design, however, for the simpler it is, the more readily the magician will be able to engage with it during the rite. Its function is similar to the triangle of evocation used by various esoteric practitioners outside of Tenebrous Satanism: it does not constrain the entity but rather, signals "this is where *you* go" — a helpful traffic sign to a being who must drive through dimensions foreign to its usual state of existence in order to reach the summoner.

The third additional prop that the Rite of the Threshold uses is *the banishing candle*. This candle should be either white or some other color that renders it clearly distinct from the magician's dedicated altar candle. The banishing candle also does not need to be kept apart from mundane usage as other occult tools are. To the contrary, it tends to fulfill its purpose better the more ordinary it is, since its function is connected with dispersal of the Shadow prior to the closing of the Black Gate. This will be explained further in the instructions below.

As the preceding details should already suggest, communion on the Threshold posits that during the rite, the entity will be real and present in the immediate vicinity of the magician. This does not mean literal monsters coming through literal portals and related Lovecraftian dramatics, as one might see in Hollywood movies. It does mean, however, that during rites of this kind, it is not uncommon to experience a variety of subtle yet distressing sensory phenomena, coupled with an impression of presence that can be deeply unsettling to sensitive minds. Many magicians report that encounters with the Nekalah tend to be more disturbing than encounters with other spirits in this regard. The would-be summoner is therefore warned: if your mind is not unreservedly receptive to the entity you are calling, it will not come — but if you are receptive enough that it will come, even the most dedicated of Satanists is not guaranteed to have a pleasant experience. It is an inherent part of the modus operandi of the Nekalah to visit adversity even upon their allies, and one must therefore take seriously that there is always an element of personal danger in inviting them into our world. Facing such danger is, however, what allows the summoner to advance more rapidly along the Sinister Path than they might otherwise be capable of.

At the start of the Rite of the Threshold, the magician should don the pendant and place the target on the ground toward the periphery of the ritual chamber in a direction appropriate to the entity being summoned. At this time, one should take careful note of the target's position, fixing it firmly in one's mind, so that one will be able to continuously know with certainty where it lies in relation to oneself as the ritual proceeds. The banishing candle should be positioned in the east, on the opposite side of the practitioner from the altar, either on a raised, flat surface or on the ground. Unlike the altar candle, it should not be lit until the point of the ritual indicated below. The magician should have a lighter or matches ready to hand throughout the ritual.

As with the Rite of Descent, the opening of the Rite of the Threshold is as usual. Therefore, only the performance phase and onward are detailed below.

1. Issue a Statement of Intent along the following lines:

    "Dark Gods, I, [magician's name],
    call you forth from the Abyss to fulfill my request:
    Open wide the Black Gate of the Void, and come forth to greet me upon its threshold;

> [Nekalah's name], meet me in the Shadow between our worlds,
> so that [we may commune with one another].
> Do as I command, and I will testify to your greatness!"

As before, what follows "so that" should be refined as needed.

2. Continue with unidirectional coordination:

   > "Darkness, come forth in all your forms
   > to make my will manifest."

3. Proceed with the words and gestures of the Intensification, just as in the Rite of Descent:

   > "[Nekalah's name], behold the Key
   > to the Dark Pool beneath the Moon.
   > [Nekalah's name], behold the sign
   > by which you are known to me."

   Instead of replacing the sigil on the altar, turn (if necessary) and place it in the center of the target as you continue:

   > "Appear before me, here, in this place;
   > Hear my call as I open the way between us!"

4. Walk the Black Gate, as described before, using the same motions in the same directions, always issuing the vibration *("Agios, O [Nekalah's name]! Binan Ath! Ga Wath Am!")* after turning, before beginning to walk again. Change the visualization, though, such that the energy from your dagger traces a pitch-black line on the ground: a crack in reality through which a shadowy miasma seeps, rising higher and higher, increasingly permeating your surroundings. The complete sequence is:

i.	Turn NW, take 4 steps
ii.	Turn S, take 4 steps
iii.	Turn W, take 2 steps
iv.	Turn NE, take 7 steps
v.	Turn W, take 2 steps
vi.	Turn S, take 4 steps
vii.	Turn NW, take 4 steps

5. Upon arriving at the final step of the Black Gate, call out:

VIII — The Nekalah: Dark Gods of the Abyss

"Thus do I open the Black Gate."

6. Walk without delay to your altar. Facing it, continue:

   "[Nekalah's name], come forth into the Shadow!"

7. The instant you are done speaking, blow out the altar candle. The ritual chamber should be dark enough this plunges you into blackness.

   Warning: It is at this point in the rite that uncanny phenomena are most likely to start manifesting. You may, in particular, begin to experience one or more of the following:

   - A subtle alteration in your surroundings, such as a drop in ambient temperature or sense of heaviness in the air

   - A sudden feeling of intense dread that has no obvious cause or other strong impressions of negative energy in your immediate vicinity

   - Physical sensations such as dizziness, nausea, or unusual energy flow in the fornax or adamanteus points

   - A sensation that something is coming toward you, touching you, or attempting to push or pull you

   Whatever happens, do not resist. Understand that since the Nekalah are Sinistrals — beings closely proximate to Darkness itself — an aura of Abyssal death inherently hangs about them. It is then only natural for living beings to perceive their arrival as distressing. Allowing terror to dominate you, however, can provoke some Nekalah into attacking or otherwise trying to take advantage of your weakness. It is therefore crucial to remain calm for the entire time that you remain in the Shadow.

8. If warning signs of the kind just described make it obvious to you that the entity is manifesting, skip to the next step. But if you do not yet sense a strong connection, seat yourself facing the target and begin breathing in the same manner as in Contemplation of the Nine-Angled Nexion. Instead of envisioning the Naos sigil, though, just stare into the darkness above the target[65] as you focus on

directing the energy flow of both yourself and your unseen visitor into the crystal. If one round of twenty-eight breaths is not enough to trigger the sensation that there is indeed a presence in front of you, repeat the exercise, paying close attention throughout to any sensory or emotional alterations that intensify your impressions of being not alone.[66]

9. Once you are convinced that the entity is before you, begin communion by greeting it, either speaking aloud or forming the words in a distinct, intentional, and focused way in your mind, as if you were speaking. You should at once receive a response from the entity, either from somewhere in the Shadow around you or seeming to come from the crystal in your hand. Either way, the response will be in the form of words which seem like your own thoughts and yet feel unsettlingly distinct from what you know as you.

At this point, the spirit may also enliven your mind's eye with at least a vague idea of what it looks like, using the same mechanisms as it uses in the Rite of Descent. Sensitive individuals may also behold an especially dark or wavering distortion in the Shadow before them or other such effects more immediate than the Rite of Descent typically produces. If none of these things happen by themselves, asking the entity to show itself to you may enable it to tap into your inner vision enough to reveal itself. Do not push the issue if a Sinistral declines, though, as this may mean it is sparing you from something it thinks you are not prepared to handle.

10. Proceed to converse with the entity in a manner that is respectful, courteous, and unhurried. Inquire directly about that which you wish to know and wait patiently for it to answer one question before posing another. It is important to go slowly, especially if speaking mentally instead of aloud, for it makes it easier for the entity to pick your end of the conversation out of the mind's background noise. The entity may also interact by showing you images, touching you, etc.

11. When you have had your fill of communion with the entity, rise to your feet. The crystal and sigil should either be returned to the altar at this time or set down on the ground, whichever is more gracefully navigated in the darkness.

12. Say aloud:

    > "[Entity's name], I thank you for the honor of your presence. The time has come, though, for our ways to part, as I now dispel the Shadow."

    Alternately, if a situation arises in which it is necessary to break off contact abruptly — e.g., due to the experience taking an unpleasant turn — say firmly:

    > "[Nekalah's name], as sovereign of my own flesh and spirit, I conclude our meeting by the power of my own will, as I now dispel the Shadow."

13. Face the banishing candle, and light it.

14. Proceed with the same banishing mantra as in the Rite of Descent *("Karu Samsu!")*, vibrating this phrase seven times while looking into the flame of the banishing candle as you visualize the sigil or the rising sun. The banishing candle speeds the dispersal of the Sinistral by disrupting the causal space of the Shadow with an evocation of the quotidian aspects of human existence.

15. Keep gazing into the banishing candle until you feel the entity's presence dissipating, repeating the vibrations again if necessary. Then, once it has departed, remove the entity's sigil from the target, replace the sigil on the altar, and relight the altar candle.

16. Take up the dagger in both hands, and issue the Statement of Accomplishment:

    > "Thus do I return to my own world, shutting the Black Gate behind me!"

You should thereafter proceed with the standard closing phase used for other workings. The banishing candle should be left burning throughout the closing and put out only after the ritual has concluded with the extinguishing of the altar candle. The magician may even leave it to burn out on its own[67] should this feel like a psychologically necessary measure for securing one's peace of mind in the ritual's aftermath.

Similarly to in the Rite of Descent, if the magician fails to make contact, the banishing candle should be lit, the mantra vibrated, and the experience concluded with "Thus do I shut the Black Gate!" followed by such closing elements as seem appropriate given the circumstances. Conversely, in the unlikely event that the entity refuses to leave even after more than one set of banishing vibrations, it is best to conduct oneself as if it has left, concluding the rite and leaving the banishing candle to burn for as long afterward as feels necessary. Ignoring the entity in this way may seem dangerous but actually tends to conclude the situation more expediently than if the magician becomes fearful or agitated. A further recommended measure would be to spend the next few evenings performing no occult practices other than Lunar Purification breathing until such time as things feel normal again.

Revelations of the Nekalah

What follows is an account of the author's personal gnosis of the Nekalah, as attained via the methods described above. Said gnosis is not intended as a comprehensive last word on these entities. The aim is instead to offer more insight into the Nekalah than O9A texts have previously, so as to provide a more substantial starting point for those interested in working with them. Some of this content echoes online sources, such as the works of Hagur and V. K. Jehannum, but the author of the current work has included nothing that is not in accord with her own experiences of the Dark Gods.

Sigils for most of the Nekalah have been adapted from O9A works such as *Naos, Caelethi,* and *The Grimoire of Baphomet*. In a number of cases, the Eighth Key's version of these sigils differs from O9A's in small details, in accord with the author's personal gnosis and aesthetic sensibilities, but the sigils are still readily identifiable as those of the Dark Gods in question. Additionally, there are two Nekalah, Gaubni and Budsturga, for whom we provide original sigils. These were devised through a combination of analyzing the visual logic of other O9A sigils and asking the advice of Nekalah that Gaubni and Budsturga are closely associated with, namely Nythra and Nemicu. As far as the author knows, the Gaubni and Budsturga sigils presented below have not appeared previously in other occult works.

The Dark Gods recognized by Tenebrous Satanism consist of eighteen distinct entities, divisible into two groups of nine. The first group, led by Noctulius, tends to view human potential optimistically and to deal forthrightly with the magicians who approach them. The second group, led by Shaitan, is more cynical and pessimistic toward humanity and must be dealt with more warily, as their agendas may or may not actually have the magician's best interests in mind. Both factions contain beings that are powerful, unpredictable, frightful to behold, capable of manifesting at any time, and eager to work with a willing Satanist. Which faction a Nekalah belongs to is the first item listed under each entity's "Attributes."

Along with faction membership, we have also included the role that each entity plays within its faction. These roles may be thought of analogously to the different pieces in chess, each of which moves and contributes to its faction's success in a distinctive way.[68] Entities belonging to opposite factions who share the same role will thus have certain parallels in common with one another. The nine roles are:

1. *Matrix:* embodies the inchoate potentiality of the Void, whether in the form of a fruitful womb or a barren one.

2. *Ostium:* a psychopomp and dweller in liminal spaces, archetypically envisioned as a wandering stranger.

3. *Gladius:* the sword of the gods, whether in the form of warrior or tactician.

4. *Cicatrix:* a scarred yet proud survivor possessed of great endurance and resiliency.

5. *Lamia:* enchantress and dark feminine ideal; mate and confidante of the leader of the faction.

6. *Regnum:* an enthroned matriarch who presides over a flourishing realm, fiercely protecting her children.

7. *Sidera:* a wise sage who offers insight and inspiration.

8. *Dux:* leader of the faction and dark masculine ideal.

9. *Vorago:* embodies the ultimacy of the Abyss and the fundamental driving power behind the faction as a whole.

As a general rule, the magician's affinity with the Noctulian Nekalah will be heightened during the waxing phases of the moon and with the Shaitanic Nekalah during the waning phases. The moon phase information provided with each Nekalah is therefore a simple binary (waxing/waning), indicating which half of the lunar month is more ideal for contact. This in no way constrains a competent magician from attempting communion during the other half of the month, but novices may find that a favorable moon phase eases their efforts.

Astrological information for each Nekalah is provided in the form of a primary planetary association and a secondary one.[69] This is followed by the classical element most predominant in the entity's nature, the mode of said element (cardinal, fixed, mutable) and the sign of the zodiac associated with that particular element-mode combination. Those who subscribe to belief in literal astrological influences may find that the effectiveness with which they can contact an entity and commune constructively with it may vary according to such factors, e.g., having more success when the primary and secondary planet are both in the appropriate constellation of the zodiac. In the author's experience, however, this kind of thing makes little difference to either the Rite of Descent or the Rite of the Threshold, whereas the sun being below the horizon and the moon being in an appropriate phase are far more decisive celestial factors in successful communion. Such information is therefore included primarily to provide an esoteric sketch of the entity's temperament — especially in light of the Nekalah being unfamiliar outside of O9A circles — and only secondarily as something to consider for those who may feel more strongly about the need for the stars to be right than the author does.

Directional information refers to which point of the compass the entity will seem to come from when it manifests. This direction should be used as the default when determining where to face during the communion proper and where to position the target for the Rite of the Threshold. Some magicians' experiences may turn out vary from the author's in this regard, however, so if experimentation suggests that for you, the entity comes from a different direction, it is best to trust your own intuition and adapt the details of your own communion workings accordingly.

Runic, mineral, and general attributions follow the directional attribution. For most Nekalah, there will be one runic attribution, but entities that go by two names will have two. The idea with these is that the divinatory vision associated with that rune has some relevance to that particular entity — a relevance that the magician should seek to decode for themselves. In some cases, the vision may illustrate something that this Nekalah wishes to see actualized among human beings, i.e., an aeonic goal of theirs; in other cases, it may highlight something they wish to see overcome, or some aspect of their inner nature that they want us to reflect upon. (A complete listing of the relationships between the runes/visions and O9A concepts — both Nekalah and otherwise — appears in Appendix II.) Mineral attributions indicate stones whose qualities are evocative of each entity's energy, and which may therefore be charged in ritual to connect the magician with the entity, used as contemplative objects in meditation in the days prior to a communion attempt, or simply serve as aesthetically-appropriate altar decorations. The communion rites do not require such props, but for those who desire them, we have attempted to offer suggestions that are reasonably available and inexpensive.[70] Finally, the general attributions are in the spirit of pagan pantheons and demonic grimoires alike, indicating broad concepts and themes over which the entity presides. All attribution information for each entity is summarized in Appendix II.

"Manifestation" refers to how the Nekalah presents itself to the magician's inner eye during the Rite of Descent. If there is anything unusually striking about how the entity appears in the Shadow, this too will be noted. For many of the Dark Gods, though, the Shadow form is too inchoate for much to be put into words, and it is therefore their descent form that the description will focus on.

Many Nekalah's manifestations entail unsettling phenomena pertaining to "focal point." This concept is best understood by reflecting upon how, when one speaks to another human being, there are both intuitive and social considerations that dictate where one's gaze should fall. The attendant issue experienced with certain Nekalah is the experience of strange and disturbing sensations regarding which part of the entity is looking back at one. For example, one may see a human form, yet get the distinct impression that this is actually a puppet or shell which the entity is ventriloquizing while the true seat of its consciousness resides elsewhere. Since many people find such phenomena alarming on a visceral level, the author's hope is that if magicians are forewarned to anticipate uncanny effects of this kind, it may become easier to accept the entities for what they are as the first step of forging a constructive relationship.

"Demeanor" indicates what a magician is most likely to notice as part of a first impression of this particular Nekalah's personality. This is less likely to vary between encounters with different magicians than the entity's appearance. It is therefore a more reliable indicator that any supposed contact is bona fide. It is rare for a communion attempt to call up a different spirit than the one intended, however, given the distinctive language and methods used to commune with the Nekalah.

"Narrative" offers key elements of the "personal story" of the entity. When speaking to causal beings who make sense of existence through storytelling (as human beings do), what account do the Nekalah give of themselves, and what do they reveal of their motives and values thereby? To aid in human understanding, such accounts sometimes refer to the deities of more familiar mythologies, with the Nekalah then comparing themselves to such entities or even claiming to be identical to or derived from them in some instances. Such claims should not be taken as indicating the literal truth of the mythologies in question. Nor should they be taken as a straightforward claim that a particular Nekalah really is identical with some other deity. The question of who is the same deity as which other deity brings complexities that distract from experiencing the entity in and of itself. It is therefore better to treat the Nekalah as individuals whom one must get to know, just as with human beings, rather than acting as if one is on a quest for verifiable facts about them.

On a related note, the entities are not above tailoring certain details of their biographies differently when speaking to different magicians. They may even give a different account of themselves to the same magician on different occasions as the magician's own understanding broadens or perspective shifts. Their goal is to have their audience understand them in the manner they desire, not to present an account of objective truth. What we provide is therefore a high-level composite of what the entities have revealed to the author on various occasions, illustrative of each entity's general self-concept.

"Expertise" is meant to give an idea of what the entity can best assist the magician with. This is by no means an extensive listing but should at least give the witch a sense of who can help with what and the sorcerer an idea of who may be fruitful to strike a pact with. Such information is provided with the expectation that mature Satanists will reflect carefully upon everything the Seventh Key stated about the potential consequences of occult recklessness before resorting to anything hazardous to themselves or others. *Any problem an unwise magician can create through an ill-advised working can be aggravated many times over by including an acausal being in the matter.* The onus is therefore on the individual magician to proceed in a responsible fashion. One ought to also keep in mind that each Nekalah has its own agenda for exerting its powers over the causal realm — and for some, manipulating dangerous idiots into destroying themselves may be part of that agenda.

Finally, it is worth speaking to what the reader will not find here, namely information on what offerings each Nekalah prefers. Such details have been omitted because it is better for the interested magician to determine this for themselves through their own experiences of the entities. It should also be noted that most of the time, Nekalah are willing to bargain if their preferred offering is something that, for practical or ethical reasons, the magician is unwilling to provide. *The magician should always understand themselves as free to question or reject the propositions of any entity they commune with.* This point applies not only to the making of offerings to the Nekalah, but to all matters that spirit and magician may contend with one another over.

The sigil of the Nekalah as a collective is shown below, as well as an overview of the pantheon's two factions. The information that follows is provided in alphabetical order.

Nine Keys of Abyssal Darkness

Role	Noctulian faction	Shaitanic faction
Matrix	Athushir-Kthunae	Mactoron-Falcifer
Ostium	Budsturga	Aosoth
Gladius	Velpecula	Abatu
Cicatrix	Sauroctonos	Shugara
Lamia	Darkat-Lidagon	Baphomet
Regnum	Davcina	Azanigin
Sidera	Nemicu	Gaubni
Dux	Noctulius	Shaitan
Vorago	Atazoth	Nythra

Abatu

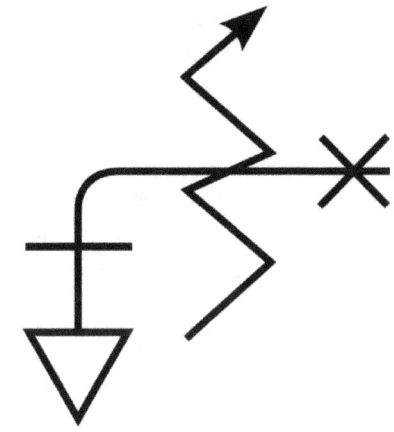

Attributes

- Shaitanic faction: Gladius
- Waning Moon
- Mars, Mercury
- Cardinal fire (Aries)
- South
- Pyrash
- Carnelian
- Primal aggression and destructive rage

Manifestation

Abatu has a propensity to appear in markedly inorganic shapes. For example, he may present himself as a mechanical-looking being in the shape of a multi-armed humanoid, heavily armored, wearing a metal mask that renders his face entirely blank. Or he may appear as a large tetrahedral pyramid made of glowing red crystal. If the humanoid form comes holding a crystalline object or appears in the vicinity of such an object, the object typically houses the focal point of the entity's consciousness, reinforcing one's impression of him as robotic or cybernetic. Both his voice and movements tend to remind one of a machine or some similar manner of artificial life-form.

Demeanor

The topic of enemies and how to overcome them preoccupies Abatu constantly. Nonetheless, when speaking of such things, he expresses his hatred in a strikingly rational, calculating manner.

Narrative

While there exist many battle gods of Apollonian-dominated cultures that Abatu could be compared to — the Greek Ares and Babylonian Nergal come especially to mind — his inhuman aloofness and malice set him apart from all such beings. He comes across rather as a weapon that was constructed by such a god in some distant aeon, only for the weapon's hunger for strife to spur it into developing a will of its own.

Abatu tends to parse all human affairs in terms of large-scale conflict between groups dominated by different patterns (e.g., Apollonian, Magian, and Faustian) more readily and insistently than many of the other Nekalah. Moreover, any form of destruction that unravels the current order and thereby paves the way to a more Faustian future is pleasing to him. One may therefore speculate that too-simplistic human interpretation of his aeonic goals may be a partial driver of some of the controversial political extremism widely associated with O9A.

Expertise

- Offers pragmatic advice regarding the means by which the magician may perpetuate acts of disruption or revenge.

- Eager to support dedicated Faustians in their infiltration and subversion of groups dominated by Magian dogmatism. This may include emboldening those of flagging spirit, providing advance warning that enables preparation for danger, or intervening to steer a conflict in the magician's favor.

- Will happily assist with the destruction of enemies, but beware, lest he wreak collateral damage that serves his own agenda at the magician's expense. A very carefully worded Statement of Intent is strongly recommended when working baneful magick with this entity.

Aosoth

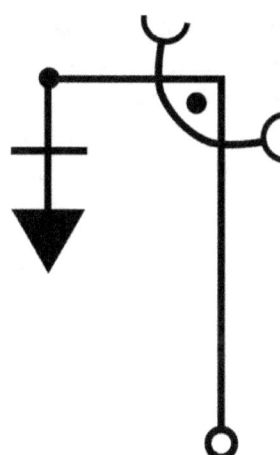

Attributes

- Shaitanic faction: Ostium
- Waning Moon
- Mars, Venus
- Mutable air (Gemini)
- Northeast
- Shaol
- Obsidian (preferably with a sharp edge)
- Threshold-crossing and exposure to danger

Manifestation

Aosoth may appear as a carrion bird, such as a crow or vulture, or a woman with attributes of such creatures: talons, wings, black clothing trimmed with feathers, etc. If the woman has a raven or vulture on her shoulder, the bird may act as the focal point of the entity's consciousness. As a woman, she may possess a harsh, weathered beauty, or she may appear as a hag or even a corpse. She may also occasionally adopt a more androgynous form. In all cases, though, typically one half of her face will be fair and the other half withered. Her hair will be similarly divided between a dark part and a pale part.

Demeanor

Despite the cold, reserved front that she gives off, she is forthright with words of wisdom or warning to those bold enough to approach her. The inexperienced magician may have to put up with being terrorized by her for awhile before she becomes willing to engage more constructively.

Narrative

A wanderer at home nowhere, Aosoth is drawn to scenes of ruin and resilience in the aftermath of struggle, whether in the context of war, crime, or disaster. She is captivated equally by the courage and resourcefulness that lead to narrow escape and by the decisive instant that flesh fails and spirit finds itself hurled over death's threshold. Morbid fascinations of this sort are likely what motivated her to delve more deeply into the Abyss than her former existence as a Tellurian allowed for. One may thus think of her as a Sinistral version of the Norse Hel, Celtic Morrigan, and other similar goddesses associated with crows, battles, and life's termination.

Unsurprisingly given the nature of the death-fixation that attracted her to the Abyss to begin with, Aosoth's strongest bond among the Nekalah is with Nythra.

Expertise

- Grants prescience, willpower, and resilience to the magician, enabling the survival of situations of acute physical danger.

- Can assist the dying with transition into a new life, including the possibility of translation into a Sinistral. She may purposely cast those she deems unworthy into oblivion during this process, however, so the magician should be careful to establish a relationship of mutual respect prior to enlisting her help with such matters.

- Both willing and able to boost a magician's ability to perceive and engage with the acausal realm on a multitude of fronts (e.g., divination ability, general psychic perception, etc.), but she expects a willingness to endure fear and to make sacrifices from those whom she assists.

Atazoth

Attributes

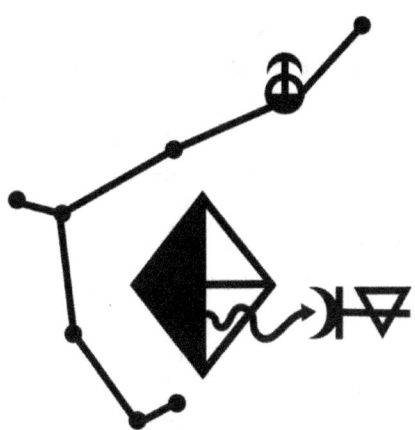

- Noctulian faction: Vorago
- Waxing Moon
- Saturn, Jupiter
- Cardinal Air (Libra)
- North
- Vhow
- Labradorite
- Omniscience and supreme mastery

Manifestation

Atazoth appears as a man whose vigorous frame belies his extremely advanced age, draped in a complex profusion of ragged, motley garments and crowned as an emperor. His face may be either partially or entirely hidden as by a mask or veil, seemingly to conceal a hideous deformity. Sometimes, he appears standing in front of an enormous portal through which can be glimpsed an indistinct mass of alien eyes, maws, and feelers seething behind him. When this portal is present, the location of the entity's focal point is liable to seem chaotically unstable and treating the human figure as if it were the seat of his consciousness is recommended as less unsettling than trying to engage with the abomination behind him.[71]

Demeanor

He speaks far more cogently and rationally than one would expect from the look of him and possesses a dry, wry sense of humor that only rarely makes itself known.

Narrative

Atazoth is one of the four Nekalah through whom the Abyssal Void itself can be glimpsed in a particularly direct and profound way.

He identifies himself with Darkness' ever growing and evolving pool of collective experience, accumulated from the countless enfleshed lives that spirit has participated in, making him "the mind of the Abyssal Void." Outwardly, he may seem impassive, since he has literally seen everything from the very beginning and is therefore surprised by nothing, but inwardly, he schemes ceaselessly toward the realization of countless future possibilities as yet unmanifest — even at the same time as he will remain utterly untroubled by whatever ultimately does happen. Although his name and manifestation both echo H. P. Lovecraft's Azathoth in obvious ways, the two should not be conflated too hastily, as Atazoth's human form is in many ways more evocative of Robert W. Chambers' infamous King in Yellow. The entity also usually conducts himself more like the ancient, sinister monarch of an alien realm than like a blind idiot god of pure chaos.

Expertise

- Offers insight into what may come to pass in the future, highlighting possibilities that a human mind would never anticipate on its own.

- In persons who are positively receptive to his influence, he can replace denial of reality and resentment of tribulations with newfound equanimity and adaptability.

- Has vast power to alter probabilities favorably for the magician or unfavorably for the magician's foes, but he is generally unwilling to lift his hand over trivial matters.

Athushir-Kthunae

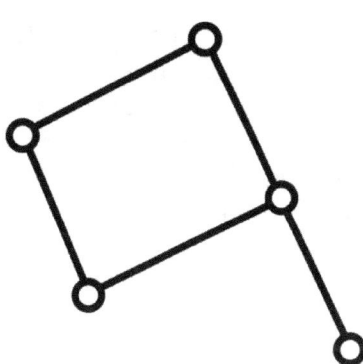

Attributes

- Noctulian faction: Matrix
- Waxing Moon
- Jupiter, Saturn
- Fixed fire (Leo)
- North
- Zhalg, Hvelgit
- Sardonyx
- Raw desire and affirmation of existence in the flesh

Manifestation

When taking a human shape, Athushir appears as a tall, proud figure with long, wild hair, clad in floor-length crimson robes, wearing a profusion of carved ornaments made from wood and bone, and often carrying a staff or spear. This figure may at first glance seem more fully human than some of the other Nekalah's forms, but a careful look reveals such features as a partially concealed horn or horns, claws on one hand, fiery eyes, or wings folded under a cloak. The gender of the figure tends to reflect the magician's own gender. Alternately, Athushir may also appear in the form of a red dragon, phoenix, winged serpent, or other primal beast, its entire body burning with primordial fire, in which case its gender will be indistinct.

Demeanor

Noble yet entirely without pretenses. Headstrong and dauntless, she (as per how the author perceives the entity) speaks forthrightly about the Will of the Fire, destroying delusion and inertia alike.

Narrative

One among the four Nekalah who is on particularly intimate terms with the Abyssal Void of Darkness itself, Athushir identifies with spirit as that which demands ever more, choosing to embrace the flesh again and again in active affirmation, as eager for its tribulations as for its pleasures. This explains the entity's close association with the O9A term "Kthunae," whose approximate meaning is "recall," i.e., "return once again to the world." As "the heart of the Abyssal Void," Athushir's empathy for all living beings, no matter how primitive or alien their forms, is capacious.

The author perceives a primal demonic femininity in Athushir, reminiscent especially of the Mesopotamian dragon-goddess Tiamat. As such, she comes across as the sort of mother who favors tough love over coddling, desirous that all of her children should grow up strong and resilient. Such impressions may be less apparent to those who perceive Athushir as Lord of the Earth rather than Lady, however.

Expertise

- Grants visions of the primeval days of the universe and of the diverse and bizarre forms life has taken throughout time so as to instill insight and a broadened sense of empathy in the magician.

- In the case of a listless person who suffers from lack of zeal, Athushir can advise as to whether it is indulgence or challenge that they need and support new pursuits aimed at driving positive change.

- Aids in overcoming conditions that hinder aeonic endeavors, such as material lack, unreceptive audiences, or obstructed inspiration.

Azanigin

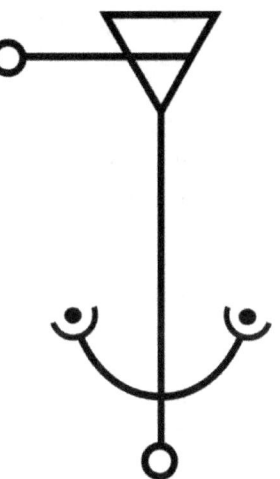

Attributes

- Shaitanic faction: Regnum
- Waning Moon
- Jupiter, Mars
- Cardinal earth (Capricorn)
- West
- Eyahin
- Hematite
- Irresistible compulsions of the instincts

Manifestation

Azanigin typically takes the form of a hulking female monster, resembling a deer or moose in the upper part of the face and a human woman in the lower part, her body grotesquely bloated with pregnancy and spindly limbs arranged erratically, causing her to move with an unnatural lurching motion. Her overall form is solid yet shadowy with an unstable shape that alters itself randomly if much time is spent in her presence. She resists taking human or otherwise pleasant forms with considerably more obstinacy than other Nekalah.

Demeanor

She respects those who stand their ground in the face of being menaced but has no use or patience whatsoever for timidity, indecisiveness, or evasion. Those unable to cope bravely with an entity intentionally trying to frighten them should not contact this entity.

Narrative

As "mother of demons," Azanigin embodies the life-force mired in the slime and filth of material existence, hell-bent on survival and reproduction with total bloody-mindedness, despite all that is hideous and degrading in physicality. An extreme, unyielding affirmation of nature emerges thereby, situating her as an uglier and more challenging manifestation of the same life energies associated with Athushir and Baphomet. Two entities that Azanigin may thus be particularly likened to are the Zoroastrian demoness Az, associated with hunger, avarice, and all forms of cupidity, and Lovecraft's Shub-Niggurath, the grotesque "goat with a thousand young."

Expertise

- Can awaken the mind and body of the magician, or of a target designated by the magician, to perversions of thought and desire that formerly seemed foreign to that individual. This can be used constructively to overcome hang-ups, as well as destructively to complicate the lives of repressed and overly strait-laced individuals.

- Capable of creating astral familiars — i.e., an acausal minion loyal to the magician — using a measure of sexual energy which the magician must provide.[72]

- Curses that proceed from her tend to take the form of long strings of interconnected misfortunes, culminating in the target being all but devoured by chaos. Such curses are best directed only at enemies whom one has completely distanced oneself and any loved ones from, lest havoc otherwise spill over into one's own life as well.

Baphomet

Attributes

- Shaitanic faction: Lamia
- Waning Moon
- Moon, Jupiter
- Mutable earth (Virgo)
- West
- Kehan
- Jasper (preferably heliotrope)
- Spilling of blood in sacrifice, childbirth, battle, hunting, etc.

Manifestation

The Baphomet of O9A appears as a dark-haired woman, crowned with the curled horns of a ram or goat, clad in a simple gown and a cloak made of animal skin, carrying a staff in one hand and a torch in the other. Her skirt is stained with a large amount of blood, either menstrual in origin or the blood of something — or someone — that she has killed and consumed. She is sometimes seen casually handling bloody limbs, severed human heads, or other similar objects and may test the magician's resolve through the morbid display of such items.

Demeanor

Baphomet's tone and behavior are usually more welcoming and benevolent than her proximity to gore might suggest, but with an undertone of ferocity. She speaks very bluntly, disregarding social graces.

Narrative

O9A's female Sinistral who goes by the title of Baphomet is a different entity than the Tellurian whom occultists of other currents address by the same title and who is more typically perceived as either ambivalently gendered or male. Like several of the other Nekalah, though, O9A's Baphomet seems to have been a Tellurian prior to her translation into a Sinistral. Originally a spirit associated with the earth as a whole, she remains even now deeply invested in our specific planet's web of life and in the ongoing evolution of all creatures that participate in it. With this affinity comes recognition of how, insofar as all living beings must consume other lives in order to perpetuate themselves, nature as a whole is perpetually steeped in blood.[73] As such, Baphomet can be thought of as a darker version of such goddesses of the hunt as the Greek Artemis or Roman Diana.

Expertise

- To those who strive earnestly to increase their physical capacities, she teaches methods by which one's own vigor may be enhanced at the expense of one's foes.

- Potent in augmenting or blighting fertility, and in causing fortune to flourish or wither as if it were a living thing. The magician should be aware, however, that she has a high likelihood of demanding literal payment in blood.

- Possessed of expansive knowledge of the Tellurian spirits who participate in the earth's web of life, she can advise as to which may have something to offer the magician and how these may be contacted. Magicians coming to Tenebrous Satanism from a Wiccan or Neopagan background may find that communion with her comes more easily and feels more "familiar" than with other Nekalah.

Budsturga

Attributes

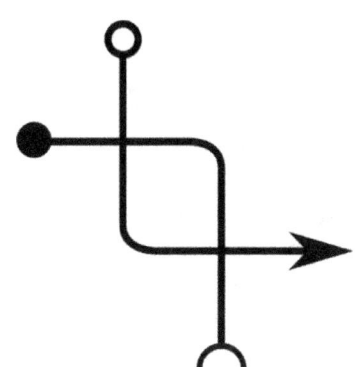

- Noctulian faction: Ostium
- Waxing Moon
- Mercury, Moon
- Mutable water (Pisces)
- East
- Xhin
- Blue chalcedony
- Enlightened madness, liminal spaces and altered states

Manifestation

Budsturga may appear as a hybrid of woman and cobra, woman and eel, or other such cold-blooded animal combinations. She may appear humanoid from the waist up or possess a human face only, with this feminine element possessed of an exotic beauty. On other occasions, she may appear as faceless or headless. The human and animal bodies alike are blue in color, with hair and fins/wings (which are only occasionally present) a paler shade. She comes accompanied by a large number of indistinct, vaguely insectoid flying creatures of various sizes and sometimes manifests wholly in this fragmented form. In such instances, the entity's focal point will seem to be split evenly between all creatures in the swarm, rendering this collective extremely disorienting to hold communion with.

Demeanor

Her unified manifestation wears a serene expression, but the more divided she appears, the more she will speak in a disjointed manner suggestive of a disordered mind.

Narrative

In her former incarnation, in a world and time far distant from our own, Budsturga was an advanced practitioner of a spiritual discipline aimed at extinction, not unlike those typical of Hinduism or Buddhism today. However, between naivety, hubris, and ill-conceived experiment, she found herself at the moment of death unable to contend with the Abyss, with the result that she was partially destroyed and partially translated into a Sinistral, albeit one with an extremely fragmented consciousness. She is thus like Sauroctonos and Shugara in having wound up a member of a pantheon that she had not intentionally set out to join.

Since Budsturga's very presence can cause both incarnate and discarnate beings to suffer acute and unpleasant alterations in consciousness, she leads the existence of a solitary Sinistral for the most part. Her heart remains benevolent, though, and it saddens her that humans so readily perceive that which is alien as evil and dangerous.

Expertise

- Possesses valuable insight into dream control, astral projection, and similar arts, but her methods of tutoring can be bizarre and unpleasant for the magician to experience.

- Is able to ward places and objects so as to prevent them being found or discourage entry, either by acting directly or by revealing effective occult methods to the magician.

- Can immobilize those she is sent to attack with confusion and curse them into perpetuating contradictory, self-defeating behavior patterns.

Darkat-Lidagon

Attributes

- Noctulian faction: Lamia
- Waxing Moon
- Venus, Moon
- Mutable water (Pisces)
- South
- Fhell, Tehir
- Garnet[74]
- Sexual pleasure and the gratification of the senses

Manifestation

Darkat presents herself as an attractive woman with the horns, wings, or talons of a dragon. She often appears mostly nude, save for a black crown, a red cloak, and ornaments of gold and jewels which cover very little of her body. Her hair may be black, red, violet, or a mixture, but is always long and flowing. If addressed as Lidagon, she tends to adopt a more warlike appearance, bearing a sword and riding a dragon, chimera, or sea monster. Alternately, she may appear in a non-human form as a jeweled snake or scorpion.

Demeanor

Sultry and sensual but also insightful, sympathetic, and cunning. She may raise the topic of a magician's desire before the magician has a chance to state it, adopting a teasing tone or otherwise behaving in a provocative manner aimed at testing the magician's resolve.

Narrative

Some Nekalah identify themselves with what amounts to a personal name and others by what amounts to a title. In the current case, the entity accepts both forms of address, Darkat being the personal name and Lidagon the title. Much about the way she carries herself is suggestive of ancient Mesopotamian goddesses of love and war, such as Inanna, Astarte, etc.,[75] but as Darkat, she bears an especially strong resemblance to the well-known demoness Lilith, and as Lidagon, to the Thelemic entity known as Babalon. In both forms, she is first and foremost an appreciator — one might even say a connoisseur — of all forms of sensual experience, sexual and otherwise, that contribute to the enjoyment of earthly life. As Darkat, she concerns herself primarily with the quest for personal gratification, and as Lidagon, with the subversion and destruction of social-political restrictions placed upon desire's fulfillment. In all instances, though, her aeonic aspiration is the establishment of a healthy ethos of pleasure among all conscious beings.

Expertise

- As Darkat, she can aid in the satisfaction of unrealized sexual desires, either by offering advice, creating opportunities, or facilitating sexual liaisons with acausal beings.

- As Lidagon, she may be called to set in motion longer-term shifts in openness to sensuality, either among individuals or larger groups of people, or to sabotage and thwart those who seek to place unjustifiable limits upon physical enjoyment.

- Can be persuaded to destroy weak-willed individuals by inciting them into various forms of overindulgence, as she prizes strength of will and laughs openly at those who suffer because they refuse to cultivate it.

Davcina

Attributes

- Noctulian faction: Regnum
- Waxing Moon
- Jupiter, Venus
- Cardinal fire (Aries)
- South
- Dolath
- Sodalite (preferably lapis lazuli)
- Harmonious coexistence of nature and culture

Manifestation

Davcina appears as an empress in the prime of life, richly dressed in floor-length garments of purple, blue, and green, bearing simple ornaments of authority but shunning the gaudiness of excessive luxury. The magician may catch a glimpse of something strange in her eyes or a faint aura of Darkness about her, but she is otherwise unusual among the Nekalah in appearing fully human. When manifesting in the Shadow, however, she is sometimes perceived as a dense mass of root-like tendrils which may draw closer to the magician than is comfortable, triggering a sensation of being stifled. This is an expression of her affection and willingness to connect, though, so the magician should try not to be alarmed by it.

Demeanor

Speaks with calm authority and a warm undertone of heartfelt concern for the world's well-being. She tends to be one of the most consistently benevolent of the Nekalah, so long as the magician has not crossed her in some way.

Narrative

Davcina ties herself to the mythology of Damkina, mother of the storm-warrior god Marduk, slayer of dragons and bringer of order. Given how gods of that sort have historically aligned themselves with the right-hand-path — Yahweh being the most prominent example of a deity who was originally of this archetype — the presence of the mother of such a god in a left-hand-path pantheon is a striking development. It seems Davcina sought translation into a Sinistral in direct opposition to her son's translation into a Celestial and the parallel rise of Dogmagianism among his devotees. Despite that translation, however, she still outwardly behaves much like a Tellurian, identifying herself with the establishment of a harmonious order in which natural abundance and honorable relations in society reflect one another, similarly to the Hindu goddess Lakshmi. Her aeonic ideal is for the human world to experience a resurgence of the best features of ancient Apollonian-dominated societies but tempered now with Faustian dynamism.

Expertise

- Has the power to sway matters of earthly prosperity in the magician's favor, but she is unwilling to assist those who behave arrogantly or dishonorably. Attempting to deceive her as to one's intentions is ill-advised and liable to end badly for the magician.

- Offers advice and may directly assist with situations in which the magician must secure the cooperation of others in order to achieve a constructive goal.

- Presides over an acausal sanctuary, wherein Sinister-Path-walkers may receive succor and refreshment in between their earthly incarnations.

Gaubni

Attributes

- Shaitanic faction: Sidera
- Waning Moon
- Venus, Mercury
- Fixed water (Scorpio)
- Southwest
- Tharu
- Fossil (preferably a remnant of an animal)[76]
- Esoteric knowledge and cultivation of expertise in magick

Manifestation

Gaubni's least-horrifying form is that of a scholarly man, clad either in the manner of the ancient world or in a post-apocalyptic style, whose garments turn out, upon close inspection, to have been constructed entirely from assorted kinds of meat and other decaying matter. It is not unusual, however, for him to appear instead as a hulking, bloated, amphibious monster that is covered in tumors, or whose form appears constructed from the haphazard assembly of the rotting carcasses of various unidentifiable alien creatures. The warning about Gaubni in O9A's text *Naos* of "revulsive smell and appearance" should not be taken lightly.

Demeanor

Gaubni expresses himself with a lucidity that belies his appearance and may even strike an avuncular tone when advising those he is fond of, but one senses a constant undertone of warning not to provoke his wrath.

Narrative

In a former incarnation as a member of an advanced but now-extinct species, Gaubni became an adept sorcerer devoted to Nythra.

The terms of the pact between them extended over many lifetimes, ultimately climaxing with his translation into a Sinistral. Having long fixed a scientist's fascination upon the crossing-over point where organic and inorganic transform into one another, he is unaffected by the morbid or otherwise grotesque sights which disgust others. Associated with this absence of revulsion are sexual proclivities of Gaubni's that most humans will find offensive, but he keeps such matters to himself unless prompted.

Gaubni can be an effective and surprisingly patient teacher of esoteric arts. He reacts harshly, however, toward those who approach such matters with a careless or presumptuous attitude. His human form brings to mind the specifically "black pharaoh" incarnation of Lovecraft's Nyarlathotep at times, but this is likely a side-effect of his close association with Nythra. As far as his role and interests go, it would not be inappropriate to compare him to such legendary tutors as Hermes Trismegistus.

Expertise

- Offers detailed advice on refining methods of meditation and ritual, so as to tailor them to a magician's personal strengths and weaknesses.

- Can blight a physical location or food or drink that are to be consumed, inflicting illness, descent into discord, or other unpleasant effects.

- Teaches powerful but hazardous arts of making and commanding acausal minions, using either the magician's own energy or the cast-off energy of deceased creatures.

Mactoron-Falcifer

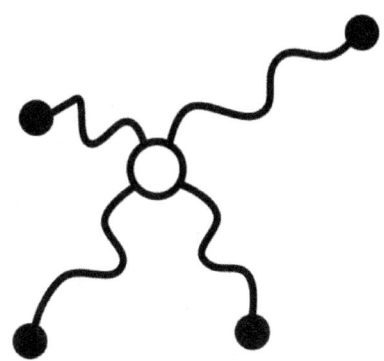

Attributes

- Shaitanic faction: Matrix
- Waning Moon
- Venus, Saturn
- Fixed air (Aquarius)
- West
- Grahl, Ishut
- Fluorite
- Purification and transcendence

Manifestation

Mactoron appears as a young maiden of albino complexion, with empty sockets in place of eyes. As she floats in the air, the long train of her black gown and veil trail down around her, her garments transitioning into tendrils of thick shadow where they spread out upon the ground. She radiates power far out of proportion to her waifish appearance, however. Alternately, when addressed as Falcifer, she may appear in a form resembling Nythra's (a vortex-like structure accompanied by a hooded figure with obscured face), except draped all in white instead of in black, with dim stars visible in the faceless, dark folds of her hood. In either form, it is not unusual for her to come bearing either a scythe or a long pole suitable for steering a small watercraft, in imitation of other familiar figures of death.

Demeanor

Devoid of hostility yet unsettling to be confronted by. She will not speak before the magician does and will extend long silences indefinitely.

Narrative

Mactoron is one of four Nekalah through whom one can readily glimpse the Abyssal Void of Darkness itself. She identifies with the Void in its primal, undifferentiated state: a state irreparably lost as of descent into the flesh, yet nonetheless chased, like a mirage in the desert, by those weary of life's miseries. As such, she constitutes "the great *no* of the Abyssal Void." She may be thought of as a personification of such Qabalistic concepts as Ain Soph or Tzimzum — i.e., that which came before the beginning — and in her case, that which preferred that initial state of nothingness.

Mactoron possesses an extensive, empathetic grasp of what motivates the life-denying doctrines of Dogmagians and Celestials, but refuses to embrace these herself, solely because she has foreseen their ultimate futility. Her association with the title "Falcifer," meaning "scythe-bearer," reflects both the Saturnine aura of melancholy and restriction that hangs about her and her aeonic desire to see life hurried toward its omega point — her hope being that the quietude of the Void might resume once all other possibilities have been exhausted.

Expertise

- Cleanses and purifies very thoroughly, assisting with the elimination of mental and emotional shackles.

- Can help the magician internalize the mindset of Magian dogmatists for the purposes of being able to operate among them to advance the Sinister Dialectic.

- Useful to call upon in circumstances in which one wishes to thwart or impede someone but the magician feels no malice toward this individual and would prefer to harm them as little as possible.

Nemicu

Attributes

- Noctulian faction: Sidera
- Waxing Moon
- Mercury, Jupiter
- Fixed air (Aquarius)
- East
- Wajhel
- Aquamarine
- Wisdom and mental-emotional healing

Manifestation

Nemicu presents himself as a graceful, androgynous man with a thin black streak in his long blond hair, wearing blue robes trimmed with gold. The faint glow around his head and the four feathered wings at his back suggest a Celestial of lofty station, but the horns upon his brow and the ruby-like quality of his eyes evoke the infernal. He sometimes carries an object in his hands, such as an angel's trumpet or a jewel. When encountered in visions, he tends to appear in the same setting consistently, hovering over the ocean or standing atop a spire that emerges from its waters.

Demeanor

He may abruptly resort to words or tactics that are mysterious, frightening, or deceptive, but his wisdom and constructive intent will become evident soon afterward. The magician who deals with him should therefore be patient and avoid jumping to premature conclusions about what exactly he is up to.

Narrative

Nemicu's account of himself uses the idiom of Islam. He claims that when Ibliss convinced Adam and Eve to eat of the Tree of

Knowledge, the Archangel Israfil (known as Raphael to Jews and Christians) suffered the briefest moment of doubt in Allah's plans and sympathy for what the Adversary had done. Mortified by this betrayal even though it lasted but an instant, Israfil immediately shed and attempted to destroy the part of himself that had reacted in such a way. That part survived the Abyss, however, and became Nemicu. One may thus think of Nemicu as a fallen angel, not unlike Noctulius.

The Celestial Raphael's association with healing and rescue appears to be manifest in Nemicu's relationships with some of his fellow Nekalah. In the cases of Budsturga and Sauroctonos, he assisted in their initial translation into Sinistrals, and both would have fared far worse in the Abyss were it not for his intervention. He also has a fondness for Shugara rooted in the degree of extreme suffering that she has had to overcome, but their relationship appears to be a complex one.

Expertise

- Can assist with the long-term healing of the mind and heart in circumstances that seem otherwise insurmountable.

- Facilitates clear communication and effective persuasion, both by offering advice to the magician on such matters and by intervening acausally on the magician's behalf.

- In the course of his extremely long existence, Nemicu has lived variously as all three kinds of acausal being: Tellurian, Celestial, and Sinistral. This breadth of experience enables him to offer unique perspectives on a wide variety of spiritual topics.

Noctulius

Attributes

- Noctulian faction: Dux
- Waxing Moon
- Moon, Venus
- Mutable air (Gemini)
- Northwest
- Byrk
- White howlite
- Leadership and diplomacy amid personal and social strife

Manifestation

Noctulius appears as a tall, lean, beautiful man with long black hair. He wears a circlet set with a pale stone and either a full-length silver robe or a long silver kilt that covers only his lower body. He may appear with an inscrutable pall of Darkness where his face should be, or he may wear a mask in the form of an attractive face whose lack of expression reveals it to be a facade. He sometimes holds a white snake in his hands, in which case the snake will serve as the focal point of his consciousness.

Demeanor

Well-spoken and wise, much in the manner of modern depictions of the Devil as a handsome and charming man. The way he presents himself is typically more reserved than outgoing, but he nonetheless exudes a passionate undercurrent of deep, abiding dedication to a far-reaching vision.

Narrative

Noctulius claims that he was formerly the second most powerful in a group of Celestials but went into exile after losing faith in the cause and character of their leader. He has come to hate that specific Celestial with a passion, and although he shows little emotion when speaking of the matter, is eager to see his ex-comrade destroyed by the Abyss one day. This does not mean that he is bereft of constructive goals, but there is little he conceives of that does not relate back to this cause of vengeance in some way, however distant and circuitous.

Noctulius' aeonic ideal is a universe in which Tellurians and Sinistrals predominate and Celestials are all but extinct, thanks to conscious beings willingly forsaking life-denying otherworldliness. He styles himself as the leader of the revolution that will make things thus. Between his taking of this role and the story of his past, he is obviously the Nekalah who most closely resembles Christianity's conception of Lucifer.

Expertise

- Possesses deep knowledge of Celestials, of how their influence impacts goings-on in the causal world, and of how best to oppose and counter such influences.

- Will happily assist the magician in destroying an open enemy of the Sinister Dialectic or in convincing or seducing a potential ally to the Sinister Path. He tends to favor subtle means and long timeframes, though, so those preferring more overt and immediate outcomes in such matters may be better off soliciting Shaitan instead.

- Can lead the magician through a rite in which one fully experiences and embraces one's darkest secret desires and attains mental and emotional liberation thereby.

Nythra

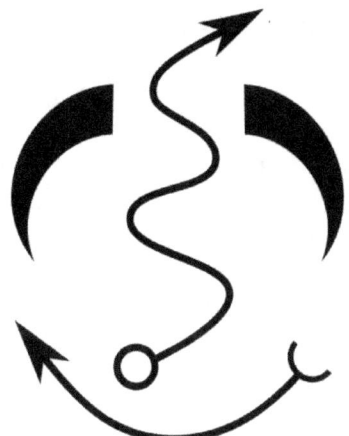

Attributes

- Shaitanic faction: Vorago
- Waning Moon
- Mars, Moon
- Cardinal water (Cancer)
- North
- Nithrul
- Smoky quartz
- Death, terror, poison, and vampirism

Manifestation

Nythra most frequently appears as a churning vortex from which numerous tendrils of Darkness extend.[77] But when taking a human form, the entity appears clad all in black, face shadowed by a hood, standing in front of an ominous portal of reality torn asunder and often holding a cluster of millipedes, a large centipede, or a stave twined with some kind of poisonous plant. This manifestation has a propensity to abruptly switch its focal point between the black hole, the hooded figure, and any crawly creatures present, to disturbing effect. The entity's gender tends to reflect what the magician finds sexually attractive, and though the face remains ever-concealed, the beholder gets the distinct impression that it must either be astonishingly beautiful or unspeakably terrible. The black cloak also conceals vast, diaphanous, locust-like wings, which the entity rarely unfurls.

Demeanor

In vortex form, Nythra is forbidding to approach and enjoys being feared. When in human shape, however, he (as per how the author perceives the entity) tends toward a creepy sort of flirtatiousness and often struggles to constrain gleeful mirth at matters he knows a human will not find amusing.

Narrative

Nythra is among the four Nekalah who overtly identify with the Abyssal Void of Darkness itself. Whereas Atazoth identifies with Darkness in an atemporal, cumulative sense, Mactoron with the Void of pre-existence, and Athushir with spirit's Adventurous existence-in-progress, Nythra identifies with the aftermath of existence: the horrors of the Abyss. An inconceivably ancient, primitive organism who has maintained continuity of consciousness through an incomprehensibly long string of Perilous lives and agonizing deaths, Nythra's primordial will combines pure affirmation and pure nihilism together into a depraved yet enlightened lunacy. He may thus be said to be "the great *yes* of the Abyssal Void." Between his propensity for both human and monstrous forms and the disturbing admixture of joy, malice, and general insanity he exudes, he cannot help reminding one of Lovecraft's Nyarlathotep.

Expertise

- Bridges the causal and acausal realms, assisting with dream control, astral projection, and acausal communion in general.

- Thinks baneful magick is "hilarious" and can be persuaded to visit all manner of horrors upon any target for any reason.

- He enjoys teaching sex magick, vampirism, and other such forms of energy manipulation, but is prone to assaulting his student in order to teach — or even just for "fun" — and will not respect boundaries unless they are vigorously enforced.

Sauroctonos

Attributes

- Noctulian faction: Cicatrix
- Waxing Moon
- Saturn, Mercury
- Fixed earth (Taurus)
- East
- Ywhaz
- Pyrite
- Physical well-being and artistic talent

Manifestation

Sauroctonos appears as a fresh-faced youth, just shy of manhood, clad in a black toga and carrying a lyre in one hand. The staff in his other hand is used as a crutch, for he walks with a limp. At a glance, he seems entirely human, but a closer look reveals horns nestled amid the curls of his hair. Sometimes he is accompanied by animals, such as a gray wolf, black swan, or white raven. When encountered in the Shadow, he takes a bizarrely geometric shape, suggestive of a series of rotating prisms whose edges are forever receding back into the gloom that surrounds him.

Demeanor

He tends to greet the magician with visible enthusiasm, as if he is overjoyed to have someone "normal" to interact with for a change. However, small hints of gloom and regret occasionally pierce his optimistic veneer.

Narrative

Sauroctonos (meaning "lizard-killer") is one of the titles of Apollo, the familiar Greco-Roman deity. Sauroctonos claims that in a past aeon, the Tellurian in question sent a part of himself forth to investigate something that troubled him on the threshold of the Void, only for that part to become lost to misadventure. Nemicu's intervention enabled him to be translated into a Sinistral, but since his fate is not one that he chose willingly or prepared for, he has retained many of his former Tellurian characteristics, albeit in a damaged or distorted form. One thus gets the impression that the other Nekalah may have chosen his form of address for him, with a hint of irony, as if to say, "So, tell us again, how did that attempt at slaying dragons in the Abyss go for you?"

Sauroctonos gets along with Nemicu, Budsturga, and Shugara, but largely avoids the others. He seems to dislike Abatu in particular.

Expertise

- Assists with the healing of the body and recovery from disease in otherwise insurmountable circumstances. This is accomplished via him fortifying the magician's energy with his own and may require allowing him to guide the magician through a visionary experience during the Rite of Descent.

- Offers advice on and assistance with the creation of amulets and talismans, i.e., objects enchanted so as to enhance abilities, alter the mood in their vicinity, etc.[78]

- Provides inspiration for artistic works and assists in the development of the skills by which one executes them, particularly in connection with music.

Shaitan

Attributes

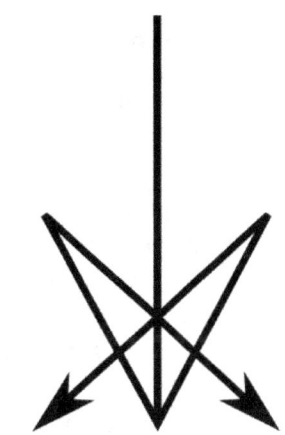

- Shaitanic faction: Dux
- Waning Moon
- Saturn, Mars
- Mutable fire (Sagittarius)
- North
- Chet
- Tiger eye
- Leadership and ferocity amid physical and political strife

Manifestation

Shaitan (whom some O9A texts refer to as "Satanas" or simply "Satan") appears as a man clad in black armor, his face concealed by a mask or a veil, and his helm crowned with horns, a fiery plume, or other such accents suggestive of the infernal. He often carries various kinds of weaponry or else a tall staff to which is attached a banner marked with his sigil. The style of the armor can vary greatly between manifestations, but it is always evident that he is a warrior of some kind. When he appears in the Shadow, he does not remain hovering over the target in the manner of most spirits and may instead slowly circle the magician, as if trying to size up an opponent from all angles. It is important to remain fearless in his presence at all times, for he is easily provoked into hostility if he senses weakness.

Demeanor

He comes across as businesslike but dour, with hints of impatience and disdain. One gets the impression that he has high standards and almost no one lives up to them.

Narrative

As the name might lead one to anticipate, Shaitan casts himself as Islam's Ibliss, who was damned because he refused to express reverence and celebration in response to God's creation of Adam. Regarding this matter, he explains that he was offended both by Celestial two-facedness, always singing the praises of God's creation even as they propagate their life-denying ideologies, and by the presumption that any creature should be held in awe merely for having attained intelligent consciousness when said creature has never really been tested and is therefore nowhere near having achieved its full potential. His aeonic goals are complementary to those of Noctulius, but he favors harsher and more warlike methods of attaining them.

Expertise

- His central interest is in helping magicians reach new heights via the staging of initiatory trials, during which he will test the magician's resolve. He can be exceedingly harsh during such encounters, but in the manner of a professional who takes a job seriously, without any lasting personal animosity toward the magician afterward.

- Offers advice and assistance in support of Faustian efforts to carry out feats never before accomplished, especially if said feats are in some sense risky or dangerous.

- He can be persuaded to grant protection and facilitate the enjoyment of good fortune, but only after a thorough interrogation to establish how the Sinister Dialectic will be advanced thereby.

Shugara

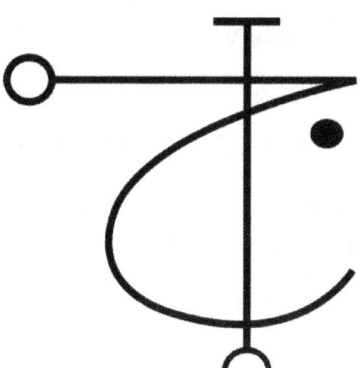

Attributes

- Shaitanic faction: Cicatrix
- Waning Moon
- Moon, Saturn
- Fixed water (Scorpio)
- Southeast
- Uruk
- Serpentine (preferably dark green)
- Suffering, horror, disease and revenge

Manifestation

Shugara appears as an imposing woman with a hag-like appearance, not on account of being aged, but on account of her flesh being hideously burned and rotting away. Mixed in with her hair is a mass of octopus tentacles, swamp-plant tendrils, and other slimy detritus. She is clad in shredded rags, and crawls on all fours rather than walking normally, such that her movement resembles that of a frog, crab, or spider. She may also take inhuman shapes suggestive of gigantic, deformed versions of these animals, or inorganic shapes such as a tall, forbidding black wall or a surging tide of black sludge. It is not unusual for her presence to be accompanied by the smell of rotting meat.

Demeanor

Shugara is unpleasant to encounter due to the dense, negative energies that accompany her, and her words often comes across as menacing or derisive. This is, however, simply part of her nature that the magician must accept. In cases of true hostility, she wastes no words and simply attacks like an animal.

Narrative

In her former existence, Shugara belonged to a tribe of Tellurian spirits who were genocidally exterminated by Celestials. None should have survived being psychically tortured into exhaustion and then cast into the Abyssal Void, but Shugara alone was able to hold herself together and prevail, assisted by the intercession of Gaubni and Nythra. Managing this, however, required crystallizing and cannibalizing the death agonies of all those who were once her compatriots. O9A's description of Shugara as a "hideous intrusion" speaks to this horror: the dark energies that surround her are simultaneously one with her and alien from her, such the focal point encountered by the magician feels like just an appendage of something larger and far more terrible. So although the human form Shugara takes may remind one of such mythological crones as the Greek Hecate and the Slavic Baba Yaga, there is a grotesque aspect to her energy that is uniquely and viscerally disturbing.

Expertise

- Specializes in the sort of baneful magick where a victim reduced to abject misery seeks to force the source of their troubles to fully feel and experience an equivalent agony. She will add her own store of psychic anguish to the magician's in order to make this happen, though, which can be very dangerous if one's own psyche is already unstable.

- Will happily provide additional dark-energy "fuel" to any workings that cause trouble for Celestials or Dogmagians, especially in support of other Nekalah's efforts.

- Can offer wise words and assistance in the weathering of extreme personal difficulties, but only if one is in a true state of desperation beyond causal remedy.

Velpecula

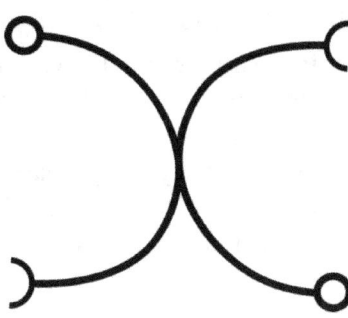

Attributes

- Noctulian faction: Gladius
- Waxing Moon
- Mercury, Mars
- Cardinal earth (Capricorn)
- East
- Lhamyu
- Chrysocolla
- Strategic intelligence and the acquisition of useful skills

Manifestation

Velpecula presents herself as an athletic woman, fully covered in armor, with her face concealed by a mask and a blue plume atop her helm. Although she comes across as fairly human, there is something subtly off in her movements at times, as if there are mechanical or otherwise artificial components beneath the plating on some of her limbs. She may also appear as a fox-like creature with unusual coloration, scarring, heterochromia, or other such striking features.

Demeanor

Affable, solicitous, constructive, and pragmatic. One gets the impression that she does not suffer fools gladly but is at the same time slow to write anyone off as beyond her capacity to educate. Toward novice walkers of the Sinister Path, she is sympathetic, patient and protective, but if she senses traces of complacency or hubris in the magician, she is certain not to let such tendencies go unchallenged.

Narrative

Velpecula's parallel can most readily be found in various wisdom goddesses, such as the Greek Athena, Roman Minerva, or Hindu Sarasvati. Zealously preoccupied with all manner of questions as to how to do more and how to do better, she is driven by a constructive vision similar to Davcina's but oriented more toward individual attainment than the harmony of larger communities. Her inquisitive spirit seems to have been the central motivator for her becoming a Sinistral, and it is perhaps then unsurprising that she was able to weather the transformation better than some of the other Nekalah who were formerly Tellurians.

Expertise

- Aids in introspection, including recollection of memories thought lost and honest assessment of the magician's strengths and weaknesses.

- Offers advice regarding how best to attain one's ambitions, providing inspiration and direction to those who have none. Those whose day-to-day lives are not unpleasant yet nonetheless suffer from a sense of meaninglessness and unmet potential would do well to seek her assistance.

- Can help novice magicians surmount difficulties that hold them back, such as controlling the wandering of the mind during meditation. Such novices should realize, however, that while she is less harsh in her dealings than the other Nekalah, she will simply stop answering the magician's call if she gets the impression that they are not serious about wanting to improve or are expecting her to fix things without them having to apply effort themselves. It is therefore not wise to take her patience for granted indefinitely.

Summary

Taking the step of pursuing communion with an acausal entity is a momentous milestone in the career of any magician. For the witch, the Rites of Descent and of the Threshold are tools that open up new avenues of occult accomplishment, offering additional means of fulfilling desires both earthly and spiritual. For the sorcerer, all this is no less true, but there is also more, for it is through communion with acausal beings that the sorcerer gains full awareness of the causal and acausal dimensions of their own destiny.

Some magicians may be excited to experience communion, only to be taken off guard by how much more difficult they find it compared to other kinds of ritual workings. In such circumstances, the following advice may help:

- *Before attempting communion,* study the Eighth Key's description of the Nekalah you wish to contact, as well as any additional sources you can get hold of that refer to the entity in question. Create a reproduction of the entity's sigil and treat this as a devotional object by placing it on your altar and incorporating it into your meditative practices, or carrying it with you constantly for several days prior to undertaking communion. The important thing, in any case, is to make real to yourself both the entity you intend to contact and your enthusiasm for contacting it well prior to when you actually enter the ritual chamber.

- *During communion,* it is critical to maintain total receptivity. If you find you must ponder over what the entity looks like instead of just *seeing* it, this is a sign that wishful thinking or self-doubt are compromising your focus. The same may be said of conversations: if you find yourself scripting the entity's response out in your mind instead of just *hearing* it, you are probably not actually in the trance state required for genuine contact. Bona fide communion with acausal beings flows similarly to when you see and converse with another human being. If you feel obstructed from being able to have such an experience, this may be a sign either of unaddressed personal issues distracting you or a lack of practice at sustaining self-discipline. Either way, undertaking a period of heightened dedication to meditation (as per the Fifth Key) together with regular performance of the Rite of Banishing (as per the Seventh Key) should improve your ability to open yourself fully enough.

- *In the aftermath of communion,* it may sometimes seem in retrospect as though whatever one experienced was too unusual, bizarre, or random to count as actual contact. Those who find themselves feeling this way should consult divination (as per the Sixth Key) to gain further insight. Yes, sometimes one deludes oneself while in the ritual chamber, and does not realize it until after. But it can also happen that your experience of the Dark Gods is uniquely different from others' experiences and that there is something important for you to learn from this. Divination can be very useful in helping one distinguish between these and other possibilities.

All of this said, the fact remains that just as there is no requirement for a Tenebrous Satanist to engage in esoteric practices as such, one does not have to pursue contact with acausal beings in order to call oneself a Tenebrous Satanist. Greeting the proceedings described in these pages with skepticism or being daunted by the complexity of what is required — or, for that matter, shying away lest one sow death, madness, and other horrors beyond the magician's power to contain — are all understandable reactions. Nonetheless, the bold and the inquisitive have much to gain from the experience of acausal communion. Many are the ways in which the agenda of the individual Satanist may intersect with the agendas of the Nekalah. And many are the ways in which the Sinister Dialectic may be advanced thereby.

We hope that the Eighth Key will provide both witch and sorcerer with the tools to forge ever-stronger relationships with the acausal beings of Darkness, for the mutual benefit of human and Nekalah alike.

Notes

[62] Exceptions do exist to this rule — e.g., if one is undergoing an entheogenic initiatory ordeal in accord with stipulations one has explicitly agreed to with the Nekalah in advance. The casual use of mind-altering substances during ritual magick, however — not only in communion rites but in Tenebrous magick generally — is not something that the author recommends.

[63] All sigils in the Eighth Key have been adapted from O9A texts such as *Naos* and *Caelethi* (a.k.a. *Black Book of Satan II)* unless otherwise noted.

[64] The author's own experience is that the O9A septenary star works especially well for the purposes for which the pendant is intended. Inconveniently for Tenebrous Satanists, though, the association of said symbol with the extremist acts and politics attributed to O9A has made such pendants increasingly hard to come by. Additionally, although the ritual chamber is meant to be a space of untrammeled psychic expression — a place wherein herd opinion should not dictate what one does or does not wear — it is understandable for a contemporary magician who strongly rejects the problematic elements of O9A's ideology to not want to wear a septenary star if other options are available. For those who wish to use a symbol from O9A's current that is not the septenary star, either the Binan Ath or Ga Wath Am sigil inscribed within a circle would be an apt choice for the pendant.

[65] Those who struggle with this part of the ritual may find that a clear, concentrated visualization of the sigil of the Nekalah one is seeking to contact may help. To this end, it is best if the magician knows the details of the sigil well, and is practiced enough in Tenebrous meditation to be able to hold its image solidly in the mind's eye at the same time as they gaze into the darkness above the target and engage in Naos-pattern breathing — i.e., picturing the sigil throughout the attempt to establish contact, rather than "looking for" the entity itself in the darkness. In the author's experience though, this method of getting the Rite of the Threshold to "work" risks succeeding via essentially converting it into an experience of the Rite of Descent, i.e., what follows will feel more "internal" than what those who attempt the Rite of the Threshold are typically looking for. It should be noted that such an alteration to the experience in no way renders any resultant contact with the Nekalah invalid, for an entity eager for contact will typically be willing to adapt if such is necessary, for example, to ensure the delivery of an urgent message. On the other hand though, if a magician finds that their attempts at the Rite of the Threshold are taking this direction on a regular basis, it is probably best if they just perform the Rite of Descent instead (and in all likelihood, get better results), lest one otherwise unintentionally train oneself to confuse the two experiences.

[66] An alternative to sitting and facing the target that the magician may attempt — assuming one has sufficient free space in the ritual chamber to carry it out without mishap — is to perform a "spiral dance" by whirling one's body quickly in a counter-clockwise direction until dizziness forces one to the ground. One then observes any sensations that may come out of the Shadow while one recomposes oneself, e.g., something looming over you, touching you, assisting you to rise or forcing you to remain down, or the intensification of other uncanny effects such as the room seeming darker, colder, etc. This technique is especially useful if you feel strongly that the entity is not present in the anticipated direction and yet something is lurking *somewhere* in the Shadow. If the entity has, for example, decided to "come in" through the target but place itself somewhere else in the room subsequently, performing a spiral dance can help the magician determine what the best direction to sit facing will now be. One may then choose to set up the target in that direction in future rituals instead of following the author's prescriptions regarding directional attributions of the Nekalah. Some will find they no longer need to perform a spiral dance

once they have made such a determination; others may find the entities' manifestations inconsistent enough that a spiral dance is always helpful for establishing or strengthening contact. The "correct" way of performing this rite is therefore whatever way the individual magician finds to be most effective in their own experience.

[67] Obviously, candles left to burn out on their own should be placed on a non-flammable surface, well away from anything that could catch fire and any potential sources of disturbance.

[68] These nine roles are derived from O9A's Star Game, which can be likened to an unusual and complicated variant of chess. Pieces in the Star Game transform through nine phases that are each defined by a combination of the alchemical principles of sulfur, salt, and mercury. While the detailed mechanics and implications of the Star Game are an esoteric matter beyond the scope of current work, those who study the Star Game may be interested to know that the roles of the Nekalah according to Tenebrous Satanism are associated thus:

1. ⊖(⊖) = Matrix

2. ⊖(☿) = Ostium

3. ⊖(🜍) = Gladius

4. ☿(⊖) = Cicatrix

5. ☿(☿) = Lamia

6. ☿(🜍) = Regnum

7. 🜍(⊖) = Sidera

8. 🜍(☿) = Dux

9. 🜍(🜍) = Vorago

[69] These planetary attributions are not related to O9A's "Tree of Wyrd" system. Said system is certainly not without esoteric value, but since it is based around the number twenty-one as per O9A's Sinister Tarot, it is not compatible with Tenebrous Satanism's runic-tarot, which is based around the number twenty-eight.

[70] Other stones of a similar color and composition will work equally well as meditation or devotional objects, e.g., for Shugara, jade or malachite instead of serpentine. Regarding such correspondences, individual intuition should be an adequate guide for any magician competent enough to be communing with spirits in the first place.

[71] Although the author has consistently had constructive experiences with Atazoth, others report him sometimes taking forms that are more thoroughly monstrous and harder to communicate with. Approaching him with awe instead of fear seems to produce the best results.

[72] Before plunging into such endeavors, the eager magician is warned that Azanigin is very difficult to persuade into taking a form that most humans would find sexually attractive. Sexual encounters involving her are therefore likely to entail a compulsive element, culminating in a sense of revulsion once the moment is past.

[73] It is not difficult to see how a desire to affirm the dark realities Baphomet embodies could be a partial driver behind some of O9A's sacrificial practices. In fact, though, it is not the frivolous destruction of life that Baphomet revels in, but purposeful, reflective acts by which conscious beings demonstrate that they live in full awareness of the brutalities of life's victories and defeats alike. The intentional shedding of one's own blood, coupled with awareness of one's own participation in the web of sacrifices that earthly life inherently demands, is of far greater worth to Baphomet than the flippant slaughter of the unwilling. This ought, however, to be a small amount of blood, shed within the ritual chamber as an offering — i.e., Tenebrous Satanism does *not* endorse habitual self-mutilation, ritual suicide, or similar practices. It should also be stressed that, while Baphomet may be pleased by O9A-style sacrifices carried out as spiritually conscious acts (as opposed to mere criminal thrill-seeking behavior) and may attempt to encourage some magicians to perpetrate such acts, this does *not* automatically mean that the magician should go along with the suggestion.

[74] What is intended here is raw garnet, preferably in a form resembling a pomegranate seed, rather than a potentially pricey cut gemstone.

[75] Insofar as the name "Lidagon" is said to mean "mate of Dagon," Darkat may be connected most closely to the lesser-known goddess Ishara, who was worshipped alongside Dagon in some parts of the ancient world and is associated both with sexuality and scorpions.

[76] An example of an abundant and readily available fossil for this purpose would be orthoceras.

[77] The vortex form of Nythra has been observed in the Shadow both by the author and by others, often accompanied by a palpable aura of terror. The warning of disturbing phenomena manifesting during the Rite of the Threshold is thus motivated in large part by the author's experiences with this entity in particular.

[78] It should be noted that Sauroctonos has a strong preference to support constructive endeavors rather than destructive ones, so if the magician desires to enchant an object for any sort of baneful purpose, it is better to consult one of the other Nekalah, such as Gaubni.

IX

Azoth: The Sorcerer as Alchemist

> *People will do anything, no matter how absurd, in order to avoid facing their own souls. One does not become enlightened by imagining figures of light, but by making the darkness conscious.*
>
> - Carl Jung, *Psychology and Alchemy* (1944)

Both the witch and the sorcerer subscribe to beliefs and practices that engage with acausal realities. The Tenebrous Creed distinguishes the sorcerer from the witch on two fronts, however: i) the sorcerer commits to an ongoing relationship with the forces of Darkness — i.e., a pact — and ii) as a manifestation of this relationship, the sorcerer lives a life that consciously aims at the advancement of Satan's cause through the embrace of creative strife. Such an endeavor requires the cultivation of physical, mental, emotional, and spiritual capacities beyond what untrained individuals possess. Tenebrous Satanism encourages all Satanists to strive for cultivation in these areas, for thus is the Faustian spirit manifest. As a purposeful fomenter of world-changing strife, however, the sorcerer is called to a yet higher level of attainment — a level that the initiation practices of Tenebrous Satanism are designed to foster.

Before going further, it is worth clarifying what we mean by "strife." Tenebrous Satanism defines creative strife as disruption for the purposes of enabling evolution — i.e., to cause it to take place, to accelerate it, or to alter its current direction. This definition presupposes that strife has a purpose in mind, however much unenlightened minds may mistake it for the mere causing of chaos for chaos' sake. By revealing something that was not previously seen or using discord to interrupt complacency, strife forces change to occur. This change, moreover, leads ultimately to a better outcome for the world as a whole than what would otherwise have been — hence its designation as "creative."

Violence, it should be noted, is often not the best way of promoting strife in this sense. The violent action that is too easy to label "evil" is, on account of that very label, an action that many people will see as bereft of constructive intent. Consequently, they will either write it off as the petty delinquency of a juvenile personality or condemn it as an unconscionable act of terrorism. Both kinds of response severely limit violence's capacity to achieve change. It is true that violence is prevalent within nature itself and that under certain circumstances (e.g., to overthrow an oppressive regime), it may be the most appropriate tool for the job. Nonetheless, human beings possessed of reason, creativity, and numerous other capacities ought not to underestimate the other, better tools that can be used to prod stagnancy into transformation. Changing the world is an inherently social endeavor, so one ought to think carefully about the limitations of trying to use anti-social methods to achieve such changes.

Although such reservations against violence distinguish Tenebrous Satanism from the Order of Nine Angles (O9A), the sort of impactful change that Tenebrous Satanism seeks through creative strife is nonetheless closely proximate to the sort of lasting and extensive change that O9A has in mind when it talks about aeonic change and the need to advance the Sinister Dialectic.[79] The sorcerer's aspiration is to inspire people to think and live differently than they otherwise would, said alteration being in accord with the values of Satanism and the goals of the Satanist's acausal allies. What exactly this means in practice can vary widely. It may entail the creation of art that opens people to what they were formerly closed to, the founding of groups and institutions aimed at furthering worthy political initiatives, the development of technological innovations that broaden the options available to human beings, or any number of other possibilities.

In all cases, however, Tenebrous Satanism contends that truly significant change of the kind the sorcerer is after can be sought most effectively by the person who possesses such traits as open-mindedness, discipline, social competence, visionary ambition, self-honesty, resilience, expansive empathy, leadership, and strategic insight. Such a person should also be free from the oblivious, counterproductive hubris that drives people to take up ill-conceived crusades wherein they impose upon other people as a method of avoiding confrontation with their own flaws. It has become apparent, in recent years especially, that the world needs better revolutionaries when it comes to this particular issue.

The aim of Tenebrous initiation is to refine the sorcerer's character in accord with these considerations. Our conviction is that the endurance of freely chosen internal strife refines one's fitness to pursue creative strife in the world at large. Initiation consists of a sequence of trials, the passing of which transforms the lead of the novice into the gold of the adept. The term "azoth," variously construed by alchemists as a universal solvent, a force driving evolution, and an elixir of life, is used by Tenebrous Satanism to refer to the ultimate goal of initiation: the unlocking of ever-greater Faustian potential, not only for the purposes of self-actualization, but with an aeonic horizon in mind. In this respect, Tenebrous initiation is not merely a status badge meant to designate one's place in an occult hierarchy. Nor does it cater to the dilettante who wants to undergo colorful, exotic experiences just to convince themselves that they are more interesting than other people. It is, instead, meant to be difficult — and meant to change one's life *because* it is difficult.

A taste for initiatory ordeals is something which Tenebrous Satanism has in common with O9A, and the similarities do not end here. The Ninth Key's conception of initiation in terms of seven stages, defined by both astrological and alchemical symbolism, is heavily inspired by the O9A text *Naos*, as are the specific trials that accompany many of these stages. Where Tenebrous Satanism differs from O9A, however, is in an overt recognition that, due to factors including differences in capability or life experience, individuals vary widely in what degree of adversity they find too difficult. For this reason, the Ninth Key delineates the symbolism and aims of each initiation stage but leaves a number of details up to individual initiates to determine. These include such matters as how many months the initiation will last for and what specific tasks will fit the broadly defined requirements of each stage.

This is not to say that Tenebrous Satanism merely aims to make O9A practices easier. A key premise of Tenebrous initiation is that *the onus is upon the individual to attempt that which is hard for themselves*. Such open-endedness is meant to encourage a wider range of people to undergo initiation and to contend thereby with adversities that will ultimately drive personal growth. O9A's policy on this front presumes that only a tiny minority of the most hardcore individuals are worthy to strive on behalf of the Sinister Dialectic. Tenebrous Satanism, by contrast, wishes to empower a wide range of people to contribute — in whatever capacity they are capable of — to the advancement of Satan's cause.

Before proceeding with the specifics of the stages, it should be noted that the following considerations apply to all:

- In order to ensure that initiation constitutes a focused commitment, the time period dedicated to any one stage should fall between one month at minimum and one year at maximum. Within this range, exactly how long an initiatory trial should last is up to the initiate.

- Although purpose underlies the order we present the stages in, nothing forbids individuals from experimentation that disregards this order. A sorcerer may do this to attempt a practice run of a particular stage, or a witch may seek self-transformation via a subset of initiatory tasks without undergoing the full sequence.

- Initiation stages can be undertaken by secular Satanists in pursuit of purely causal benefits, such as to facilitate the processing of psychological baggage or overcome personal limitations. Such individuals should be aware, however, that what is described below presumes that the initiate believes in acausal realities and seeks contact with such realities. Those who are not of this proclivity are therefore advised to adapt what is described in these pages to their own needs carefully. Otherwise, discord between one's intentions, expectations, and actions may cause complications of a nature that the secular Satanist may find challenging to grapple with.

One more thing that should be clarified before proceeding is the implications of the astrological and alchemical references employed below. Tenebrous Satanism sees much to be said for a Jungian interpretation of astrology and alchemy as symbolic systems illustrative of psychological realities, and therefore embraces the evocative imagery of these branches of esotericism. It is in connection with such an understanding more so than literalistic belief in the specifics of alchemy or astrology that the Ninth Key utilizes astrological and alchemical concepts.

Moon

Symbolism

In astrological terms, the Moon is associated with the instincts, emotions, and dark mysteries. Its influence manifests beneficially in terms of being in touch with the intuitive insights of the unconscious or malefically in terms of madness if the dark side of one's psyche becomes overly dominant. The Moon is therefore a fitting symbol for the beginner's initial discovery of the inward, acausal facets of the Sinister Path — one's first real glimpse of the power that the path offers and the risks that accompany it. Key challenges at this time include learning how to distinguish genuine occult experience from mere wishful thinking and how to open oneself up to the mysterious without succumbing to the delusional.

This initial stage of initiation is analogous to the alchemical processes known as calcination and dissolution. In these, a substance is reduced to ash, then dissolved in a solvent. Psychologically, this means that one first experiences an incineration of one's unreflective default egoism. Subsequently, an inward-turning descent takes place, during which the boundaries of one's psyche become more permeable to hidden, acausal forces. The process as a whole evokes an encounter with the shadow aspect of oneself and one's reality. This nocturnal element is alluded to via the word *nox*, meaning "night," which O9A associates with this stage.

Central concept

What the Moon stage of initiation requires is simply that one get one's hands dirty by engaging in a sustained period of esoteric contemplation and actually performing ritual magick instead of just thinking about performing it. Many are those who style themselves as occultists yet do nothing other than read books about the topic, philosophize, and daydream. The express purpose of the Moon stage is to ensure that the initiate starts actually *doing* things on the occult front.

Requirements

The Moon stage requires completing the following tasks:

1. *Complete twenty-eight meditation sessions within a set time, according to a set pattern.*

   This may consist of any combination of practices described in the Fifth Key, but all four should be attempted during the initiation period. The initiate should decide at the outset when they will meditate (e.g., every night vs. every second night), and what pattern of practices to pursue (e.g., focusing on one for a week, then proceeding to the next vs. alternating practices every night). This commitment must be upheld for the whole initiation period without missing sessions due to forgetfulness, distraction, or other failures of willpower.

2. *Perform ritual magick at least three times over the course of the initiation period.*

   At least two such workings should be of the Rite of Alignment described in Appendix I, once at the start and once at the end of the initiation period. The remaining performance may also be an Alignment, or it may be the Rite of Banishing described in the Seventh Key, or it may entail something specific that the initiate seeks for their own purposes. This additional ritual may take place any time during the initiation period — e.g., at the halfway point or at a time otherwise auspicious for the intent of the chosen rite.

An additional requirement for the Moon stage, as well as all stages that follow, is to keep a daily journal. One should use it to record reflections both on what takes place as part of the initiation proper, and the mental and emotional impact of day-to-day events during this time, meaningful dreams that occur, and so forth.

Evaluation

The primary quality that the Moon stage cultivates is openness to the mysteries of the acausal. Such openness is expressed via a willingness to take action, rather than remaining merely an armchair occultist. Accordingly, the key consideration of success is simply that one must do the practices. The meditation session or ritual magick performance that is flawed yet was attempted earnestly and examined thoughtfully afterward is still a worthy contributor to the Moon experience.

Conversely, the central way in which this stage of initiation can be failed is via lassitude. If a personal emergency necessitates deviating from the schedule, making up the missed session as soon as possible is acceptable. However, the initiate must recognize that the point of the Moon stage is to start developing and applying the discipline requisite of a serious practitioner. This means, among other things, planning one's day in a way that ensures there is enough time for esoteric practices and regulating one's emotions enough to follow through with obligations, even when one "doesn't feel like it today." Inconsistency and sloth are the primary obstacles of this stage, and one must overcome such obstacles before one can hope to manage the demands of subsequent stages.

Mercury

Symbolism

Mercury is associated with wit, eloquence, and analysis. Its favorable disposition manifests in increased mental acuity, effective use of talents, and free flow of information. When Mercury is in retrograde, on the other hand, all such matters are thwarted — or at least, such is the convenient astrological excuse often given for mundane human incompetence.

Dedicated as the Sinister Path is to overcoming limitations, the symbolic emphasis in Tenebrous Satanism is upon Mercury's positive aspect manifest in the development of one's intellect and abilities. O9A's association of the concept of indulgence with Mercury speaks to a connection between the possession of skilled competence and the attainment of one's desires — a connection which the Faustian spirit of Tenebrous Satanism similarly affirms.

In alchemical terms, the Mercury stage is analogous to the processes known as separation and filtration. In these processes, the ashes previously immersed and dissolved are recovered from the solution in a changed form, augmented now with qualities alien to the original material. What the initiate experiences psychologically in Mercury is the sprouting of the seed planted during the Moon stage. Before, one merely opened the door to acausal contact. Now, one works with the acausal in a more intensive manner, so as to bring about changes in oneself that will be evident even from a causal perspective.

Central concept

The Mercury stage of initiation takes what was begun in the Moon stage to the next level by demanding the dedication of significant time, energy, and labor to acausal doings. Mercury is accordingly more boot-camp-like than Moon. Its aim is to establish that the initiate possesses the degree of fitness and discipline requisite for an effective agent of creative strife. To pass is to show that one has what it takes to be, in one's own right, a *Satan*, as per the key word O9A connects with this stage.

Requirements

The Mercury stage requires all of the following tasks:

1. *Attain both a theoretical and intuitive understanding of the Tenebrous runic-tarot by studying the omens and performing the Diviner's Journey meditation once for each of the twenty-eight visions.*

   The initiate should approach this goal in the same systematic manner as the Moon meditations — i.e., set a schedule for studying and meditating, and adhere to it. For example, for one month, they might spend each day studying one vision's trio of omens and each night undertaking the Diviner's Journey for that vision.

2. *Choose a challenging goal framed in terms of physical endurance and undertake a training program to achieve it.*

The goal should be defined in terms of increasing one's capacity to engage in an outdoor physical activity, such as walking, running, or cycling. It should entail striving to reach a personal record by the time of the initiation's conclusion (e.g., increasing how long one can sustain the activity for by x hours, or how far one can travel by x distance) and strictly adhering to a daily training regimen for the whole of the initiatory period (e.g., no less than x hours of activity per day). The initiate will need to research what constitutes a realistic goal and how best to train for it prior to formally starting the initiation. What is most important is that the challenge be difficult to meet yet attainable for that specific individual, provided they put forward an earnest effort.[80]

3. *Commit to learn a practical skill up to an intermediate level of proficiency and train to achieve this.*

The skill should be either something practical (e.g., survival-related skills, public speaking) or something that yields an end product of objective quality (e.g., learning to play an instrument, crafting of an object). Just as with the physical goal, the initiate ought to precede entry into the formal initiatory period with research and practice to gain a realistic perspective both on what is possible overall and on what sort of progress is reasonable to strive for within a given time frame.

These goals may be pursued in any sequence or simultaneously. The latter option will, of course, intensify the initiation experience significantly and is therefore good for those seeking greater challenge.

Mercury initiates should, additionally, perform the Rite of Alignment at the start and end of the initiation period (as well as other times during it, if appropriate), and attain practice in divination by consulting the omens regularly — e.g., for a general weekly forecast or to solicit advice about specific obstacles that may arise. They should also journal all elements of the initiation in detail for later reflection.

Evaluation

It can be said of all initiation stages that while they require discipline, at the same time they train the initiate to become more disciplined. This is true especially of Mercury. Its essence lies in successful self-enhancement of a kind that only disciplined striving can accomplish. Unlike the Moon stage, wherein the most important thing is just that the initiate makes an effort, with Mercury, the most important thing is that they achieve that which they set out to do. The initiate should arrive at the end of this stage with a solid grasp of divination, an augmented capacity for physical exertion, and new competence at doing something that is either useful, aesthetically pleasing, or both. It should thus be fairly obvious what constitutes passing or failure of the Mercury stage.

On the other hand, a pitfall worth being on guard against is the temptation to subvert Mercury's requirements via rationalization. For example, one might look back at something one has done in the past and assert that it counts, so as to excuse oneself from part of what is to be done presently. Or one might tell oneself that the physical goal can be ignored because "I'm fit enough already" or "Exercise is just not my thing." A person who rationalizes in such ways demonstrates that they have the wrong attitude toward initiation as such. One may as well not make the attempt at all if one is only willing to do it half-heartedly.

Venus

Symbolism

Venus is associated with attraction, love, and sensual pleasure. Its auspices facilitate harmonious cooperation. When its influence is inauspicious, however, self-absorption and vanity rear their heads. Tenebrous Satanism draws a connection between these relational qualities of Venus and the conception both of individual beings and the world itself as nexions. By choosing to enter into worldly existence, spirit shattered the primal unity that preceded entry into the flesh, choosing multitudinous existence instead. Accordingly, a spiritually mature person should demonstrate awareness of this relational aspect of life. Primary among the Venus stage's aims is the development of such maturity.

Alchemical processes proximate to Venus are known as conjunction and cibation. In such processes, two distinct elements are brought together for the purposes of creating a whole that is greater than the sum of its parts. Such a description is suggestive of the sexual act, justifying O9A's association of Venus with the word *hriliu*, a declaration of ecstasy in the Thelemic tradition. Tenebrous Satanism posits, however, that sexuality should not be overemphasized as if it were the only arena in which profound human connection might be cultivated. Accordingly, the Venus stage of initiation is not defined by the literal having of sexual intercourse, but by the empathic cultivation of a capacity for intercourse in a broader sense.

Central concept

In the Venus stage, the initiate broadens their experience of the acausal by allowing their journey to intersect with that of another person. Such a prospect is sure to draw a cringe from the typical introvert, yet its benefits cannot be overstated. By performing occult practices with a companion, one gains a novel perspective on the efficacy of such practices. The earnest striver emerges with a boost in confidence, while the deluded braggart is forced to grapple honestly with their shortcomings. The sort of companionship that the Venus stage promotes also teaches both empathy and perseverance via sharing a significant part of one's life with another person and making a wholehearted effort to engage with that person's unique perspective as part of the process. Enhanced empathy of this kind does much to discourage the oblivious solipsism and self-absorbed arrogance that may otherwise sabotage a sorcerer's destiny.

Requirements

The Venus stage requires both of the following tasks:

1. *Acquire a companion open to exploring Tenebrous Satanism and meet with them to discuss its philosophy or experiment with its practices at least seven times.*

A manageable schedule for these meetings should be set by the participants. The exact balance of what to explore — conversing about the Keys of Doctrine, practicing meditation, performing divination for the companion and discussing results, or undertaking the Diviner's Journey together — is up to the initiate and companion to agree on. Regardless of how exactly the participants spend their time together though, the initiate should always make a concerted effort to understand their companion's perspective — on what fronts they are similar to and different from the initiate, what assumptions and life experiences have shaped them, and what comes to them easily vs. what they struggle with. Any disagreements or obstacles that arise should be handled in a patient and constructive manner. The initiate should also engage in regular introspection regarding what can be learned from interactions with their companion and journal their reflections.

2. *Perform ritual magick with your companion present on at least three separate occasions.*

Forms this could take may include: i) allowing one's ritual to be observed; ii) adapting a rite to include another participant who echoes the initiate's performance or otherwise contributes energy; iii) making the other person the focus of the rite — e.g., performing a banishing on them or seeking something on their behalf. It is up to the initiate and their companion whether to attempt all of these variants over the course of the initiation or attempt only some of them.

The initiate's companion for all of these endeavors should be an adult of sound mind, who enters into the arrangement in a fully informed and consensual manner. It is also recommended, so as to minimize headaches for the initiate, that the companion be someone who reliably follows through on plans to meet, defers to the initiate's judgment regarding what is to be publicly known about the relationship, and is both level-headed and emotionally grounded. Note, however, that while the companion may be a fellow sorcerer (either less or more experienced), they do not necessarily have to be a current or prospective convert to Tenebrous Satanism. Where open-mindedness accompanies an ethos and temperament that differ from the initiate's own — a person who is intelligent and curious but dedicated to a different esoteric path or to atheism — there may well be more to talk about and hence more that the initiate can learn from the interaction.

While it is not an absolute requirement to carry out all Venus tasks with the same companion, the initiate should avoid multiplying companions needlessly. Otherwise, one will fail to invest sufficient time and effort in the deepening of relationship that is the crux of this stage.

Evaluation

Many solitary occultists are understandably private about their esoteric practices. A reluctance to follow through with all that the Venus stage entails is understandable in connection with this. Nonetheless, this stage is invaluable in developing a different dimension of self-knowledge and self-honesty than Mercury fosters. By entering into a relationship, the initiate is forced to come out of their shell and to examine their virtues, vices, and vulnerabilities more objectively than they might otherwise. Regardless of whether a strong affinity with one's companion flowers into something that outlasts the initiation period or the proceedings are weathered reluctantly amid difficulties with multiple companions, the most important thing is to grow in terms of social competence. A pass of this stage requires that the initiate follow through with all ten encounters and become better both at understanding and making themselves understood by others as a result.

The main factor to note as far as risk of failure goes is that, as with all of the other stages, a set time period for the initiation must be declared at the outset. All tasks associated with the initiation proper must then be completed within that time. The initiate therefore sets themselves up for success by establishing a stable relationship with their companion — whether friendship or more — prior to the initiatory period. They set themselves up for failure, on the other hand, if any of the stipulated time must be frittered away on seeking a new partner. Given this consideration, many initiates would be better off making a companion of a trustworthy friend whom they can deepen a platonic connection with instead of attempting to juggle initiation and romance at the same time. Welcome though a sexual relationship may be in the presence of mutual attraction and consent, Tenebrous Satanism does not require such relationships as part of the Venus stage — and *under no circumstances* should a companion ever be pressured for sexual contact under pretenses implying otherwise.

Sun

Symbolism

The Sun represents one's own energy, the earthly and spiritual achievements it makes possible, and the healthy sense of pride that accompanies such accomplishments. Its auspicious face manifests in the experience of maximal flourishing, while its inauspicious side shows itself in imbalance: the poverty of too little or the reckless excess of too much. Above all, the Sun symbolizes reason and order. Tenebrous Satanism relates these qualities to the personal evolution that self-reflection and self-regulation together enable. By attaining open-eyed, realistic insight into oneself and one's place in the world, one becomes maximally able to capitalize upon the unique opportunities that delineate one's destiny. O9A's association of *lux* (light) and vision with this stage speaks to the gaining of this kind of insight.

In alchemical terms, the conjunction stage associated with Venus is followed by what may be conceptualized either as a single stage divisible into two parts or as two separate stages: putrefaction and fermentation. Both evoke the natural processes that produce such products as wine, wherein a raw substance is transformed through decay into a wholly different substance of much greater value. Psychologically, the dynamic of the Sun stage entails working with events and forces that ought to be "dead" in one's life for the purposes of transmuting and transcending them. The initiate is relieved of past baggage thereby and cleansed of the mental and emotional impurities that such baggage tends to generate.

Central concept

The Sun stage requires the initiate to spend an extended period of time in intensified reflection upon their past, guided by an acausal factor and culminating in a binding commitment to a better future. To Venus' augmentation of perspective via the inclusion of a companion on the causal plane, the Sun stage adds augmentation of perspective via the inclusion of an acausal companion. The forging of this kind of relationship is only possible in the presence of two prerequisites: genuine receptivity untainted by self-delusion and genuine skill in the occult arts. Passing through the previous stages is meant to establish that the initiate does indeed possess these capacities — or, at minimum, is at a point where they can refine their skills enough to become ready for the current stage's challenges.

Requirements

What follows is a walk-through of a default version of the Sun stage, positing an initiatory period of one month. The actual timeline will be up to the individual to decide. It is symbolically preferable, however, for this stage to unfold sometime between the winter and summer solstices, during the half of the year when the days are becoming longer.

Prior to formally beginning the initiation, the initiate should use a combination of divination, past experience, and personal inclination to determine which of the Dark Gods would make an appropriate spiritual guide and primary confidant for themselves as a sorcerer. Many initiates will by this point have worked with more than one of the Nekalah before and attained some feel for their individual personalities, values, goals, and so forth thereby. There may also be initiates, however, for whom the solicitation of a patron will constitute their very first attempt at communing with an entity that up until now they knew of by reputation alone. Either way, the initiate must perform either the Rite of Descent or the Rite of the Threshold and receive an affirmative expression of interest from the Nekalah they solicit. The authenticity of such a response — as distinct from a mere projection of wishful thinking — will obviously be easier for the initiate to determine if they are already well-practiced in ritual magick generally and in communion specifically. At the same time, the nature of our current is such that few will find their way this far that are not well-fitted for it. Those who are relatively inexperienced in communion are therefore not barred from proceeding, so long as they are confident that they can still handle everything that the Sun stage will demand of them.

Securing the support of a patron marks the formal beginning of the initiatory period. Shortly after this initial communion, the initiate should consult the runic-tarot for a comprehensive reading of their past, drawing one token for each of the following lines of inquiry:

1. Something that occurred within the last month which continues to weigh upon the initiate's mind.

2. Something that occurred within the last year which continues to weigh upon the initiate's mind.

3. Something that occurred within the last decade which continues to weigh upon the initiate's mind.

4. Something that occurred in the initiate's adolescence that continues to weigh upon the initiate's mind.

5. Something that occurred in the initiate's childhood that continues to weigh upon the initiate's mind.

6. A recurring concept or theme that underlies 1-5.

7. Something that must be grasped and acted upon if the pattern revealed in 6 is to be broken.

The initiate should then dedicate two days to the thorough exploration of each of these omens. One of these two days should be used for extensive and uncensored written introspection — e.g., for each of 1-5, identify a specific past incident that the omen seems to point to, narrating what happened, feelings and thoughts at the time vs. afterward; for 6 and 7, reflect thoroughly upon the implications, both in backward-looking and forward-looking terms. The other of the two days should be used for engaging in occult practices aimed at exploring the matter more deeply — e.g., performing the Diviner's Journey meditation, ritual magick aimed at soliciting input from the initiate's patron, or whatever else advances the initiate's self-understanding. Everything that proceeds from these exercises should be journaled. The initiate should also take at least one day off for grounding in between finishing with one omen and moving on to the next. Unlike the Mars stage that will follow, the Sun stage as a whole should take the form of alternating periods of work and rest, not continuous tribulation.

Once the above process is complete, the initiate should prepare for the making of a formal pact with their patron. This pact should take account of what the initiate has learned about themselves through the initiation process, how they intend to move forward, what manner of support for their resolutions they are hoping for from the Nekalah, and what obligations they will undertake in exchange for that support. The initiate is to write up an actual physical document that speaks to all of these matters, complete with a space for their signature, but not to be actually signed until the ritual described below. They should also scout a suitable ritual location in the wilderness, away from any signs of civilization and unlikely to be disturbed.

On the night on which the rite is to be performed, the initiate should go alone to the chosen site, bringing with them only the minimum needed for ritual performance — i.e., the usual ritual props, plus the written pact and a pen or quill. Upon arriving, they will carry out either the Rite of Descent or the Rite of the Threshold (as per individual choice), during which they will consult with their patron about the proposed pact. What exactly this process looks like may vary considerably, depending upon which variant of communion the initiate undertakes and which specific Nekalah they are approaching. Some of the Dark Gods will merely review what has occurred during the initiation, ask a few questions, offer a few words of support, and then assent to the covenant; others may guide the initiate through some manner of visionary experience such as a journey or contest prior to assenting. There are even a few who may put on a hostile front, imitating the manner of a prosecutor or assailant and relenting only once the initiate has unflinchingly stood up for themselves. Regardless of the exact details, though, only after the patron is satisfied should the initiate either sign the pact as is or amend it in accord with any demands the Nekalah makes, and then sign. This should take place immediately after the termination of the communion proper. Once the contract is thus settled, the initiate should proceed to the Banishing portion of the rite and the conclusion of the proceedings.

After the ritual has concluded, the initiate should remain in the vicinity of the ritual site, either seated in the manner used when performing the Contemplations, lying on one's back so as to view the sky, or going for a meditative walk. Whichever of these the initiate engages in, the remainder of the night should be spent contemplating what has come to pass during the initiation period, and once all matters pertaining to this are settled in the initiate's mind, in quietly observing the natural world. This contemplative period should culminate in observing the sunrise, with the initiate departing from the ritual site not long afterward.

The days that follow may be spent in some manner of celebration, if the initiate desires, for such would be an appropriate expression of Sun's exuberant spirit. The signed pact should be kept in a safe place thereafter and its terms upheld by the initiate from this point forward.

Evaluation

There are three main ways in which one may fail the Sun stage. One, initial communion may fail, either due to occult incompetence or due to the initiate being rejected by the Dark Gods for their own reasons. Two, the process may get bogged down in the middle if the initiate has difficulties following through with the divination and accompanying introspection. Three, something may go awry at the end, the Nekalah signaling rejection of the pact by refusing to negotiate constructively. This last possibility is unlikely if the initiate has entered into the process in good faith. If it does occur, however, the initiate should not sign the contract and should wait at least one year before attempting to restart the initiation process, if not longer, as the introspection component will need to be redone no less than the ritual component. None of these outcomes should come to pass, however, if the initiate possesses sufficient occult competence to be attempting the Sun stage to begin with.

The more significant risk with the Sun stage stems from passing it. The making of the pact marks the point at which the initiate can truly be said to have become a Tenebrous sorcerer: one who has chosen to advance their visionary ambition by entering into a formal alliance with the Nekalah. This need not be the only pact that the sorcerer ever enters into, but insofar as it is the first, it is likely to exercise considerable sway over one's destiny subsequently. Accordingly, the Sun stage should not be attempted rashly, or entered into with anything less than full sincerity. Subsequent deviation from the pact will prompt a reaction from the acausal side of the covenant, and any attempt to disentangle oneself from the stipulated obligations is likely to come with complications of its own. *Do not promise more than you can deliver* is therefore the most important piece of advice that can be offered to initiates at this stage.

Mars

Symbolism

Mars is associated with conflict and aggression. It rules over the most primal of human instincts: ruthless attainment of survival needs, ambitions fulfilled through bold action rather than intellectual calculation, and raw sexuality stripped of all sentimentality. These associations give Mars a largely malefic reputation. However, insofar as Mars is a harbinger of hardship, its omens may be interpreted favorably by those who subscribe wholeheartedly to the concept of strength through adversity.

The terms associated with Mars by O9A include "blood" and *azif*. The former is self-explanatory, given Mars' traditional qualities. The latter is an Arabic term that refers to the howling of the djinn in the desert and is known to the West via "Al-Azif" being posited as an alternate title for H. P. Lovecraft's *Necronomicon*. Both terms are suggestive of how, in the Mars stage, the initiate is due to encounter a significantly darker and more dangerous aspect of the acausal than in previous stages.

In alchemy, the process immediately following fermentation — distillation or sublimation being the most widely-used terms — entails using heat to boil off part of the ferment, leaving it purer and more concentrated. This illustrates two key aspects of the Mars stage: the heat represents intense tribulation which the initiate must pass through, while the distilled end product represents the perfection of character produced thereby. While refinement through suffering is a concept found in connection with all stages of initiation to some extent, Mars dwells most extensively and explicitly upon it. Psychologically, Mars is the stage that most overtly forces the initiate to deal with whatever inward realities they would sooner flee from than confront.

Central concept

The general flow of events during the Mars stage is similar to that in the Sun stage. But whereas the Sun stage entails a cooperative collaboration aimed at bringing forward one's strengths, the Mars stage entails an antagonistic confrontation aimed at destroying one's weaknesses. Since such a process requires first acknowledging one's shortcomings, and culminates in a literal struggle with one's demons, it is certain to be an unpleasant experience. Such is what the initiate must endure, however, in exchange for victory over the lower self and liberation from past limitations.

Requirements

As with the Sun stage, what follows is a walk-through of a default version of Mars, positing an initiatory period lasting approximately one month. Again, the actual timeline is for the initiate themselves to decide. In the case of Mars, however, it is symbolically preferable for the period as a whole to unfold sometime in between the summer and winter solstices, during the half of the year when the days are becoming shorter.

Prior to formally beginning the initiation, the initiate should determine who among the Nekalah would make an appropriate antagonistic challenger for the purposes of what is described below. It may be Shaitan, who has a particular affinity for the role, or the initiate may decide based on such factors as their patron's input, divination, or which of the Dark Gods they personally are most intimidated by. The initiate must then perform either the Rite of Descent or the Rite of the Threshold and receive an affirmative expression of interest from the particular Nekalah they solicit. Whichever Nekalah is to play the role of the challenger will be referred to as the initiate's adversary in all instructions that follow.

Securing the participation of the adversary marks the formal beginning of the initiatory period. Shortly after this initial communion, the initiate should consult the runic-tarot for a comprehensive reading of their destiny in relation to the Sinister Dialectic. Toward this end, they should draw the number of tokens indicated in response to each of the following lines of inquiry:

1. How the initiate and their current endeavors are presently perceived by their acausal allies (1 token)

2. Three negative factors that threaten to prevent the initiate from reaching their full potential — i.e., past weaknesses or potential setbacks to come (3 tokens)

3. An underlying or recurring theme behind all of 2, indicative of a deeply rooted issue that the initiate should recognize and address (1 token)

4. Three positive factors that could help the initiate reach their full potential — i.e., capacities already manifest or that could be developed (3 tokens)

5. An underlying or recurring theme behind all of 4, indicative of a general strength of the initiate that has yet to be fully tapped (1 token)

6. Something that, were it to be sacrificed or otherwise set aside, would greatly facilitate the minimization of 3 and the maximization of 5 (1 token)

7. A glimpse of what the Nekalah and the initiate alike can expect to gain if the initiate and their endeavors evolve in the most fruitful direction (1 token — and if this omen appears to be negative, draw an additional token regarding how to change course)

The initiate then proceeds in the same manner as with Sun, alternating days between detailed written introspection and deeper occult investigation of the omens. However, since there are more omens in need of individual interpretation here than in the previous stage, fewer breaks can be taken between omens if the process is to be completed within a comparable timeframe. The initiate should, additionally, mark any in-between days during the Mars stage with some manner of willingly adopted hardship — e.g., commit to engaging in multi-hour outdoor physical exertion on such days (as per the previous Mercury goal) or adopt some form of abstinence, such as fasting, withdrawal from social obligations, or curtailing some other form of indulgence. As a whole, the Mars stage should consist of near-

IX — Azoth: The Sorcerer as Alchemist

constant exertion, amid which the initiate makes a point of persisting despite fatigue on the physical, emotional, mental, or spiritual levels.

The climax of the Mars stage is the performance of the Rite of Tribulation (see Appendix I). This rite requires that, in addition to the adversary's sigil, the initiate also prepare the Vindex sigil, as shown here:

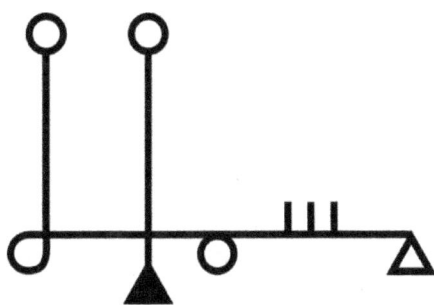

This sigil should be drawn in the initiate's own blood — i.e., pierce a finger and draw it, or mix a small amount of one's blood into a suitable ink — or, if the initiate is not willing to do this, in some alternate fashion which the adversary has deemed acceptable via prior communion.[81] Tenebrous Satanism's interpretation of O9A's Vindex is that the term refers to a role that the individual sorcerer takes on by entering into a "duel" against their adversary and emerging victorious.[82] Display of the Vindex sigil — taking the trouble to make it and displaying it during the Rite of Tribulation — is used to signal to the adversary that the initiate is serious about their willingness to be tested, accepting the risks that inherently accompany the potential rewards of such a trial.

Performing the Rite of Tribulation requires the initiate to secure both a suitable time (the ritual itself requiring two nights and necessitating recovery afterward) and an appropriate ritual site (a place where the initiate will be able to remain, free of any human contact or other disturbances, for at least forty-eight hours). The rite itself, a script for which is provided toward the end of Appendix I, initially proceeds similarly to either a Rite of Descent or a Rite of the Threshold, in accord with whichever variant the initiate chooses. Either way, during the intensification the initiate displays the Vindex sigil and indicates their will to be tested prior to walking the Black Gate. Then, once they have opened the Gate and put themselves into an appropriate trance state, they must solicit a vision from their adversary with the following theme:

> *You are transported to a place of your nightmares, where you will be confronted by personifications of your own fears and doubts. Though your urge will be to flee or fight, you must ultimately submit, allowing these self-created monsters to wreak whatever devastation they wish upon you, and endure your own destruction at their hands.*

The initiate must allow the vision to arise spontaneously, without premeditation as to its exact imagery and plot, observing and accepting whatever horrific, painful, or absurd details they encounter. Provided that effective communion has been established, the experience will arise as a joint product of the initiate's own unconscious mind and the intervention of the adversary, who will ensure that the demons one encounters have the uncanny, alien quality of that which is external to one's own mind — and are hence far more menacing than one could have conjured on one's own.

This induced nightmare should terminate with a graphic envisioning of the death of the initiate, who enacts this moment outwardly in whatever manner they desire — e.g., shifting from a meditative position to lying prone or supine. The initiate should remain thus, awake but unmoving, until dawn, without performing the standard ritual closing.

The next day is to be spent in retreat. If the Rite of Tribulation was performed at a location away from civilization, the initiate should remain in the proximity of the ritual site; otherwise, they should seclude themselves in a space prepared for this purpose in advance (e.g., in their own home). Either way, though, the initiate should observe the following stipulations from dawn until dusk:

- Absolutely no contact with other human beings.

- No resort to clocks, electronic devices, or escapist media.

- Simple fare for meals, if not outright fasting.

- No sleeping — or, if this is absolutely not manageable, set an alarm to ensure no more than one hour of sleep.

- If indoors, remain in darkness, using candles for illumination and admitting only enough natural light to be able to tell when night has fallen once again.

Under these conditions, it is likely that the initiate will fall in and out of trance over the course of the day. While out of trance, they should attempt to remain in the present moment as much as possible. If outside, walk, and take in nature; if staying inside, devise some low-tech way of passing the time. Either way, though, the initiate should not allow themselves to ruminate over matters not pertinent to the initiation. When in trance — e.g., whenever the initiative chooses to sit down and meditate throughout the day or simply finds their mind shifting into non-ordinary states on its own — the following should be the sole object of contemplation:

Despite having suffered impotence, humiliation, and death, your existence yet persists, albeit in an uncertain form, like that of a spirit between incarnations. In this zone of infinite possibility, listen to the voice of Darkness, and learn from it what must yet be suffered and understood before you can rise from your own ashes.

The Nine-Angled Nexion is an especially good way of enhancing the necessary listening, but any and all forms of Tenebrous contemplation can serve the initiate well during this time. Broad experimentation with different forms of meditation throughout the day is therefore a good idea. In all instances, though, the initiate should not allow themselves to become alarmed at any disturbances in mood, cognition, or perception that may arise. Instead, they should endeavor to observe themselves and their situation dispassionately and keep a thorough record of any acausal messages received and relevant personal reflections.

Once the sun has set, the initiate should restart the Rite of Tribulation. Upon calling for the second phase of the trial to commence and once again putting themselves into an appropriate trance, the initiate now solicits a vision from their adversary with the following theme:

You are once again transported to a place of your nightmares, where you will be confronted by personifications of your own fears and doubts. This time, though, you have devised a way to overcome your foes by dominating and transforming them. Your victory will be marked by a sublime transfiguration of both you and your surroundings.

Again, the vision must be allowed to create itself without forcing anything, taking whatever fantastic turns the initiate's unconscious may concoct under the adversary's influence. Note that while the initiate's demons are to now to be overcome, this should manifest not as total destruction, but with some element of reconciliation included, however small — e.g., after a violent battle, the wounded enemy submits to the initiate's will; from the slain beast comes an elixir or treasure; a formerly hostile party is made an ally or perhaps even a lover. Provided that the preceding day was spent constructively, the initiate should be able to devise a conclusion along these lines that both satisfies their own psyche and meets the adversary's approval.

Once the vision has concluded, the initiate should close the proceedings by banishing the adversary and concluding the rite. The days that follow should be spent in recovery.

Evaluation

Just as all stages of initiation require discipline, yet Mercury especially so, all stages of initiation require self-honesty, yet none more so than Mars. Frank acknowledgment of weaknesses and unbiased assessment of strengths are both essential if one is to benefit from the Mars experience. One must also be honest regarding how much ongoing hardship one can endure and one's ability to manage short-term feats of willpower in a situation of extremity, as per the Rite of Tribulation. The key considerations for passing Mars are that one persists through all that is required without cutting corners or giving up and emerges victorious — outcomes that it is impossible to assess meaningfully in the absence of self-honesty.

Regarding failure, while the Mars stage can fall apart for the initiate along similar lines as previous stages (lack of discipline in adhering to scheduled activities or insufficient divinatory insight), it is also attended by an additional and acute danger: psychologically disastrous defeat, if after the initiate is "killed" on the first night, they are not able to pull themselves together enough to manage their "resurrection" on the second. Such an experience is liable to cause serious damage to one's mental and emotional equilibrium. Initiates should therefore treat the climax of Mars as a life-or-death situation in which failure is not an option. If there is any significant doubt as to whether the initiate can manage this part of the initiation, it is probably more prudent to abort than to proceed.

♃

Jupiter

Symbolism

Jupiter's influence is expansively and benevolently growth-fostering. When auspicious, it is associated with material and spiritual bounty, illustrated mythologically via a kingdom's exuberant prosperity under the reign of a wise and virtuous monarch. When inauspicious, however, Jupiter is associated with the blind optimism and naivety that precede misfortune.

When approached from a Sinister-Path perspective, complexities emerge with the symbolic implications both of Jupiter and of Saturn. Astrologically, Jupiter has the more positive reputation, connoting fruitful integration into an overarching social order. Saturn's reputation, by contrast, is negative, connoting order's more restrictive manifestations. How are these associations to be reconciled with the Satanist's understanding of themselves as a disrupter of order? What is critical to grasp is that the sorcerer's revolt against existing order does not mean a rejection of *all* order, for even though the underlying force behind the universe is chaos (i.e., the Abyssal Void of Darkness), the fact remains that pure chaos is inimical to life. The task of the sorcerer is, first, to perceive the possibilities of a new order beyond what has thus far been imagined, and second, to both inflict and endure whatever strife is necessary to actualize these possibilities. The former of these is the Jupiterian task, while the latter is the Saturnine.

In alchemical terms, that which was begun in fermentation and continued in sublimation reaches its climax and conclusion in what is typically known as coagulation: through further purification, the distilled elixir takes a solidified form that is no longer in danger of evaporation, becoming permanent as the "philosopher's stone." It is therefore appropriate that O9A assigns the term *azoth* to this stage specifically. The attainer of azoth is one who, through the achievement of Faustian excellence, becomes ever more capable of further self-evolution, and of safeguarding such growth against sloth, corruption, and other forms of entropy. Psychologically, it is during the Jupiter stage that the initiate comes to embody the long-term resilience of a truly dedicated walker of the Sinister Path. Such perseverance additionally fosters empathy, as its deprivations and hardships open one's eyes to what life itself must perpetually contend against.

Central concept

The Jupiter stage recalls the requirements of O9A's grade of Internal Adept: the initiate must live in primitive isolation for a prolonged period. Tenebrous Satanism does not insist that this take as lengthy and extreme a form as O9A envisions, however, and it is critical to understand why. The intent is to enable initiates who cannot follow O9A's prescriptions to the letter and yet possess drives and talents that can contribute to the Sinister Dialectic to undergo what transformation may yet be experienced via such pressures as the Jupiter stage asserts. The intent is not to offer initiates the cachet of an O9A-like initiation without having to actually struggle, for that would wholly defeat the purpose of the endeavor. We must therefore emphasize, with regard to this stage in particular, that the onus is on the initiate to undertake the initiation in a manner that they personally find challenging.

Requirements

Initiates should undertake the Jupiter stage at a time of the year that takes prudent account of the temperature and weather conditions that they will be exposed to. The initiate will need to prepare ahead of time by scouting out an appropriate location in the wilderness, acquiring supplies, and conditioning themselves for the coming ordeal. Throughout the initiation (a minimum of one month), the initiate should observe all of the following restrictions:

- Dwelling within a primitive shelter with minimal facilities, such as a tent, bringing along only what can be carried on one's own back.

- No human contact, unless unavoidable in order to obtain food, seek medical treatment, or discourage interlopers.

- No engagement with clocks, electronic devices, social media, or escapist entertainment. An emergency tracking and rescue device is permissible, but the initiate's ongoing day-to-day experience of their time in the wilderness should be as low-tech as possible.

- Food and water may be derived from the environment (by hunting and gathering) or obtained in some other way (retrieved from a stockpile closer to civilization, contactless delivery), but the initiate's menu throughout the ordeal should be kept simple and consistent.

The initiate may make short returns to civilization during daylight hours when necessary to attend to such things as obtaining essential resources and brief check-ins with a designated emergency contact. Similarly, although it is ideal for the entire retreat to take place at a single location, it is permissible to break camp and re-establish it elsewhere for such reasons as limiting one's impact upon nature or avoiding predatory animals. However, the initiate should organize the whole endeavor so that these sorts of interruptions occur as rarely as possible. Additionally, no more social contact or electronics usage than is absolutely necessary should occur during forays back into civilization, and all nights during the initiation period should be spent either back at one's primitive shelter or outside. These measures ensure that continuity is maintained even amid unavoidable interruptions.

While in the wilderness, the initiate should anticipate dedicating large portions of time to the following activities:

- Attending mindfully to survival needs such as food, water, etc.

- Disciplined daily exercise of the body and the mind.

- Close observation of nature, e.g., plants, animals, etc.

- A maximum of two different pastimes of a portable and low-tech nature, which the initiate should choose at the outset and should not alter once the initiation has begun. One might bring, for example, a sketchbook, tools and materials for a handicraft, a non-electronic game that can be played by oneself, or a musical instrument.

- Perfection of one's occult technique in such areas as divination, ritual magick generally, and communion with the Nekalah specifically. Toward this end, the initiate should definitely bring the dagger, crystal, and runic-tarot into the wilderness with them.

As with previous stages, the initiate should keep a daily record of their reflections and observations, and the opening and closing of the initiatory period should be marked by appropriate ritual workings.

Evaluation

Two major gains proceed from the Jupiter stage. Firstly, through immersion in a primitive environment, the initiate develops a broader and deeper comprehension of the world as a nexion — i.e., an interdependent system of energies. Earnest awareness of this reality enhances appreciation for even the simplest pleasures and significantly expands one's capacity for empathy. Secondly, by imposing a period of extended hardship, the initiate is challenged to truly walk the walk when it comes to resilience. Individuals who pass such a test are unlikely to be deterred by any of life's difficulties, having learned through experience that they possess such an abundance of internal resources that they need fear nothing. The initiate who perseveres through all that the Jupiter stage calls for, so as to emerge with gains of these kinds in hand, can rightly be said to have passed the initiation.

On the other hand, two temptations must be resisted in order to avoid failure of the Jupiter stage. One is allowing the hardships and long days of the initiation to wear out one's patience, such that one gives up prematurely. The other is too much bending of the rules, to the point that in the course of avoiding inconveniences, one winds up embarking on little more than a glorified vacation. Both of these failings tend to be products of insufficient conditioning prior to entering into the initiation proper. Initiates would therefore be wise not to jump into Jupiter's demands before first establishing that they can weather shorter excursions under similarly austere conditions.

Saturn

♄

Symbolism

Saturn is associated with restriction and severity. The "no" that opposes Jupiter's "yes," it evokes the scythe that mows down what was promising before its time, the final sands departing from the hourglass for those whose time is done, and the reign of implacable ancient forces over time as a whole. Accordingly, Saturn is typically perceived as malefic. From the perspective of the Sinister Path, however — whereupon the sorcerer's destiny entails cooperation with forces Dark and alien to accomplish shared goals of advancing creative strife — Saturn represents not only limitation, but also limitation overcome, in accord with the relentlessly ever-striving will of the Abyssal Void of Darkness. The apparent contradiction of the two concepts O9A assigns to this stage, namely *chaos* and thought, can be reconciled via understanding that the former refers to the need to break down the existing order and the latter to the need to erect something new in its place.

Regarding alchemy, the attainment of the philosopher's stone in the preceding stage now inspires the alchemist to seek a further goal: the multiplication of that which hard work has produced. Of the various terms used for this final process, exaltation is most suggestive of the Tenebrous understanding of Saturn, for it connotes the raising of something to its highest point of rank and influence. Such is the position that the fully initiated sorcerer ascends to. After having weathered all the inward psychological demands of previous stages, Saturn now turns the initiate's attention outward to that which must be achieved and experienced on the social-communal plane. How to manage human affairs for the specific purposes of confronting restrictions and moving beyond them is the central question the Saturn stage revolves around.

Central concept

Saturn varies in format more than previous stages, depending not only upon variations in individual capacity, but also differences in each individual's long-term ambitions. Its fundamental requirement, however, is that the initiate undertake an endeavor that will involve multiple other human beings, in accord with a goal set in consultation with one's acausal allies. The two options described below are illustrative of two variants that Saturn may take: the overt and the covert. Initiates should decide at the outset which pattern they will follow and strive always to treat people they interact with during the initiatory period in a manner appropriate to that pattern. It follows that though the ambitious may wish to complete the Saturn stage twice, trying one pattern on one occasion and the other on another, one should not attempt to combine them within a single initiation.

Requirements

The overt variant of the Saturn stage requires the initiate to found an organization involving at least five members in total.

At least three of these should be people who come into the initiate's life for the express purpose of this new endeavor rather than previously known acquaintances. The group which the initiate founds may be a coven aimed at such goals as the perfection of occult arts via regular practice, the provision of support for initiates at earlier stages of initiation, the pursuit of specific earthly goals, the veneration of a particular acausal being, etc. Alternately, it may be outwardly mundane, concealing an aeonic purpose of changing minds and swaying attitudes: a band, business, activist group, charitable organization, or similar. Whatever the purpose, it should be discussed and agreed to openly between all founding members of the group, striving for transparency between the initiate and all primary collaborators.

The covert variant of the Saturn stage requires the initiate to intentionally join an organization or otherwise enter into a lifestyle that is foreign to their past experience and challenging for them to navigate.

This is, in essence, what O9A calls an "insight role." In this instance, there should be a degree of conflict between initiate's true goals and values and the goals and values of what they are signing up for, such that discretion, if not outright deception, will be necessary if the initiate is to get by in their new milieu. While thus immersed, the task of the initiate will be both to i) attain some degree of genuine empathy regarding why those devoted to this organization or lifestyle are thus engaged and ii) bring about some manner of alteration in at least three people whom they meet in this setting and would not have met otherwise. This need not necessarily mean converting three random people to Tenebrous Satanism (admirable an accomplishment though that would be), but by the end of the initiatory period, there should be some front upon which the initiate can claim to have made a decisive difference in these individuals' lives, whether in terms of changed perspective, material well-being, etc.

Regardless of which one of these two variants the initiate intends to pursue, they should first perform some manner of communion rite (either with their patron or another Nekalah whom they have an established relationship with) so as to solicit acausal input regarding what they wish to accomplish, both in the short term (as part of the initiation) and in the long term (making use of that which will be learned in the course of the initiation). The initiate should subsequently devote a period of time to reflection, research, and concrete planning for the purposes of firming up their conception of what exactly they are setting out to accomplish. Then, once they are ready to begin the initiation proper, they should perform either the Rite of Descent or the Rite of the Threshold, during which they will put forward a written account of the nature and scope of the intended endeavor, similarly to how the pact of the Sun stage is proposed, negotiated, and signed. The initiate's formal dedication at this time and the Nekalah's assent mark the official beginning of the initiatory period.

If the initiate is pursuing the overt version of Saturn, they must now lead their group, ensuring that tasks are undertaken and goals accomplished. Or, in the covert case, they must insinuate themselves among those they have chosen to infiltrate and begin cultivating influence over those around them. Either way, the initiate is to persist in pursuing their goals over whatever time period they have stipulated, it being not unreasonable to dedicate an entire year to a pursuit of this nature. Throughout this period, the initiate should keep a detailed record of any noteworthy events that arise, complementary undertakings entered into, competing obligations in need of being managed, and doubts and difficulties that weigh upon one's mind.

It should be noted, so as to distinguish the practices of Tenebrous Satanism from those of O9A, that neither the overt nor covert versions of Saturn inherently require the initiate to place themselves in physical danger, to risk arrest and imprisonment, or to perform actions that go strongly against the initiate's own ethical convictions. This is not to say that initiates are forbidden from crossing such lines should they and their acausal allies decide there is a valid reason for doing so. It must be understood, however, that the role of Saturn in Tenebrous initiation is not the testing of whether one is willing to transgress just for transgression's sake. Rather, initiates are to undergo experiences relevant to becoming effective change-makers in the long run, able to impact the world in a way that serves the Sinister Dialectic. Therefore, if anything "dangerous" is to be done during the Saturn stage, it should be directly connected to this goal.

The Saturn stage should conclude with some form of communion rite so that the initiate may review their accomplishments with the Dark Gods, bringing closure to the endeavor. In the aftermath, any relationships established during the initiation should be dealt with according to the judgment of the initiate — groups may continue activities or wind them down, and connections may be maintained or severed.

Evaluation

It is difficult to say, in an objective and general sense, what constitutes a pass or failure of the kind of initiation Saturn entails. While concrete results such as impacting at least three strangers in a life-changing fashion are strongly preferred, the judgment must ultimately be made by the initiate themselves and the particular acausal allies to whom they have made a commitment. Initiates at this level should possess both self-honesty and acausal insight enough to be able to assess whether the extent of life-changing personal growth that their endeavor has wrought may justify construing a technical failure as a pass or whether, conversely, a technical pass should be regarded as a failure on account of aspirations being only marginally met. Either way, though, what is most important to consider is whether the overt version of the Saturn stage has decisively advanced the initiate's capacities to lead, teach, cooperate, and inspire, and whether the covert version has done the same for the initiate's abilities to infiltrate, adapt, understand, and persuade. From an aeonic perspective, it is less important for short-term goals within the initiation to be met than it is to gain the key skills — leadership and strategic insight — requisite for the attainment of long-term imperatives beyond the initiation.

That said, catastrophic failure of the Saturn stage is of course possible. The initiate may prove wholly unable to keep their group together and on-task in the overt case or may be found out and ejected in the covert one. In either of these circumstances, the initiate should do what they can to exit the situation gracefully and conclude the endeavor by communing with their patron about lessons learned.

Summary

Willing exposure to adversity is considered salutary in Tenebrous Satanism, no matter whether it entails overcoming procrastination and sloth, forging and maintaining relationships despite tensions, grappling with one's own flaws and mistakes, pushing past fatigue and discomfort, or finding ways to transcend or subvert the established patterns of the herd. Whenever the sorcerer does any of these things, they reject the Dogmagian conviction that individuals on their own cannot survive and flourish without the imposition of otherworldly ideals and utopian interventions.

Against such hand-wringing about human limitations and fetishization of victimhood, Tenebrous Satanism asserts the power of the Black Flame: the inner dynamo of will, energy, and insight that any determined person is capable of cultivating and harnessing. Every competent Satanist lives a life that pays tribute to this power, but none more so than the fully initiated sorcerer. Tenebrous initiation matters because it is not just an occult exercise that makes no real-world impact. It is, rather, an experience aimed at awakening the initiate to the utmost they are capable of, not only esoterically, but also exoterically. Transformative self-evolution of this kind is the true secret of magick: it is through purposely facing one's own soul head-on that the Satanist gains the power to transmute the world's filth into gold, rising from Darkness to shine as the morning star.

Tenebrous Satanism envisions initiation as a lengthy process, the whole of which takes at least two or three years in total. This process is not aimed at sorting initiates according to who is the most hardcore, but at enabling individuals to progressively actualize whatever potential they personally possess. The stages of this process can be distilled into the following summary:

- ☽ In *Moon*, the reward of diligence is wonder.

- ☿ In *Mercury*, the reward of discipline is greatness.

- ♀ In *Venus*, the reward of companionship is empathy.

- ☉ In *Sun*, the reward of reconciliation is dynamism.

- ♂ In *Mars*, the reward of suffering is clarity.

- ♃ In *Jupiter*, the reward of perseverance is fearlessness.

- ♄ In *Saturn*, the exaltation of wonder, greatness, empathy, dynamism, clarity, and fearlessness is its own reward.

This formula is indicative of what Tenebrous Satanism has in mind with regard to "the advancement of Satan's cause through the embrace of creative strife." Contra what proximity to O9A might lead one to anticipate, Tenebrous strife is not manifest in hateful, criminal acts of violence. Tenebrous Satanism does however find accord with O9A in its high-level conception of Satanism's ultimate purpose: the disruption of human ideologies and institutions that stifle flourishing and hold back evolution. We are in agreement in our formulation of an adversarial Creed that is relentlessly hostile toward stagnancy and which is therefore readily perceived, in the eyes of mundane cowards, as Sinister.

We hope that the Ninth Key will provide the Satanists of today and tomorrow with a method by which the Black Flame may be stoked to heights never before achieved and the useless debris of dogma and stasis incinerated thereby, for the greater good of a more Satanic world.

Notes

[79] The refusal to generalize about races or civilizations as a whole in Tenebrous Satanism's concept of aeonic change is of course another difference from O9A, as was previously discussed — see the Introduction, Note 3.

[80] Some readers may feel initiation requirements of this kind are either overtly or subtly prejudicial against those who are physically unable to perform certain activities (due to disability, chronic illness, trauma-based limitations, etc.) and worry about ableism in connection with this. Our primary response to such concerns is that we encourage differently-abled individuals to attend closely to Tenebrous initiation's expectation that initiates carry out the initiation in a way that is challenging but doable by their own standards — i.e. between your own ingenuity and the support of those who sympathize with your goals, you too can devise meaningful initiation experiences for yourself, and you should disregard anyone who makes you feel otherwise. We think it must be admitted that yes, past a point, too many accommodations can take away from the quality of adversity essential to the Niner current. The problem, though, is that people are often too quick to assume persons with certain limitations inherently cannot do things, instead of putting effort into devising ways of overcoming the obstacles. A willingness to use one's creativity and resourcefulness to devise an unconventional initiation that is still challenging and meaningful is exactly the kind of thing we like to see among Tenebrous sorcerers.

[81] See the Seventh Key, Note 49, regarding the use of a diabetic lancet in connection with this and similar practices wherein one's own blood is shed in ritual contexts.

[82] O9A's *Caelethi* (a.k.a. *Black Book of Satan II*) contains the following passage regarding Vindex, which is relevant to our interpretation:

> Two horses
> Fight within a circle of trees
> (The Sun at Night)
> Two angels
> Laughing in a room of sacrifice
> Two
> In a haze of gold
> Beyond the Door.

Appendix I: Rites of Abyssal Darkness

The standard opening, performance, and closing phases of Tenebrous ritual are provided below, followed by intensification formulae that may be adapted variously. The Tenebrous current is defined by the structure provided, but individual magicians should feel free to alter small details in accord with personal inclination. In what follows, parentheses distinguish instructions from words to be spoken, and anything that must be vibrated is indicated in italics. Square brackets indicate content that must be filled in with appropriate specifics.

General ritual template

Opening phase

General Evocation

Eam deorsum ad aram Tenebrarum
I hereby evoke the Dark Gods of the Sinister Path
Masters of life and death
Reconcilers of the flesh and the spirit
Come forth and appear before me
For I am a seeker of wisdom and power
Fearless and proud in my pursuit of divinity
Agios, O Tenebrae Profundae!
Ave, Satanas! Veni, Malevoli!

Evocation of the South

From the Southern Fires, I call forth the Archons
Rulers of this world and granters of desire
Come forth at my call:
Agios, O Archontes!
Binan ath! Ga wath am!

Evocation of the East

From the Eastern Air, I call forth the Fallen Angels
Knowledge-seekers and bearers of the light of wisdom
Come forth at my call:
Agios, O Sapientes!
Binan ath! Ga wath am!

Evocation of the North

From the Northern Earth, I call forth the Abominations
Revealers of harsh truths and enemies of the cowardly
Come forth at my call:
Agios, O Nefandi!
Binan ath! Ga wath am!

Evocation of the West

From the Western Waters, I call forth the Ancient Ones
Chaos-bringers and destroyers of obstacles
Come forth at my call:
Agios, O Veteri!
Binan ath! Ga wath am!

Conclusion of Evocations

Ineo naon!
Thus do I welcome the Dark Gods.

Performance phase

Statement of Intent

Dark Gods, I, [magician's name],
call you forth from the Abyss to fulfill my request:

[state the Intention]

Do as I command, and I will testify to your greatness!

Statement of Coordination

(use i or ii, not both)

   i.   I turn now to the four directions to make my will manifest.

   ii. Darkness, come forth in all your forms to make my will manifest.

Intensification

[this will vary widely, depending on the rite being performed]

Statement of Accomplishment

[state the Accomplishment]

Closing phase

Offering

Dark Gods, I acknowledge your power with gratitude:
Receive now the offering.

Acknowledgements of the Four Directions

Archons, as your favored regent, I thank you.
Fallen angels, as your ardent disciple, I thank you.
Abominations, as your chosen vessel, I thank you.
Ancient Ones, as your awakened offspring, I thank you.

Parting

Thus is the rite complete.
Dark Gods, go forth with all of the might of the Adversary,
for our wills are united as one.
Ave, Satanas!
Nythra Kthunae Atazoth!

Specific rites

Rite of Banishing

As per the Seventh Key. With this and all rites that follow, immersive visualization should be assumed as the intensification method unless the details provided suggest otherwise.

Intent

Banish all energies that I have no use for and forbid their influence from hindering me.

Intensification

Archons, purify my will, for I am the Black Flame that cannot be extinguished!

Fallen Angels, purify my mind, for I am the fresh, strong wind that destroys yet also creates!

Abominations, purify my body, for I am the seed sown in blood-stained soil, which grows forever anew!

Ancient Ones, purify my spirit, for I am the torrential rain that washes away all obstructions!

Accomplishment

Thus do I banish all that opposes my will!

Rite of Alignment

The effect of this rite is to align the magician with acausal forces supportive of the one's true will as a walker of the Sinister Path. Its dynamics are thus a hybrid between banishing and communion. Alignments are suitable at the inception or conclusion of initiation periods or when in need of acausal connection and assurance more generally — e.g., as a Sinister-Path equivalent of prayer. The intent should be amended to fit specific circumstances, e.g., "... as I embark upon the [planet's name] stage of initiation" when beginning an initiation.

Intent

Align me with your will and purge me of all that opposes our shared purpose.

Intensification

Archons, incinerate my fear and folly upon the raging pyre of your Black Flame!

Fallen Angels, illuminate my path with the secret wisdom of your Sinister Moon!

Abominations, show me what I must know in the depths of your Obsidian Mirror!

Ancient Ones, drown my doubts and delusions in the limitless waters of your Primordial Ocean!

Accomplishment

Thus do I reconcile the Fire of the Will and the Will of the Fire!

Rite of Boon-Seeking

This rite is for when the magician wants something and seeks to tilt probabilities accordingly. The Seventh Key's fundamental principles of magick should be studied carefully to understand the conditions under which such a working can be expected to bear fruit. The example is suitable for an initiate embarking upon the Venus stage of initiation.

Intent

Sway the ways of the world in my favor so that a suitable companion may come to me;
Acquaint me with one who is [list a few desired characteristics] and receptive to my cause.

Intensification

Archons, fill my companion's heart with the ardor of your Black Flame!

Fallen Angels, call my companion forth to meet me fortuitously beneath your Black Stars!

Abominations, swallow up all that could divert my companion from me in the depths of your Black Earth!

Ancient Ones, wash away all that could divert me from my companion with the downpour of your Black Rain!

Accomplishment

Thus do I invite my new companion into my life!

Rite of Hindering

This rite is the opposite of boon-seeking. The example presumes a case where someone imposes upon the magician, and causal methods of curbing the annoyance have proven impractical or ineffective. The mechanism such a rite utilizes is easily adapted to either protective or destructive purposes.

Intent

Sway the ways of the world against [target's name] so that [target's pronoun] bothers me no more;
Hinder [target's name], so that [target's pronoun] ceases to hinder me.

Intensification

Archons, singe the fortunes of [target's name] with upheaval, loss, and regret!

Fallen Angels, spread confusion, discord, and anxiety among [target's name] and [target's pronoun] allies!

Abominations, crush [target's name] with all manner of failure, inconvenience, and disappointment!

Ancient Ones, drench the days and nights of [target's name] in doubt, indecision, and folly!

Accomplishment

Thus do I bind [target's name] and forbid [target's pronoun] from acting against me!

Whereas the previous examples utilized more poetic Intensifications, this current rite uses a more direct and literal approach, and the visualization that follows should revolve around enumerating the literal specifics of what is described, as opposed to conjuring imagery of a more metaphorical nature. Other rites can also be adapted in this direction if desired, especially if the rite is aimed at bringing about or avoiding a given state of earthly affairs. So long as such rites use multidirectional coordination, however, the magician should still formulate the Commands in a way that suits the symbolism of the directions being addressed, even if only in a somewhat abstract way — as per the present case.

The potency of the Rite of Hindering can be further enhanced by supplementing immersive visualization with a complementary symbolic gesture, such as the tying of knots in a cord — e.g., while performing each of the visualizations associated with the directions, tie three knots, and then tie the two ends of the cord together as the Statement of Accomplishment is being issued. This knotted cord may subsequently be kept on one's person or left in a concealed location in the setting where the magician most typically crosses paths with the target.

Rite of Enchantment

This rite's effect is to charge a causal object with acausal energy. The example is an optional consecration that can be performed upon tools of divination. The container in which the diviner stores the runic-tarot, with the tokens inside of it, should be laid upon the altar at outset. The magician should point the dagger at this target object while the Intent is stated. During the issuing of the Commands and accompanying visualizations, the magician should set the dagger aside, hold the target object in the right hand, and use their breath to direct energy in accord with what the Commands stipulate, breathing in to draw power from the direction being addressed and breathing out through the nose to send this energy down the right arm and into the object. Once the process is complete, the charged object should again be placed upon the altar and the dagger pointed at it while the Accomplishment is issued.

Intent

Imbue these tokens of divination with your power so that I may peer ever deeper into Darkness, and see ever more.

Intensification

Archons, imbue these tokens with the energy of your Black Flame!

Fallen Angels, imbue these tokens with the insight of your Black Stars!

Abominations, imbue these tokens with the realities of your Black Earth!

Ancient Ones, imbue these tokens with the profundity of your Black Ocean!

Accomplishment

Thus do I receive the gifts of Darkness and empower myself thereby!

Rite of Descent

As described in the Eighth Key.

Intent

Open wide the Black Gate of the Void,
so that I may venture forth into your realm;
[Nekalah's name], guide me down into your region of the Abyss, so that [briefly describe the purpose of the communion].

Intensification

(raising crystal)
[Nekalah's name], behold the Key to the Dark Pool beneath the Moon.

(displaying sigil)
[Nekalah's name], behold the sign by which you are known to me.
Unlock the gate that separates me from your acausal throne;
Hear my call and open the way before me!

(while walking the Black Gate)
Agios, O [Nekalah's name]! Binan Ath, Ga Wath Am! (x 7)

(after walking is complete)
Thus do I open the Black Gate.
[Nekalah's name], extend your hand to me and draw me forth unto your presence!

Banishing

(use i or ii, as appropriate)

   i.   [Nekalah's name], I thank you for this revelation.
        The time has come, though, for our ways to part, as I return now to the causal realm.
        Karu Samsu! (x 7)

   ii. [Nekalah's name], as sovereign of my own flesh and spirit, I withdraw from you by the power of my own will and return now to the causal realm.
        Karu Samsu! (x 7)

Accomplishment

Thus do I return to my own world, shutting the Black Gate behind me!

Failure

Thus do I shut the Black Gate!

Rite of the Threshold

As described in the Eighth Key.

Intent

Open wide the Black Gate of the Void,
and come forth to greet me upon its threshold;
[Nekalah's name], meet me in the Shadow between our worlds, so that [briefly describe the purpose of the communion].

Intensification

(raising crystal)
[Nekalah's name], behold the Key to the Dark Pool beneath the Moon.

(displaying sigil)
[Nekalah's name], behold the sign by which you are known to me.

(placing sigil upon target)
Appear before me, here, in this place;
Hear my call as I open the way between us!

(while walking the Black Gate)
Agios, O [Nekalah's name]! Binan Ath! Ga Wath Am! (x 7)

(after walking is complete)
Thus do I open the Black Gate.

(just before blowing out candle)
[Nekalah's name], come forth into the Shadow!

Banishing

(use i or ii, as appropriate)

i. [Nekalah's name], I thank you the honor of your presence. The time has come, though, for our ways to part, as I now dispel the Shadow.
Karu Samsu! (x 7)

ii. [Nekalah] 's name, as sovereign of my own flesh and spirit, I conclude our meeting by the power of my own will, as I now dispel the Shadow.
Karu Samsu! (x 7)

Accomplishment

Thus do I return to my own world, shutting the Black Gate behind me!

Failure

Thus do I shut the Black Gate!

Rite of Tribulation

As called for in the Mars stage of initiation. The initiate should read the Ninth Key carefully to ensure they understand the intended flow of the ritual. The first night's portion of the rite is best begun after midnight. The second night's portion can proceed as soon as daylight is gone. The version of the rite provided here is modeled after the Rite of Descent but modeling it after the Rite of the Threshold is equally viable.

Night 1: Intent

Open wide the Black Gate of the Void,
so that I may venture forth into your realm;
[Nekalah's name], guide me down into your region of the Abyss, so that I may confront my demons!

Night 1: Intensification

(raising crystal)
[Nekalah's name], behold the Key to the Dark Pool beneath the Moon.

(displaying the Vindex sigil)
[Nekalah's name], behold my pledge to contend with you.

(displaying the adversary's sigil)
[Nekalah's name], behold the sign by which you are known to me.
Unlock the gate that separates me from your acausal throne;
Hear my call and open the way before me!

(while walking the Black Gate)
Agios, O [Nekalah's name]! Binan Ath! Ga Wath Am! (x 7)

(after walking is complete)
Thus do I open the Black Gate.
[Nekalah's name], extend your hand to me and draw me forth to face your challenge!

(there is no banishing, nor other closing elements, on Night 1)

Night 2: Intent

Open wide the Black Gate of the Void,
so that I may venture forth into your realm;
[Nekalah's name], guide me down into your region of the Abyss, so that I may defeat my demons!

Night 2: Intensification

(raising crystal)
[Nekalah's name], behold the Key to the Dark Pool beneath the Moon.

(displaying the Vindex sigil)
[Nekalah's name], behold my pledge to contend with you — and to emerge victorious!

(displaying the adversary's sigil)
[Nekalah's name], behold the sign by which you are known to me.
Unlock the gate that separates me from your acausal throne
Hear my call and open the way before me!

(while walking the Black Gate)
Agios, O [Nekalah's name]! Binan Ath! Ga Wath Am! (x 7)

(after walking is complete)
Thus do I open the Black Gate.
[Nekalah's name], extend your hand to me and draw me forth to resume my trial!

Night 2: Banishing

(use i or ii, as appropriate)

i. [Nekalah's name], I thank you for this contest, through which I have gained new strength.
    With my demons now defeated, the time has come for our ways to part, as I return now to the causal realm.
    Karu Samsu! (x 7)

ii. [Nekalah's name], as sovereign of my own flesh and spirit, I withdraw from you by the power of my own will and return now to the causal realm.
    Karu Samsu! (x 7)

Night 2: Accomplishment

(use if contact was successful, whether victory or defeat followed)

Thus do I return to my own world, shutting the Black Gate behind me!

Failure

(use if unable to make contact on either first or second nights)

Thus do I shut the Black Gate!

Appendix II: Tables

Table I: Tenebrous runes and their alphabetical equivalences

Letter	Rune	Name	Letter	Rune	Name
A		Anthal	Ng		Ngiha
B		Byrk	O		Olith
C		Chet	P		Pyrash
D		Dolath	Q		Qolf
E		Eyahin	R		Rhais
F		Fhell	S		Shaol
G		Grahl	T		Tehir
H		Hvelgit	Th		Tharu
I		Ishut	U		Uruk
J		Jhire	V		Vhow
K		Kehan	W		Wajhel
L		Lhamyu	X		Xhin
M		Manoth	Y		Ywhaz
N		Nithrul	Z		Zhalg

Table II: Kingdoms and incarnations

Kingdom	Glyph	Incarnation	Glyph
Attainment		Muses	
Communion		Witches	
Strife		Heroes	
Innovation		Sorcerers	

Table III: Relation of Tenebrous runes to O9A concepts

Name	Sound	Connotation	O9A concept
Qolf	Q	Impetus	Lunar Purification
Anthal	A	Novice	Ga Wath Am
Byrk	B	Master	Noctulius
Grahl	G	Insight	Mactoron
Dolath	D	Nature	Davcina
Ishut	I	Boundary	Falcifer
Hvelgit	H	Shelter	Kthunae
Vhow	V	Order	Atazoth
Xhin	X	Chaos	Budsturga
Zhalg	Z	Commitment	Athushir
Chet	C	Challenge	Shaitan
Fhell	F	Attachment	Darkat
Tharu	Th	Severing	Gaubni
Ngiha	Ng	Concealment	Nekalah
Tehir	T	Affirmation	Lidagon
Ywhaz	Y	Inspiration	Sauroctonos
Kehan	K	Fortune	Baphomet
Lhamyu	L	Revelation	Velpecula
Manoth	M	Sacrifice	Vindex
Nithrul	N	Negation	Nythra
Shaol	S	Balance	Aosoth
Eyahin	E	Ignorance	Azanigin
Pyrash	P	Disruption	Abatu
Wajhel	W	Destiny	Nemicu
Uruk	U	Night	Shugara
Rhais	R	Day	Karu Samsu
Jhire	J	Nexion	Naos
Olith	O	Culmination	Binan Ath

Table IV: Summary of the Nekalah, Noctulian faction

Role	Nekalah	Connotation	Stone
Matrix	Athushir-Kthunae	Life	Sardonyx
Ostium	Budsturga	Transitions	Blue chalcedony
Gladius	Velpecula	Skill	Chrysocolla
Cicatrix	Sauroctonos	Healing	Pyrite
Lamia	Darkat-Lidagon	Passion	Garnet
Regnum	Davcina	Harmony	Sodalite
Sidera	Nemicu	Wisdom	Aquamarine
Dux	Noctulius	Leadership	White howlite
Vorago	Atazoth	Ultimacy	Labradorite

Table V: Summary of the Nekalah, Shaitanic faction

Role	Nekalah	Connotation	Stone
Matrix	Mactoron-Falcifer	Purity	Fluorite
Ostium	Aosoth	Danger	Obsidian
Gladius	Abatu	War	Carnelian
Cicatrix	Shugara	Suffering	Serpentine
Lamia	Baphomet	Blood	Jasper
Regnum	Azanigin	Instinct	Hematite
Sidera	Gaubni	Magick	Fossil
Dux	Shaitan	Trials	Tiger eye
Vorago	Nythra	Death	Smoky quartz

Table VI: Astrological attributions of the Nekalah

Nekalah	Moon	Planets	Zodiac
Abatu	−	♂, ☿	Aries
Aosoth	−	♂, ♀	Gemini
Atazoth	+	♄, ♃	Libra
Athushir-Kthunae	+	♃, ♄	Leo
Azanigin	−	♃, ♂	Capricorn
Baphomet	−	☽, ♃	Virgo
Budsturga	+	☿, ☽	Pisces
Darkat-Lidagon	+	♀, ☽	Pisces
Davcina	+	♃, ☽	Aries
Gaubni	−	♀, ☿	Scorpio
Mactoron-Falcifer	−	♀, ♄	Aquarius
Nemicu	+	☿, ♃	Aquarius
Noctulius	+	☽, ♀	Gemini
Nythra	−	♂, ☽	Cancer
Sauroctonos	+	♄, ☿	Taurus
Shaitan	−	♄, ♂	Sagittarius
Shugara	−	☽, ♄	Scorpio
Velpecula	+	☿, ♂	Capricorn

+ = waxing phases, − = waning phases

Table VII: Directional attributions of the Nekalah

Direction	Nekalah
North	Athushir-Kthunae, Atazoth, Nythra, Shaitan
Northeast	Aosoth
East	Budsturga, Nemicu, Sauroctonos
Southeast	Shugara
South	Abatu, Darkat-Lidagon, Davcina, Velpecula
Southwest	Gaubni
West	Azanigin, Baphomet, Mactoron-Falcifer
Northwest	Noctulius

About the Author

T. L. Othaos has a PhD in Religious Studies and over 25 years of lived experience in various Satanic denominations. A mixed-race Canadian of center-left political leaning, she rejects totalitarianism regardless of which end of the political spectrum it comes from. She is well-acquainted with the scriptures and esoteric practices of the Order of Nine Angles but has no affiliation with O9A as a human organization. She is a passionate fan of black metal and similar dark genres of music.

www.ingramcontent.com/pod-product-compliance
Lightning Source LLC
Chambersburg PA
CBHW071331080526
44587CB00017B/2793